PAYROLL

Update Service

BECOME A SUBSCRIBER!
Did you purchase this product from a bookstore?

If you did, it's important for you to become a subscriber. John Wiley & Sons, Inc. may publish, on a periodic basis, supplements and new editions to reflect the latest changes in the subject matter that you *need to know* in order to stay competitive in this ever-changing industry. By contacting the Wiley office nearest you, you'll receive any current update at no additional charge. In addition, you'll receive future updates and revised or related volumes on a 30-day examination review.

If you purchased this product directly from John Wiley & Sons, Inc., we have already recorded your subscription for this update service.

To become a subscriber, please call **1-877-762-2974** or send your name, company name (if applicable), address, and the title of the product to:

mailing address: **Supplement Department**
John Wiley & Sons, Inc.
One Wiley Drive
Somerset, NJ 08875

e-mail: **subscriber@wiley.com**
fax: **1-732-302-2300**
online: **www.wiley.com**

For customers outside the United States, please contact the Wiley office nearest you:

Professional & Reference Division
John Wiley & Sons Canada, Ltd.
22 Worcester Road
Etobicoke, Ontario M9W 1L1
CANADA
Phone: 416-236-4433
Phone: 1-800-567-4797
Fax: 416-236-4447
Email: canada@wiley.com

John Wiley & Sons, Ltd.
The Atrium
Southern Gate, Chichester
West Sussex PO 19 8SQ
ENGLAND
Phone: 44-1243-779777
Fax: 44-1243-775878
Email: customer@wiley.co.uk

John Wiley & Sons Australia, Ltd.
33 Park Road
P.O. Box 1226
Milton, Queensland 4064
AUSTRALIA
Phone: 61-7-3859-9755
Fax: 61-7-3859-9715
Email: brisbane@johnwiley.com.au

John Wiley & Sons (Asia) Pte., Ltd.
2 Clementi Loop #02-01
SINGAPORE 129809
Phone: 65-646 32400
Fax: 65-64634604/5/6
Customer Service: 65-64604280
Email: enquiry@wiley.com.sg

PAYROLL

A Guide to Running an Efficient Department

Vicki M. Lambert, CPP
and
IOMA

WILEY

JOHN WILEY & SONS, INC.

For general information on our other products and services, or technical support, please contact our Customer Care Department within the United States at 800-762-2974, outside the United States at 317-572-3993 or fax 317-572-4002.

Wiley also publishes its books in a variety of electronic formats. Some content that appears in print may not be available in electronic books.

For more information about Wiley products, visit our Web site at www.wiley.com.

Library of Congress Cataloging-in-Publication Data

Lambert, Vicki.
    Payroll : a guide to running an efficient department / Vicki M. Lambert.
        p.   cm.
    Includes index.
    ISBN 0-471-70223-4 (cloth)
    1. Payrolls--Management. 2. Office management. I. Title.
    HG4028.P5L35 2005
    658.3'21--dc22

2004022231

Printed in the United States of America

10 9 8 7 6 5 4 3 2 1

Dedicated to my late father, Master Gunnery Sergeant Harold F. Jaster, the family's other technical writer.

Contents

IMPORTANT NOTE:

Because of the rapidly changing nature of information in this field, this product may be updated with annual supplements or with future editions. **Please call 1-877-762-2974 or email us at subscriber@wiley.com to receive any current update at no additional charge.** We will send on approval any future supplements or new editions when they become available. If you purchased this product directly from John Wiley & Sons, Inc., we have already recorded your subscription for this update service.

Preface

Payroll: A Guide to Running an Efficient Department is a guide to improving the payroll department through increasing its efficiency and compliance. It combines the tasks the payroll department must do with the most efficient ways available to do them. With the demands made upon today's payroll department—to do more work in less time without sacrificing compliance or customer service to the company's employees—it is essential for payroll professionals to look for smarter and faster ways to accomplish the multitude of tasks that encompass running a payroll department.

Payroll: A Guide to Running an Efficient Department is a book that is designed to meet the needs of all levels of payroll professionals who want to increase the efficiency of their functions. From the payroll clerk who is a "party of one" to the vice president of payroll operations who oversees dozens of payroll staff members, this book will help in redefining and reshaping how the critical processes of payroll are performed.

The format of this book is designed for easy use. The functions of a payroll department have been broken down and each has been given its own section. Then the related tasks or topics for that function are discussed in depth. When spreadsheets, forms, letters, or memos are suggested, a sample copy is provided as a demonstration, where possible.

Payroll: A Guide to Running an Efficient Department was developed over the years by helping numerous payroll professionals who have strayed from efficient methods of running a payroll department or who have been taught "we've always done it this way." This book strives to pass on the proper methods for achieving and maintaining department-wide efficiency.

Vicki M. Lambert, CPP

CHAPTER 1

Basic Function
of the Payroll Department

1.1 TIME RECORDS

One of the essential and core functions of any payroll department is the processing of time records. It does not matter what they are called, time sheets, time cards, or time reports or whether the records are written by hand on paper time sheets, punched on a time clock, or created by the most sophisticated computerized time and attendance system, they are vital to producing the payroll. Because the information is so critical, the payroll department must make sure that it handles the processing of the time records in the most efficient manner available to it. But capturing time can be a very labor-intensive job requiring massive staff and time, especially if paper or manual time records are used. So a payroll department may decide to skip the auditing of time records in order to speed up the processing of the time records and to cut down on staff. It relies instead on letting the managers or supervisors who approve the time record to "check the math" and so on. But cutting corners when preparing and processing time records does not always equate to saving time and money. Many times it just may mean more work after the payroll is processed to correct the errors that should have been caught prior to inputting the employees' time. What the efficient payroll department must find is the proper balance between quick processing and accurate processing to achieve an efficient and effective method of handling time records.

(a) Capturing Time Effectively

Sometimes to increase efficiency in this labor-intensive area, a payroll department may believe that by implementing an electronic timekeeping system it will solve all of its problems concerning time record entry. This appears logical on the surface. If the computer captures the time and inputs it into the payroll system, how could that not speed up the process? But technology alone does not make a task more efficient. A software package is not a silver bullet because the processing of time records begins and ends outside of any system that may be used. What the payroll department should be concerned with before the format of the time records is the procedures used to capture and process the data before it ever goes into the payroll system. Is this the most efficient method available? When auditing the time record procedures to increase efficiency, the following areas should be examined:

- *Unnecessary Steps*. Eliminate any unnecessary procedures that have been put in place over the years but really do not make any sense now (procedures that are just being done because "they have always been done that way"). This may include tasks such as alphabetizing the paper time cards prior to input. Unless this is necessary to increase input speed, it could be a wasted step.
- *Multipurpose Time Records*. Eliminate using time records for any other purpose than recording of time. Employees should not be permitted to attach notes or requests to time records or to write on time records except to record time. This type of request could include a vacation check in advance that applies to the time record.
- *Data Flow*. Streamline the data flow. The more pay codes, the more separate runs of the system, the more unique the details, the more opportunity for errors. Because payroll code conforms to compliance guidelines, the payroll department should have refined codes. However, the number of pay and time codes it relies on should be simplified to push data through the system more efficiently. For example, a data code should not be created every single time a unique one-time pay occurs or for few and far between uses.

- *Exempt Employees.* Streamline the chain of command for exempt employee time records. Exempt employees' time records may need minimal or no supervisory review as the employee is paid on salary. It is even possible to eliminate the need for time reporting for exempt employees with the exception of anomalies such as benefit leaves.

- *Don't Half and Half Any System.* Hybrid systems, those that are half paper and half electronic, are neither efficient nor do they create a good audit trail. If the payroll department has an electronic timekeeping system, it should improve the front end time capture mechanisms to allow employees to input their own time and to be responsible for its accuracy. For example, the employee inputs all the time punches, is notified if punches are missing, and, using a PIN, submits the time record directly to the payroll department. Some payroll departments are under the false impression that creating a paper time record is required. All government agencies accept electronic records if done properly. There is no need to produce a paper record. Nor is it required by law for an employee to sign a time card. If banks can accept transactions via a PIN then so can payroll. This also prevents employees and supervisors from making quick changes on paper time records but not making those changes to the electronic record and expecting the payroll department to implement the changes.

- *Chain of Command.* Streamline the chain of command used to approve the payroll process. It should not be set up so that one department inputs the master file while another inputs the time records and each must wait for approval before proceeding. It is common for Human Resources to input to the master file all changes to rates, benefits, and so on, but these changes should be continuous and not held up for final approval before implementation to the payroll system.

(b) Auditing Procedures Prior to Processing

No matter what method a payroll department uses to collect time—electronic or manual or a hybrid of the two—it is the responsibility of the department to conduct the final audit of the record. This audit can be done through the electronic system or manually. Of course, the department's efficiency is greatly enhanced if the computer system is allowed to handle the task of checking the math and compliance issues on time records. This capability, along with the elimination of the data entry step, is the major selling feature for electronic time and attendance systems. The audits a payroll department needs—wage and hour law, tax law, company policy—are built right into the system when it is installed and are updated as required. However, no such audit will be done if the time records are done manually or as a hybrid.

But why should the payroll department have to do this audit? Basically it is either pay now or pay later. Unless company management holds managers, supervisors, or whoever submits time records responsible for the total accuracy and compliance of the records, any errors on the time records will reflect back on the payroll department and will have to be corrected by the payroll department. Thus, it is much more efficient and cheaper to catch any errors before processing rather than to have to void and reissue a check if the employee was overpaid, or cut a second check if he or she was underpaid.

Each time record should be audited in the following areas (again, for automated systems, this would be incorporated into the system during setup):

- *Are All Punches Present and Accounted for?*
  - For each day is there a time listed for in, one for out, and if required by state law or company policy, times to reflect meal periods?
- *Math (in General).*
  - Do the times in minus the times out equal the total hours for the day?
  - Do the total daily hours equal the weekly totals listed?
- *Overtime.* After checking the math and the punches, check to see if the overtime has been calculated correctly according to the applicable federal or state law, union contract, or company policy.

- *Leave Benefits.* If leave benefits such as vacation, sick, or Family and Medical Leave Act (FMLA) leave is requested, does the employee have sufficient time and/ or has provided any required company forms?
- *Signature.* Although not required by law, most companies require both the employee's and the supervisor's signatures on paper time records.

Once this audit is complete, the time record can be processed into the computer system. Of course, if an error has been found it must be corrected before proceeding further.

(c) Correcting Errors Prior to Processing

If an error was found on a time record prior to processing, the proper method for correcting it depends on the type of error found.

The following are areas where errors might occur and suggestions for how to either avoid the error altogether or to correct it.

- *Missing or Illegible Time Punches.* These do occur on a regular basis. Employees forget to punch back from lunch or before going home, or double punch over another time and so on. When this occurs, the employee or supervisor needs to furnish the missing time. If it is an automated timekeeping system, the edit reports to reflect time information can be run daily to prevent massive backlogs during the payroll processing time. Sending reports to the supervisors or directly to employees on a daily basis in order to complete the missing punches greatly increases the efficiency of the system as all pertinent information is updated whenever it is needed. In fact, many time and attendance systems will not allow a time record to be submitted if any time punches are missing. For manual systems, the record itself can be sent back for correction or it can be done via e-mail if the printed copies of the e-mails are kept with the time record for an audit trail. Using e-mail generally speeds up the process considerably.
- *Math or Other Errors.* If a math or another type of error occurs, it must of course be corrected. But remember that

time records are legal documents in the sense that they can be subpoenaed by courts or government agencies and are retained as documentation for any audits for that payroll. Therefore, a complete audit trail of all changes must be maintained. If the payroll department is required to make a change to a time record, it must be documented as to when and why the change was made as well as who made it. With an automated system, this would be automatically recorded by the password assigned to the payroll staff member and notations would be made on the edit reports. If a paper time record is used, then the audit trail must be done manually. If payroll is required to make a change on a signed and submitted time sheet, the staff member should never use white out or any type of method that obliterates the original number. Instead the incorrect number should be neatly lined through once, the new number inserted next to the old number, initialed to show who made the change, and a notation made as to why the correction was made. This should be done even if there is only one person in the payroll department. Noting why a correction is made is a critical step. This allows anyone, including the payroll staff member who made the correction, to clearly see why the change was made if it should ever come up weeks, months, or years later, which can happen. If the employee is requesting a benefit leave and does not have sufficient leave, the same system is used as described above to correct the time record to reflect the new hours to be paid.

(d) Auditing Procedures after Processing

After processing the time records it is a standard custom and certainly a best practice to audit (more commonly referred to as "edit") the time records that have been input. A general edit is also done on other remaining input information during this time. This edit ensures that what should have gone in, did go in— nothing more and certainly nothing less. Edit reports are critical to an efficient time record process. These edit reports are generally built right into the payroll system and should at least include:

- *Batch Totals.* The total hours input in batch totals should match the total hours the system accepted. This is usually edited during the data entry phase of the editing.

- *Exceptions to Any Norms.* The edit should list exceptions to any norms established by the department. For example, an employee may not be paid more than 90 hours of straight time in one payroll period. If the employee is receiving 91 hours of straight time, the edit will list this for verification by the payroll department. Other norms that can be tested include overtime hours, vacation hours, holiday pay, jury duty, and sick time.

- *New Hires.* All new hires should be listed on the edit report. This lets whoever is editing the processing know that a new employee has been entered into the system and a time record should also be included for this employee. This is especially critical if payroll does not input new hires directly but instead it is done by a separate department, such as human resources.

- *Terminated Employees.* Any employee who is terminated on this payroll should be listed to let payroll know that a final check is necessary. Also, any terminated employee who receives a check or hours should be flagged for verification as well. This helps prevent terminated employees from accidentally being paid.

- *Non Hours for Current Employees.* Any employee who is not terminated or on unpaid leave status and does not have hours input for them should be listed on the edit report. This helps catch missing time records that may have not been turned in or were not processed by the system.

- *Masterfile Changes.* Whether or not payroll does the input for masterfile changes such as pay raises or department changes, these should be listed on the edit reports. It is the best way to establish an audit trail.

Edit reports should be done after all time records and masterfile changes and additions have been made but prior to the actual processing of the payroll. The purpose of this edit run is to catch any errors prior to producing the payroll and printing checks.

Once this edit run is complete, the payroll can then be processed. If a final edit report is not created as part of the payroll reporting system after the payroll has finished processing, then the last edit report used should be kept for audit purposes.

(e) Record Retention

Federal laws stipulate specific record retention periods for employee-related data. In fact, each individual agency or act has its own record retention requirements. However, because most of the information that is required by these agencies is identical, it is not too difficult for the payroll department to enforce an efficient record retention program. Before addressing the question of how long to keep certain payroll records, companies must first decide who is responsible for retention of the employee data. While payroll and human resources may share common information, only one should be held accountable for the accuracy and timely update of critical system information.

In general, the payroll department is the keeper of transactional information related to payroll, such as hours worked, wages paid, and garnishments withheld. However, payroll also needs access to information on employees' salaries and rates, withholding status, work locations, and the like. Where both the payroll department and the human resources department use the same information, one must be designated as the primary keeper of that information, and be accountable for its accuracy. The other party may use a copy of the information, but not change it.

The basic federal record retention laws applying to the payroll department are:

- *Fair Labor Standards Act (Department of Labor).* All records used to support the making of a payment to an employee must be kept for two to three years. Most payroll departments interpret this to mean three years, as the information requiring two years' retention is usually combined with information that must be retained for three years. See Exhibit 1.1 for a full list of the record retention requirements.

Exhibit 1.1

Record Retention under the Fair Labor Standards Act

Records that should be kept at least three years after the last date of entry
- Name, as it appears on the employee's Social Security card
- Complete home address
- Date of birth, if under age 19
- Gender and occupation (for use in determining Equal Pay Act compliance)
- The beginning of the employee's workweek (time and day)
- Regular rate of pay for overtime weeks, the basis for determining the rate, and any payments excluded from the regular rate
- Hours worked each workday and workweek
- Straight-time earnings (including the straight time portion of overtime earnings). Overtime premium earnings
- Additions to and deductions from wages for each pay period (e.g., bonuses, withheld taxes, benefits contributions, garnishments)
- Total wages paid each pay period
- Date of payment and pay period covered

Records that should be kept at least three years from the last date they were in effect
- Collective bargaining agreements
- Certificates authorizing the employment of industrial home workers, minors, learners, students, apprentices, and handicapped workers
- Records showing total sales volume and goods purchased

Records that should be kept at least two years from the last date of entry
- Basic employment and earnings records supporting the data for each employee's hours of work, basis for determining wages, and wages paid (time cards)
- Order, shipping, billing, and delivery records
- Records substantiating any additions to or deductions from employee's wages

Records that should be kept at least two years from last effective date
- Wage rate tables and piece rate schedules
- Work time schedules establishing the hours and days of employment

- *Internal Revenue Code.* All records used to support the issuance of payroll related forms (e.g., deposits, Form 941, Form 940, Form W-2) must be kept for at least four years after they were filed (basically, four years plus the current year). See Exhibit 1.2 for a full list of the record retention requirements.

- *State Laws.* The payroll department must remember that it must also comply with the state record retention requirements.

EXHIBIT 1.2

Basic Record Retention Requirements for the Internal Revenue Service

---

The following are records that should be kept for four years after the due date or the date the tax is actually paid, whichever is later:

- Employee name, address, occupation, and Social Security number
- Total amount and date of each compensation payment and amount withheld for taxes or otherwise, including reported tips and fair market value of noncash payments
- Amount of compensation subject to withholding for federal income, Social Security, and Medicare taxes and amount withheld for each tax
- Pay period covered by each payment of compensation
- Reasons that total compensation and taxable amount for each tax are different
- Employee Form W-4
- Beginning and ending dates of employee's employment

Some examples of federal record retention requirements for the payroll department are:

- Any record that supports tax withholding (e.g., Form W-4) should be kept for at least four years from the last time the record was used because if any instructions against them are still active. The payroll department cannot start the record-retention limit clock.

- Direct deposit information is part of the FLSA two- to three-year withholding requirement because this information supports payment to the employee.

- Anything that reduces net pay falls under the FLSA's two- to three-year record-keeping rules, and anything related to gross pay or tax calculations falls under the IRS's four-or-more year record-keeping rules.

There are no requirements dictating the exact method for record retention. Paper documents are acceptable of course. But the federal requirements also accept electronic storage if the record is the equivalent of the paper record and reasonable controls are in place to protect the integrity of the data so that unauthorized alterations cannot occur. Microfiche or film is also still acceptable but the payroll department must make sure that the equipment used to read the data is available as long as the records are retained. The department needs to verify the state requirements as well.

1.2 FORM W-4

To process an employee's paycheck correctly, the payroll department must calculate and deduct the appropriate federal income tax. Payroll systems are designed to take an employee's marital status and number of allowances into account to determine the proper taxation. The employee gives this information to payroll on the Form W-4, Employee's Withholding Allowance Certificate. Because this form is vital to processing the employee's paycheck correctly, it is important to make sure the form is processed efficiently and properly.

(a) Receiving the Form from the Employee

The payroll department must have a Form W-4 on file for every employee it pays. A Form W-4 could be a part of the new hire packet in order to expedite the process. The form should be filled out in time to process it with the first payroll for the new employee. However, the IRS has made allowances if the form is not received in time. If the payroll department does not have an employee's valid Form W-4 on file, the marital status of Single with zero (or no) allowances must be used until the form is received.

Once the first form has been processed, it remains in effect until the employee submits a new form. The form does not expire unless the employee claims exempt on the form. Exempt forms expire each year and a new form must be submitted by the employee. If the employee does not submit a new form by February 15th of the new year (this date does fluctuate slightly from year to year depending on whether it falls on a weekend or not), the payroll department reverts the employee's status back to that of not having a valid form on file until a new form is received.

Employees must be allowed to change their Form W-4 as often as they find it necessary. It is conceivable that an employee could change his or her Form W-4 every payroll. The IRS regulations do allow the payroll department up to 30 days to process a new Form W-4, however, it is not advisable to use this time frame for processing the forms. The forms should be processed for the payroll in which they are received for maximum efficiency.

Employers may establish a system to receive Forms W-4 from their employees electronically. Employers need to refer to IRS Regulation Section 31.3402(f)(5)-1(c) for more information.

When a form is received from an employee who is employed in a state that also requires state income tax withholding, the payroll department needs to determine if a state certificate is needed as well. There are 41 states that require state income tax to be withheld. Some of the states allow the Form W-4 to be used as the state form if the employee is claiming the same marital status and number of allowances. Some require their own form be used, regardless of what the employee is claiming and others do not have a state form. It is the responsibility of the payroll department to make sure that the proper forms are received for state and local taxation as well as the federal Form W-4. If the payroll department is multi-state, a list should be created noting each state and its requirements for certificates.

(b) Auditing the Form for Processing

When the payroll department receives a Form W-4 from an employee, there is an auditing process that should be performed to ensure that the form is indeed a valid form. There are three ways a form could be considered invalid. The payroll department must audit all Forms W-4 to determine if they contain the following:

Any Unauthorized Change or Addition. Any unauthorized change or addition to the form itself makes the form invalid. This includes taking out any language by which the employee certifies that the form is correct.

Statement the Form Is False. The form is also invalid if, by the date an employee submits the form to payroll, he or she indicates in any way that the form is false. For example, Employee A comes to the payroll office to drop off a new Form W-4 for the upcoming payroll. The form lists nine allowances. The employee currently claims one allowance. While handing the form to the payroll clerk, Employee A casually mentions that he is not really allowed to claim nine allowances but that he wants to make sure he has a little extra money for his upcoming vacation. This should be considered an invalid form.

Form Is not Completed Properly or Completely. This includes any missing information or improper information. An example of missing information is: Employee B submits a Form W-4 but does not complete his address or date the form. This is an invalid form. The form is considered to have improper information if the employee requests something other than what the form allows. For example, Employee C submits a Form W-4 requesting that 15 percent be deducted from each paycheck. The amount of any income tax withholding must be based on marital status and withholding allowances. An employee may not base his or her withholding amounts on a fixed dollar amount only or a percentage. Therefore, the payroll department cannot accept a form as valid if the employee only puts a dollar amount on line six or enters a percentage amount anywhere on the form. See Exhibit 1.3 for samples of this type of invalid form.

It is the payroll department's responsibility to ensure that they accept only valid forms. So if the form does not contain any unauthorized changes or additions, the employee has not made any statement indicating the form is false, and the employee is not requesting a flat dollar amount only or a percentage, then all payroll must do to complete the validation is to audit the form to verify that it is filled out properly and completely. The following steps will help to make sure the form is audited in the fastest and most efficient way. See Exhibit 1.4 to apply these steps.

Step 1. The form must be for the current year unless the employee is submitting in December for the upcoming new year.

Step 2. The employee's complete first name, middle initial, and last name must be listed on line 1 along with his or her complete address including city, state, and zip code. It is a common practice to omit some of these items in smaller companies, especially if the payroll department knows the employee. But efficiency is based on consistency, so the department must have a complete form for each employee with no exceptions.

EXHIBIT 1.3

Examples of Invalid Forms W-4

STF FED8105F.1 ‑ ‑ ‑ ‑ ‑ ‑ ‑ ‑ Cut here and give Form W-4 to your employer. Keep the top part for your records. ‑ ‑ ‑ ‑ ‑ ‑ ‑ ‑ ‑ ‑

Form **W-4** | **Employee's Withholding Allowance Certificate** | OMB No. 1545-0010 **2004**

Department of the Treasury
Internal Revenue Service
▶ Your employer must send a copy of this form to the IRS if: (a) you claim more than 10 allowances or (b) you claim "Exempt" and your wages are normally more than $200 per week.

1 Type or print your first name and middle initial *Amanda V* Last name *Russo*   2 Your social security number *123 45 6789*

Home address (number and street or rural route) *123 Main St*

3 ☐ Single ☐ Married ☐ Married, but withhold at higher Single rate.
Note: If married, but legally separated, or spouse is a nonresident alien, check the "Single" box.

City or town, State, and ZIP code *Anytown NH*

4 If your last name differs from that shown on your social security card, check here. You must call 1-800-772-1213 for a new card. ▶ ☐

5 Total number of allowances you are claiming (from line H above or from the applicable worksheet on page 2) | 5
6 Additional amount, if any, you want withheld from each paycheck . . . . | 6 $*150.00*
7 I claim exemption from withholding for 2004, and I certify that I meet **both** of the following conditions for exemption:
 • Last year I had a right to a refund of **all** Federal income tax withheld because I had **no** tax liability **and**
 • This year I expect a refund of **all** Federal income tax withheld because I expect to have **no** tax liability.
 If you meet both conditions, write "Exempt" here . . . . ▶ | 7

Under penalties of perjury, I certify that I am entitled to the number of withholding allowances claimed on this certificate, or I am entitled to claim exempt status.
Employee's signature
(Form is not valid unless you sign it.) ▶ *Amanda V. Russo*   Date ▶ *11-17-04*

8 Employer's name and address (Employer: Complete lines 8 and 10 only if sending to the IRS.) | 9 Office code (optional) | 10 Employer identification number (EIN)

For Privacy Act and Paperwork Reduction Act Notice, see page 2.
ISA
Form **W-4** (2004)

STF FED8105F.1 ‑ ‑ ‑ ‑ ‑ ‑ ‑ ‑ Cut here and give Form W-4 to your employer. Keep the top part for your records. ‑ ‑ ‑ ‑ ‑ ‑ ‑ ‑ ‑ ‑

Form **W-4** | **Employee's Withholding Allowance Certificate** | OMB No. 1545-0010 **2004**

Department of the Treasury
Internal Revenue Service
▶ Your employer must send a copy of this form to the IRS if: (a) you claim more than 10 allowances or (b) you claim "Exempt" and your wages are normally more than $200 per week.

1 Type or print your first name and middle initial *Amanda V* Last name *Russo*   2 Your social security number *123 45 6789*

Home address (number and street or rural route) *123 MAIN Street*

3 ☐ Single ☐ Married ☐ Married, but withhold at higher Single rate.
Note: If married, but legally separated, or spouse is a nonresident alien, check the "Single" box.

City or town, state, and ZIP code *Anytown NH*

4 If your last name differs from that shown on your social security card, check here. You must call 1-800-772-1213 for a new card. ▶ ☐

5 Total number of allowances you are claiming (from line H above or from the applicable worksheet on page 2) | 5
6 Additional amount, if any, you want withheld from each paycheck . . . . | 6 $*15%*
7 I claim exemption from withholding for 2004, and I certify that I meet **both** of the following conditions for exemption:
 • Last year I had a right to a refund of **all** Federal income tax withheld because I had **no** tax liability **and**
 • This year I expect a refund of **all** Federal income tax withheld because I expect to have **no** tax liability.
 If you meet both conditions, write "Exempt" here . . . . ▶ | 7

Under penalties of perjury, I certify that I am entitled to the number of withholding allowances claimed on this certificate, or I am entitled to claim exempt status.
Employee's signature
(Form is not valid unless you sign it.) ▶ *Amanda V. Russo*   Date ▶ *11-17-04*

8 Employer's name and address (Employer: Complete lines 8 and 10 only if sending to the IRS.) | 9 Office code (optional) | 10 Employer identification number (EIN)

For Privacy Act and Paperwork Reduction Act Notice, see page 2.
ISA
Form **W-4** (2004)

Step 3. The employee must fill in his or her Social Security number on line 2.

Step 4. The employee must indicate marital status by checking the appropriate box on line 3.

Step 5. The employee must indicate the number of allowances he or she wishes to claim on line 5. This cannot

EXHIBIT 1.4

What to Look for When Auditing a Form W-4

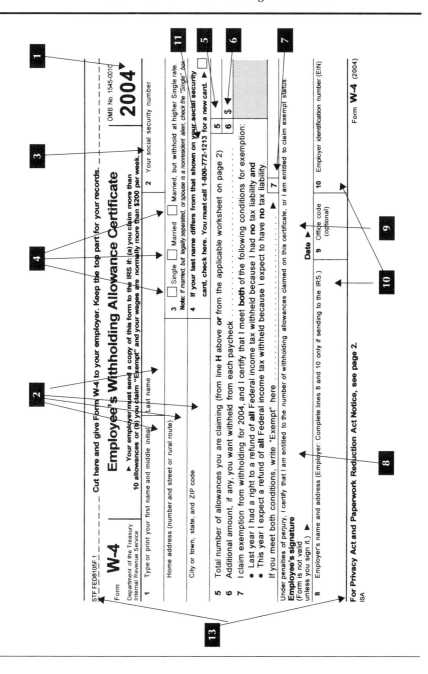

be left blank to indicate zero. If the employee wishes to claim zero allowances then a "0" must be written on line 5. The payroll department must never assume an empty line indicates zero on this line.

Step 6. Line 6 requests an additional dollar amount if desired. A blank line here is acceptable to indicate zero dollars to be withheld.

Step 7. If the employee wishes to claim exempt and he or she has determined that they are qualified to do so, then "exempt" is written on line 7 and lines 3, 5, and 6 do not need to be completed. If they are and line 7 is also completed, the form should be returned to the employee for clarification.

Step 8. The employee must sign the form using his or her full name where indicated.

Step 9. The form must be dated by the employee. The payroll department should never complete any portion of the employee section of the form, even the date. The payroll department may, however, complete the items listed below.

Step 10. The employer's name, address, and EIN need to be completed only if the form is going to be submitted to the IRS. Many payroll departments find it faster and easier to complete this portion prior to distributing the forms to employees.

Step 11. Line 4 is the IRS's attempt to call attention to the fact that the name on the Social Security card and the name on the form must match. If the employee does check this box, the payroll department will need to flag the employee's file to make sure that the new name and Social Security card are verified prior to processing the Form W-2 at year end.

There are special rules for nonresident aliens when it comes to the Form W-4. When completing the Form W-4, nonresident aliens are required to:

- Not claim exemption from income tax withholding.
- Request withholding as if they are single, regardless of their actual marital status.

- Claim only one allowance (if the nonresident alien is a resident of Canada, Mexico, Japan, or South Korea, he or she may claim more than one allowance).

- Request an additional income tax withholding amount, depending on the payroll period, as follows:

Payroll Period	Additional Withholding
Weekly	7.60
Biweekly	15.30
Semimonthly	16.60
Monthly	33.10
Quarterly	99.40
Semiannually	198.80
Annually	397.50
Daily or Miscellaneous (each day of the payroll period)	1.50

Note: Nonresident alien students from India are not subject to the additional income tax withholding requirement.

Once the audit of the form is complete and no changes are needed or errors found, it can be processed in the payroll system. If the form is invalid, it cannot be processed and must be sent back to the employee to complete any missing information or a new form submitted. If the department does not receive a new form, it should continue to use the information from the last valid form.

Returning invalid forms that are missing information or are improperly completed can be time consuming if done on a personalized or individual basis. However, a fast and efficient method is available. The payroll department should create a master memo that explains to the employee that his or her Form W-4 is being returned as incomplete and that the employee will need to provide the missing information before it can be processed by the payroll department. The form letter, along with the Form W-4, should be sent back to the employee. Missing information should be highlighted and the memo should instruct the employee to complete the highlighted areas. A sample memo is shown in Exhibit 1.5.

EXHIBIT 1.5

Sample Memo for Missing Information on the Form W-4

From: The payroll department
To: Insert employee's name here
Re: Incomplete Form W-4

Dear: Insert employee's name here

The payroll department has received your Form W-4, dated (insert date of form here). However, we are unable to complete the processing of the form due to missing information. Please provide the required information where we have highlighted the form in yellow.

When you have finished providing the missing information, please return the form to the payroll office.

Thank you for your prompt attention to this matter.

A separate form letter should be written for a Form W-4 that cannot be accepted at all due to improper completion. This memo should request that the employee submit a new Form W-4 and explain why the present one cannot be accepted as is. A sample memo is shown in Exhibit 1.6.

The payroll department must keep in mind that as long as the employee has submitted a valid form, it is not the duty of the department to determine whether the employee has requested the correct marital status and number of allowances. This is strictly between the employee and the Internal Revenue Service.

(c) Processing the Form

Once the Form W-4 has been validated, it needs to be processed through the payroll. Although every payroll department has its own methods and requirements for inputting a Form W-4 to the payroll system, there are several tasks that all departments must do regardless of the type of payroll system:

Date Stamping. The form should be date stamped several times during the course of processing the form. These should include the date the form is received in the payroll department, the date the audit of the form is completed, and the date it is processed in the payroll system itself. All of

EXHIBIT 1.6

Sample Memo for Invalid Form W-4

From: The payroll department
To: Insert employee's name
Re: Invalid Form W-4 submitted to payroll

Dear: Insert employee's name here

It is necessary for the payroll department to return your Form W-4, dated (insert date of form here). We are unable to process the form. IRS regulations do no allow us to accept and/or process any Form W-4 that claims a fixed dollar amount only or a percentage.

According to the IRS:

The amount of income tax withholding must be based on marital status and number of allowances only. You may specify any additional dollar amount as well.

If you still wish to change your withholding, please complete a new Form W-4 and submit it to payroll at your earliest convenience.

these date stamps are highly recommended as they create an excellent processing trail. But where to put the date stamp is important as well. The face of the form should never be marred with any type of marks by payroll including date stamping. The face of the form is basically the area between the two black lines at the top and bottom of the form. See item 13 in Exhibit 1.4 for an example of this area. The date stamp may be placed on the back of the form, or above or below the face of the form. For larger departments where more than one employee may be involved in the processing of the form, initials should accompany the date stamps to keep track of who handled which tasks. Again, this also creates an excellent processing audit trail.

Sending Forms to the IRS. Generally, the payroll department must send to the IRS copies of certain Forms W-4 that are received during the quarter from employees still employed by the company at the end of the quarter. The payroll department must send copies of Form W-4 when the employee claims (1) more than 10 withholding allowances or (2) exemption from withholding and his or her wages would normally be more than $200 per week. The copies should be sent to the IRS office where the Form 941 is filed. The payroll department is not required to send any other Forms W-4 unless the IRS notifies it in writing to do so. The forms should be sent with the Form 941, if possible. The payroll department should complete boxes 8 and 10 on any Forms W-4 that are sent in. The department may use box 9 to identify the office responsible for processing the employee's payroll information. If the employee submitted any written statements in support of the claims made on his or her Forms W-4, these statements should be sent as well, even if the Forms W-4 are not in effect at the end of the quarter. The forms may be sent to the IRS more often if the department chooses to do so. When sending in Forms W-4 to the IRS without the Form 941, the department should include a cover letter giving the company's name, address, EIN, and the number of forms included. The department should use the "Return Without a Payment" address on the Form 941 when sending forms to the IRS separately from Form 941. In certain cases, the IRS may notify the company in writing that it must submit specified Forms W-4 more frequently, separate from the Form 941.

Base any employee income tax withholding on the Forms W-4 that are sent in unless the IRS notifies the payroll department in writing to do otherwise. If the IRS notifies the department about a particular employee, base his or her income tax withholding on the number of withholding allowances shown in the IRS notice. The employee will get a similar notice directly from the IRS. If the employee later gives the payroll department a new Form W-4, follow it only if: exempt status is not claimed or the number of withholding allowances is equal to or lower than the number in the IRS notice. Otherwise, disregard it and do not submit it to the IRS. Continue to follow the IRS notice.

If the employee prepares a new Form W-4 explaining any difference with the IRS notice, he or she may either submit it to the IRS or to the payroll department. If submitted to the department, send the Form W-4 and an explanation to the IRS office shown in the notice. Continue to withhold based on the notice until the IRS tells the department to follow the new Form W-4.

(d) Record Retention

The Form W-4 is covered under the IRS regulations concerning all tax records. These are:

- Keep all records of employment taxes for at least four years. These should be available for IRS review. Records should include:
  - Employer identification number (EIN)
  - Amounts and dates of all wage, annuity, and pension payments
  - Amounts of tips reported
  - Records of allocated tips
  - The fair market value of in-kind wages paid
  - Names, addresses, Social Security numbers, and occupations of employees and recipients
  - Any employee copies of Forms W-2 and W-2c that are returned as undeliverable
  - Dates of employment
  - Periods for which employees and recipients were paid while absent due to sickness or injury and the amount and weekly rate of payments you or third-party payers made to them
  - Copies of employees' and recipients' income tax withholding allowance certificates (Forms W-4, W-4P, W-4S, and W-4V)
  - Dates and amounts of tax deposits made and acknowledgment numbers for deposits made by EFTPS
  - Copies of returns filed, including Form 941 TeleFile Tax Records and confirmation numbers
  - Records of fringe benefits provided, including substantiation

The forms can be maintained in the employee's personnel or payroll file, as a group with all the forms together or by year. It is up to the payroll department to determine the method of filing. Records may be kept electronically or on paper, whichever the department's preference. Bear in mind that once a Form W-4 has been submitted to the payroll department, it is to be kept until it is replaced by another Form W-4. The replaced Form W-4 must then be kept for four years.

1.3 NEW HIRES

Hiring new employees is a basic fact of life in the business world. Employees are terminated or resign voluntarily and new ones must be hired to take their place. This process of hiring new employees has a direct result on the payroll department. Each new hire must be processed into the payroll system in time to receive his or her first payroll check. Quick and accurate input of a new employee's information is vital to running an efficient payroll department.

(a) Should Payroll Process New Hires?

This question has been argued for decades. Is it better, faster, and more efficient for payroll to input new hire data or should human resources do the input to help with separation of duties and to ensure that the information they need (e.g., benefits, EEO, etc.) is input? In fact, in companies where payroll reports to one department head (e.g., finance) and human resources to another, establishing who is responsible for new hire input has turned into a power play. Interdepartmental squabbles aside, the question is simple: is it more efficient for payroll to input new hire data? In fact, there are both pros and cons to having the payroll department do the input. As demonstrated in the following points, there are very valid arguments to both sides of this issue:

- *Pro:* Control over input by payroll helps ensure that the data will be input on time and on schedule for processing each payroll.
- *Con:* Having the same department and possibly the same employee who is responsible for both set up of new hires and processing of paychecks could be a potential prob-

lem. This could lead to fraud and theft and does not pass standard internal auditing procedures.

- *Pro:* Having payroll input the new hire data limits access of employee data to only one department.
- *Con:* Payroll must input all data needed by all departments. This would include data on masterfiles and screens in the payroll system that it does not use or need. This adds extra work for the department.
- *Pro:* Payroll is responsible for reporting data to outside government agencies and is under threat of stiff penalties for inaccurate data. Having the payroll department input its own data assists in the verification process of the data.
- *Pro:* Input to the payroll masterfile does require knowledge of the system and payroll. This knowledge is not always available in other departments that may do this input (such as human resources).

As demonstrated by the pros and cons listed above, the argument can be made for both methods of input. So no matter which department does the actual input, efficiency of input and accuracy of the data must be the foremost consideration for the payroll department.

(b) Auditing New Hire Data for Processing

When an employee is hired, he or she usually must complete a whole battery of paperwork and forms—information the human resources department must have to process items such as the employee's benefits, EEO reports, and so on. The payroll department also needs this information to perform its function and begin paying the employee. But the collection of the necessary data differs slightly for the payroll department. Before payroll can accept such basic information as name and Social Security number, the information must be verified by comparing it to official government records.

The IRS requires that the employee's name and Social Security number on the Form W-2 and the name and number on the Social Security card match exactly. If they do not match when the Form W-2 is submitted at year end, penalties may be incurred by the company. The most accurate way to perform this task is to compare the physical social security card to the employee's information provided in the new hire paperwork. Unlike years ago, most people now who are reporting for work for the first time and know they will need to complete the new hire paperwork bring along their social security card. The reason for this is simple. When the human resources department completes the new hire package one form that must be done is the Form I-9 that verifies the employee's eligibility to work in the United States. One of the forms of identification that may be presented is the social security card, but it is not the only one. Therefore, the payroll department needs to have whoever is verifying the Form I-9 to also verify the employee's name and social security number to the social security card information if the card is presented. If it is not done then, the payroll department must make arrangements for this verification to be done independently of the new hire process.

In fact, if the Form I-9 is handled by the human resources department, the H.R. staff member may be reluctant to handle this verification because regulations concerning the Form I-9 specify that the employer can not require a certain form of identification but must accept what the employee offers, as long as it falls within the regulation's guidelines. One way to circumvent this situation is to have the staff member who is processing the new hire wait until the Form I-9 has been completed, and then do the social security card verification as an independent process. A very efficient method to ensure this step is done is to add it to the new employee paperwork processing. If a checklist is used to verify that all steps have been completed on a new hire packet, this verification could be added to the checklist. If a new hire packet is considered ready for input when all forms are verified as complete, then a form could be added that requests this verification and confirms it with a signature line.

There is an alternate method that may be used to at least determine if the physical verification of the social security card is necessary. This method may be helpful if the department handling the Form I-9 is hesitant about verifying the social security card or if the payroll department cannot physically verify each card due to location or logistics. This method is offered by the Social Security Administration and is known as EVS (Employee Verification Service). This is a free service offered to employers to assist companies in verifying the employee's name and social security number prior to it being reported to the Social Security Administration (SSA). EVS is simple. The payroll department contacts the Social Security Administration (for contact information, see the bulleted list that follows). The department furnishes the employee's name and social security number as shown in the payroll records. The SSA then compares the data to its files. If the records match, the SSA will give the payroll department a "yes." However, if the records do not match, the payroll department will receive a "no" but the SSA will not give the employer the correct information. It is up to the payroll department to contact the employee directly to physically verify the employee's social security card against the payroll records. With this method, the only time payroll would need to physically verify a social security card is when a "no match" indicator is returned by the SSA. This saves staff time and energy verifying all new hire packets. The submission to the SSA could be done on a regular basis, such as submitting all new hires for the month of June so that they are verified by July 1. With a regular submission system in place, the payroll department can make sure that all employee information will be verified prior to year end processing.

The three methods for contacting the SSA and providing them with the employee's name and social security number are:

- *Phone:* Up to 5 Names/SSNs—They can be verified over the phone. Call 1-800-772-6270 and have available the Company Name and Employer Identification Number and the employee's full name, SSN, date of birth, and gender.

- *Fax:* Up to 50 Names/SSNs—Contact the local Social Security office for the fax number. It can be found on the SSA website or in the local phone book.

- *Electronic:* Over 50 Names/SSNs—They can be submitted on magnetic tape, cartridge, diskette, or paper. A simple registration process is required. See the Social Security's Publication *Employee Verification Service Instructions* for registration information, file format instructions, and more. This publication is also on the SSA website at www.socialsecurity.gov.

(c) Processing New Hires

Once the company has decided which department will input new hires, a new hire processing schedule must be established to ensure that all new hires are set up in the payroll system in time to receive the first paycheck. It is extremely inefficient and costly to have the payroll department constantly cutting manual checks for newly hired employees whose paperwork was not processed on time.

How this schedule is set up depends on which department does the input. If the payroll department is handling the input, it must receive all the new hire paperwork on or before the day the masterfile input is done. This requirement must be determined for the calendar year and then the dates must be supplied to human resources or to whoever is responsible for processing new hires. It is imperative that this department understands that these deadlines are not merely suggestions if the payroll is to be processed efficiently and in the most cost effective manner possible.

If a department other than payroll is inputting the new hire information, the same type of calendar must be established. But in this case it will need to reflect the deadline for when the new hire input must be completed in order to meet payroll's processing deadline.

(d) Record Retention

The record retention for the information contained in the new hire packet is extremely complicated. Numerous government agencies and regulatory acts each have requirements for what to retain and for how long. As the information applies to payroll, the record retention requirements follow the same guidelines that are discussed in Section 1.1, Time Records. It is important to note that if the payroll department is responsible for retaining the entire new hire packet, it will need to verify the record retention requirements for all records (such as Form I-9) not just those that are payroll related.

1.4   ERRORS AND CORRECTIONS

No matter how efficient a payroll department is or how accurate it attempts to be, occasionally errors will occur on an employee's paycheck. These errors could be caused by underreporting time on a time record, overpayments of time, or late submission of time records. No matter what the reason for the error, the payroll department must correct the employee's paycheck.

(a) When to Issue a Manual Check: Setting a Policy

It is very important for an efficient payroll department to have a manual check policy. Manual check is a term that is used to indicate any check that is issued off a normal payroll cycle. Although nowadays most payroll departments use their computer systems to issue these types of checks, it is still widely referred to as a manual check. This type of check takes time and extra work for a payroll department including the actual calculations and processing in addition to tax deposits and updates to payroll systems that may have to be performed. This policy basically states in writing when a manual check may be issued and essentially eliminates any confusion as to when one can be requested. Of course, exceptions do occur, but it is helpful to have this policy established beforehand with all the parties concerned. When it comes to underpayments to employees, federal and state regulations address how and when an employee must be paid, so consult and these laws before establishing any manual check policies. The following is an outline of a typical manual check policy:

When to Issue

For all new employees who are due wages but, due to time restraints, could not receive system-generated checks.

For all terminating employees on date and time of termination. Many states now require payout on date and time of termination by statute.

For vacation advances, if policy allows and sufficient time was given to the payroll department. One time frame used is three days.

Errors made by the payroll department or other company entities on time sheet, etc., that resulted in underpayment to the employee. Usually issued on a material worth basis.

Example of policy: if over $45.00 or one day's pay then issue; if not, correct on next available payroll.

Bona fide emergency situation. Definition of bona fide emergency situation: The employee is in a situation that would affect life, health, or environment for himself or his family. For examples, (1) family emergency out of state; (2) to pay for medical treatment for self, family, or pets; or (3) loss of home or personal property.

If the policy is issued in writing, then it is easier for the payroll department to turn down a request for a check if it falls outside of these guidelines. That said, the payroll department should deny emergency requests *only* after careful consideration. To each employee, his or her need for a manual check is a matter of life and death, even if the rest of the world does not see it that way. To retain goodwill among employees, always listen to each employee and base the decision to cut a manual check on the individual case. Remember, although efficiency is important in the payroll department, compassion and confidentiality are equally important.

(b) Handling Late Time Records and Underpays

If a payroll department has communicated its needs correctly to all other departments, the late submission of time records should be kept to a minimum. Of course, there are always a few habitual exceptions to this rule and these will be discussed later in this section. Occasionally, however, a time record will be submitted late due to circumstances beyond anyone's control—the employee was suddenly out sick, there was an honest oversight, and so on. Whatever the reason, every so often a time record will be submitted too late for processing with the current payroll cycle. However, the late submission does not change one basic fact—the employee must be paid on time. Failing to do so constitutes a violation of wage and hour laws. One quick note here is needed. The payroll department must be on the constant alert for any supervisor or manager who wants to use the payroll department as a "personnel training" tool. It was very common years ago and still sometimes occurs today: A supervisor believes that he or she can punish an employee by delaying his or her paycheck. This is especially true for employees who habitually submit late time records to the supervisor. The supervisor may then feel justified in holding up the employee's paycheck. Make it department policy: Withholding an employee's wages is not a training method and should never be used as such.

As payroll has no other recourse but to process a manual check for any employee whose time record is submitted late, the payroll department must make sure that all other departments understand the processing schedule and when time records must be submitted. How to do this is discussed in depth in Section 2.4. However, as mentioned earlier, there always seem to be one or two departments or supervisors who do not follow the submission timetable and who habitually submit time records late. When this occurs, it is best to handle the matter on a higher level than manager to manager. Supervisors and managers who habitually submit late time records cost the payroll department its efficiency and the company money on the needless expense of preparing manual checks. So if the payroll department has made its processing submission schedule clear to all other departments, it must not back off from its responsibility to keep the company in compliance and maintain its own efficiency. Of course, as stated previously, the occasional late time record will happen and is just part of the cost of doing business. But if more than 1 percent of time records must be habitually processed via a manual check, then this is unacceptable. The payroll department should begin tracking which supervisor or employee or department is responsible. The matter should then be handled through the appropriate channels within the company guidelines. Remember that this is not the time to complain about the amount of extra work that is being created but about the extra costs involved. It is always better to focus on the bottom line.

What should the payroll department do if the employee's time record is submitted on time and processed through the system but the record itself is incorrect? Perhaps the employee did not record all the regular hours worked, left off overtime, or forgot to request vacation or sick time. Whatever the reason, when an employee is underpaid, the payroll department must handle the situation immediately. But does that mean a manual check must be prepared? Not necessarily. In the case of overtime, federal law and most states allow overtime to be paid on the following payroll check, so the missing time could be added to the next payroll. Maybe the amount of time that was omitted is very small and not really worth a separate check. This is exactly why a manual check policy should be in effect. This way, management has agreed when manual checks will be issued, supervisors and employees have been informed under what circumstances manual checks will be issued, and all the regulations have been thoroughly researched before the situation arises.

(c) What to Do When Payroll Overpays an Employee

On occasion, a mistake will be made and an employee will be overpaid. This could be the result of a processing error that went undiscovered during the edit process, an error in recording time on a time record, or a terminated employee being issued a payroll check in error. No matter what the reason for the overpayment, as soon as the error is discovered it needs to be corrected immediately. As with underpayments, wage and hour laws on the state level as well as federal regulations could also address how overpayments should be handled. These regulations should be consulted before establishing any policy. But a policy does need to be established along with the manual check policy. Exhibit 1.7 demonstrates how an efficient payroll department might handle overpayments. Again, an official policy should be established, documented, and conveyed to the employees *before* the situation arises.

If the department decides to withhold the overpayment out of the employee's next paycheck, the employee should be informed in advance of any deductions. It is best to have a preset form (that has been approved by legal advisors) that clearly states the amount of the overpayment, the amount of each deduction (if being done on more than one payroll) and the paydays involved. The employee should sign the form, if possible. In most states and under federal law, an overpayment is considered an advance on wages and may be recovered. But the payroll department will be adjusting the employee's

EXHIBIT 1.7

Examples of How to Handle Overpayments

Possible Situation	Suggested Solution
The employee is overpaid but the physical check has not been cashed.	The employee should return the check to the payroll department. The check is then voided and a check for the correct amount is issued.
The direct deposit has not been processed and can be recalled.	This should be done at once. Time is of the essence when handling direct deposits. The correct payroll check could be given to the employee as a paper check. Or, if possible, the correct payroll check could be wired into the employee's bank account.
Either the direct deposit cannot be recalled or the employee has cashed the payroll check.	If this occurs, the payroll department can recoup the money in three ways: 1. Deduct the entire overpayment from the next payroll check. 2. Have a set amount deducted from the next certain number of payroll checks. 3. Have the employee return just the overpayment amount via a personal check.

wages, so a very clear audit trail is essential. All overpayments should be documented down to the last detail and attached to the processing paperwork. The audit trail should also include proof that the employee is aware of the overpayment and the solution being used by payroll to retrieve the monies.

If the payroll department decides to have the employee return the overpayment via a personal check, an adjustment in the payroll system will be required to ensure that the employee's Form W-2 is correct and that all taxes have been adjusted as well. The employee returns the net pay of the overpayment, but the taxes and gross pay must be calculated and this also must be adjusted in the system.

All of the methods discussed should be written in the company's procedures manual. The procedures should be cleared by the legal department and by management in advance. This way when an overpayment does occur, the procedure has been documented and known to all parties involved from the outset.

If the overpayment is the result of a terminated employee being paid by mistake, the recovery of the monies is much more difficult. Some employers make the conscious decision not to pursue the return of overpayments to terminated employees, the logic being that it would cost more in staff labor costs than the amount of the overpayment. Other companies believe that any overpayment needs to be recovered. Some companies make the decision on a case-by-case basis, taking into consideration the amount of the overpayment and the individual circumstances. Whatever the policy, it should be formalized and documented in writing.

How to collect overpayments of wages from terminated employees is a difficult question to answer. Many factors affect the outcome. These include under what conditions the employee left the company and how long ago. Errors discovered at year end (one of the more common times to discover such errors) may affect an employee who has been gone from the company for months. Other times, it may be the next payroll after the employee has departed. But one of the most efficient methods for collecting overpayments to terminated employees is to simply write a letter to the employee, explain the situation in simple terms, provide thorough backup to prove the overpayment, and request that the overpayment be returned via a personal check. The letter should be polite and should contain an apology for the error and inconvenience. A self addressed stamped envelope should also be included so the employee can send the check back to payroll without incurring any costs. If there is no response, the letter is returned because the employee has relocated, or a refusal is received, then the matter should go straight to the legal channels available to the company. These may include using in house counsel to send a more strongly worded letter, or perhaps the matter will be taken up in small claims court. The recourse chosen depends on the policy the employer has in place.

1.5 PAYROLL RECONCILIATION, TAX DEPOSITS, AND QUARTERLY REPORTING

The payroll department devotes a great deal of time and energy to producing the payrolls including handling employee requests, interacting with human resources over new hires or benefits, and racing to finish all the time record input. But once the payroll is processed and the paychecks are disbursed, the department must concentrate on the accounting side of payroll. The payroll must be reconciled; tax deposits posted and paid; and if it is quarter end, quarterly reconciliation duties need to be handled.

(a) Reconciliation of the Payroll

Reconciliation has been described as bringing two or more items into agreement. This can be applied to payroll as well. The time has long passed since the payrolls were computed by hand and huge reports had to be created manually to record the payrolls. The computer system now handles all the report creation and posting of the payroll. However, it is possible that the integrity of the accumulator information or the integrity of the data could be compromised, so the payroll department should still be creating a spreadsheet to reconcile the payroll. It is to the payroll department's advantage to reconcile the payroll regularly and to avoid the "January 941-W-2 reconciliation crunch." Because the computer system tracks this necessary information, there is no reason to wait until January. The following reconciliations should be regularly prepared by the payroll department as follows:

- *Current Payroll.* The total amounts of the current payroll are input into the spreadsheet. These totals are then added to the month to date, quarter to date, and year to date totals. These totals are then compared to the payroll totals. They should match. The amounts to be included in this review are:
  - Gross wages
  - Social security taxable wages
  - Medicare taxable wages
  - Federal income taxable wages
  - Federal income tax withheld
  - Social security tax withheld
  - Medicare tax withheld

- ○ State taxable wages
- ○ State tax withheld
- ○ Payroll deductions that reduce taxable wage can also be tracked, if desired
- ○ *Garnishments* (discussed in Section 1.6)
- ○ *Tax Deposits* (discussed in the next subsection)

A sample spreadsheet is shown in Exhibit 1.8.

Because payroll transactions flow through a company's entire accounting system, the reliability of payroll data affects the accuracy of overall financial reporting. Payroll transactions hit the books in other corporate departments for further reconciliations and reporting. Hence, do not overlook the payroll department's role in contributing to the accurate measurement of corporate profitability. For example, a mistake in labor hours could affect the cost of goods sold on the income statement and ultimately the value of inventory on the balance sheet.

While payroll managers do not have to be CPAs, they do have to be conversant with basic payroll accounting to make sure that all withholding and deductions are accurately accounted for and properly reported. In reconciling the payroll, the department must also include reconciling the general ledger. It is important for an efficient payroll department to make sure that the information it feeds to the other departments is accurate. It must also make sure that the general ledger accounts the department is responsible for have been reconciled. Most companies today have integrated payroll and G/L systems so that once the payroll is produced, the amounts paid are automatically disseminated to the pertinent G/L accounts. Still, all payroll-related G/L accounts should be reviewed each month. Immediately after month end, any required adjusting entries should be made.

(b) Setting Up a Tax Deposit Schedule

A spreadsheet to track tax deposits is also very useful in keeping the payroll department efficient. Each tax deducted from payroll is listed. In addition, the computed taxes are calculated. These include social security and Medicare. This is done by list-

EXHIBIT 1.8

Payroll Reconciliation 2005

Payroll Date	FIT Wages	FIT Withheld	Social Security Wages	Social Security Withheld	Medicare Wages	Medicare Withheld	Total FICA Wages	FIT To Be Paid	FIT Paid	Social Security To Be Paid	Social Security Paid	Medicare To Be Paid	Medicare Paid	Total FICA To Be Paid	Total FICA Paid	Total Tax Due	Total Deposit (EFT Amount)	Check Number	Check Date
Payroll Totals																			
Manual Corrections																			
Corrected Payroll Totals																			
Reported 941 Totals																			
Discrepancies																			

EXHIBIT 1.8 (CONTINUED)

Quarter	FIT Wages	FIT Withheld	Social Security Wages	Social Security Withheld	Medicare Wages	Medicare Withheld
1st						
2nd						
3rd						
4th						
Year						
Adjustments:						
1st Quarter						
2nd Quarter						
3rd Quarter						
4th Quarter						
941c						
Final Total	$0.00	$0.00	$0.00	$0.00	$0.00	$0.00

ing the taxable wages for each tax and having the spreadsheet do the math. The spreadsheet then tells the payroll department what the deposit should be. Then the deposit due dates and amounts are listed. When the deposits are made, this information is then noted on the spreadsheet. This includes the check numbers or EFT confirmations for the deposits. This comes in very handy when completing the Form 941 Schedule B and in reconciling and IRS notices. A sample spreadsheet is included in Exhibit 1.8. If desired, the payroll reconciliation spreadsheet and the tax deposit spreadsheet can be combined.

(c) Setting Up a Quarterly Reporting Schedule

If a company has only one employer identification number and is located in one state, it probably does not need to set up a quarterly reporting schedule. But if the payroll is multi-state or has multiple EINs, then the most efficient method for tracking quarterly returns is to create a spreadsheet. On the spreadsheet, list each EIN for the federal return. Then list each state and each return due for that state. Indicate when each return is due. Note the source of the report if it is not received through the mail. Include the date when each preprinted return is received. List the date each report is completed and when it is mailed. This spreadsheet is extremely helpful to ensure that all quarterly returns are completed on time. It is especially helpful if the preparation of the quarterly returns is outsourced. This list can be used to track when the preprinted quarterly returns are received and when they are forwarded to the vendor.

(d) Quarterly Reconciliations

Before making the final federal tax payment for the quarter, the payroll department should complete a draft version of the Form 941. This draft version becomes the worksheet to verify the totals for the quarter. The spreadsheets are then used to reconcile the tax deposits to the draft Form 941. Any errors can be discovered quickly. If an error is discovered, a deposit should be made immediately. This deposit is then included on the final version of Form 941.

1.6 GARNISHMENTS

One of the more labor-intensive tasks the payroll department must tackle is handling garnishments. Whether it is for child support, a tax levy, or a creditor garnishment, keeping the company in compliance with the myriad laws, rules, and regulations that govern garnishments is a daunting challenge for the payroll professional. This is especially true for the payroll department that wants to do it efficiently. But it can be done. The key to handling garnishments efficiently is communications. The payroll department needs to communicate with the employee as well as with the issuing party from the time the garnishment is received up until it is satisfied or rescinded.

When a garnishment is received in the payroll department it must be handled immediately. This is one task that cannot wait for the dozens of other tasks that may have come before it. Garnishments are time sensitive and failure to process the garnishment within the allotted time frame can lead to penalties for the company. With the increase in the number of garnishments that payroll departments are receiving, it has become a full-time position or a sub-department within many payroll departments (similar to how benefits departments have begun to break away from human resources).

When a garnishment is received by the payroll department it must be examined, set up, processed, and reconciled. For a department to do this efficiently, each garnishment must be handled in the exact same manner to prevent any required steps from falling through the cracks. The payroll department should create written procedures for handling garnishments. This is not a task that should be done by memory or rote, even if the staff member handling the garnishment has "20 years of payroll experience." A checklist should be used with each garnishment to ensure that every step has been completed and then the checklist should be filed with the garnishment for a complete audit trail.

(a) Setting Up Garnishment Files

It does not matter if the company receives only a few garnishments a year or thousands; all of them still must be handled the same way. The steps for setting up a garnishment for processing include:

Step 1. Payroll First. All garnishments (or what appears to be a garnishment or what could be a garnishment) should always come to the payroll department first. Hand delivered garnishments are very rare; most garnishments are mailed to the employer these days. So when the garnishment is received in the mailroom, this is the first opportunity for it to go astray or for security to be breached. Therefore, the payroll department must set up a list of all possible return addresses that could signal a garnishment is inside the envelope. First, the payroll department needs to create a list of the exact names and addresses of the federal and state agencies it knows has, will, or could send a garnishment to them. This list should include all the agencies for the states in which the company is located that issue state tax levies, the IRS, and all child support agencies the department is currently aware of. In addition, the list of agencies for each state that handles defaults on student loans should be included. A copy of this list is included in Exhibit 1.9, but it is usually furnished with the student loan garnishment. Then the payroll department needs to create additional generic names for garnishments that may come from agencies or states with which the department has not yet had first-hand contact. This list could include names and addresses such as:

- Anything with "Child Support" in the address
- Any state agencies with the word "Revenue" in the title
- Anything with the words "sheriff," "marshal," "wage attachment," "wage assignment," or "clerk of the court" in the address

EXHIBIT 1.9

Student Loan Address List for the Mail Room

The directory below lists the names and mailing addresses of the various guaranty agencies for each state that are authorized to collect on defaulted student loans.

ALABAMA
See Kentucky

ALASKA
See USAF*

ARIZONA
See USAF*

ARKANSAS
Agency: Student Loan Guarantee
   Foundation of Arkansas
Mailing address: 219 South Victory
Little Rock, Arkansas 72201-1884

CALIFORNIA
Agency: California Student Aid
   Commission

Mailing address: P.O. Box 510845
Sacramento, California 94245-0845

COLORADO
Agency: Colorado Student Loan
   Program
Mailing address: Denver Place
999 18th Street, Suite 425
Denver, Colorado 80202-2471

CONNECTICUT
Agency: Connecticut Student Loan
   Foundation
Mailing address: P.O. Box 1009
Rocky Hill, Connecticut 06067

DELAWARE
See PHEAA (Pennsylvania)

Exhibit 1.9 *(CONTINUED)*

Student Loan Address List for the Mail Room

DISTRICT OF COLUMBIA
See ASA (Massachusetts)

FLORIDA
Agency: Florida Department of Education, Office of Student Financial Assistance
Mailing Address: 325 West Gaines Street
255 Collins Building, Room 255
Tallahassee, Florida 32399-0400

GEORGIA
Agency: Georgia Higher Education Assistance Corporation
Mailing address: 2082 East Exchange Place
Suite 200
Tucker, Georgia 30084

HAWAII AND THE PACIFIC ISLANDS
See USAF*

IDAHO
Agency: Northwest Education Loan Association (NELA)
Mailing address: 811 First Avenue
500 Colman Building
Seattle, Washington 98104

ILLINOIS
Agency: Illinois Student Assistance Commission
Mailing address: 1755 Lake Cook Road
Deerfield, Illinois 60015

INDIANA
See USAF*

IOWA
Agency: Iowa College Student Aid Commission
Mailing address: 200 10th Street, 4th Floor
Des Moines, Iowa 50309-3609

KANSAS
See USAF*

KENTUCKY
Agency: Kentucky Higher Education Assistance Authority
Mailing address: 1050 U.S. 127 South
Frankfort, Kentucky 40601-4323

LOUISIANA
Agency: Louisiana Office of Student Financial Assistance
Mailing address: P.O. Box 91202
Baton Rouge, Louisiana 70821-9202

MAINE
Agency: Maine Education Assistance Division, Finance Authority of Maine
Mailing address: #119 State House Station
One Weston Court
Augusta, Maine 04333

MARYLAND
See USAF*

MASSACHUSETTS
Agency: American Student Assistance (ASA)
Mailing address: 330 Stuart Street
Boston, Massachusetts 02116-5292

MICHIGAN
Agency: Michigan Higher Education Assistance Authority
Mailing address: P.O. Box 30047
Lansing, Michigan 48909

MINNESOTA (NORTHSTAR)
See Wisconsin (Great Lakes)

MISSISSIPPI
See USAF*

EXHIBIT 1.9 *(CONTINUED)*

Student Loan Address List for the Mail Room

MISSOURI
Agency: Coordinating Board for Higher
    Education
Mailing address: 3515 Amazonas Drive
Jefferson City, Missouri 65109-5717

MONTANA
Agency: Montana Guaranteed Student
    Loan Program
Mailing address: P.O. Box 203101
Helena, Montana 59620-3101

NEBRASKA
Agency: Nebraska Student Loan
    Program
Mailing address: P.O. Box 82507
Lincoln, Nebraska 68501-2507

NEVADA
See USAF*

NEW HAMPSHIRE
Agency: New Hampshire Higher
    Education Assistance Foundation
Mailing address: P.O. Box 877
Concord, New Hampshire 03302-0877

NEW JERSEY
Agency: New Jersey Higher Education
    Assistance Authority
Mailing address: 4 Quakerbridge Plaza
CN 540
Trenton, New Jersey 08625

NEW MEXICO
Agency: New Mexico Student Loan
    Guarantee Corporation
Mailing address: P.O. Box 27020
Albuquerque, New Mexico 87125-7020

NEW YORK
Agency: New York State Higher Education
    Services Corporation
Mailing address: 99 Washington Avenue
Albany, New York 12255

NORTH CAROLINA
Agency: North Carolina State Education
    Assistance Authority
Mailing address: P.O. Box 2688
Chapel Hill, North Carolina 27515-2688

NORTH DAKOTA
Agency: Student Loans of North Dakota–
    Guarantor
Mailing address: P.O. Box 5524
Bismarck, North Dakota 58506-5524

OHIO
Agency: Ohio Student Aid Commission
Mailing address: P.O. Box 16610
Columbus, Ohio 43216-6610

OKLAHOMA
Agency: Oklahoma Guaranteed Student
    Loan Program
Mailing address: P.O. Box 3000
Oklahoma City, Oklahoma 73101-3000

OREGON
Agency: Oregon State Scholarship
    Commission
Mailing address: 1500 Valley River Drive
Suite 100
Eugene, Oregon 97401

PENNSYLVANIA (PHEAA)
Agency: Pennsylvania Higher Education
    Assistance Agency
Mailing address: 1200 North 7th Street
Harrisburg, Pennsylvania 17102-1444

RHODE ISLAND
Agency: Rhode Island Higher Education
    Assistance Authority
Mailing address: 560 Jefferson Boulevard
Warwick, Rhode Island 02886-1320

EXHIBIT 1.9 *(CONTINUED)*

Student Loan Address List for the Mail Room

SOUTH CAROLINA
Agency: South Carolina State Education
    Assistance Authority
Mailing address: P.O. Box 210219
Interstate Center, Suite 210
Columbia, South Carolina 29221

SOUTH DAKOTA
Agency: Education Assistance Corporation
Mailing address: 115 First Avenue, SW
Aberdeen, South Dakota 57401

TENNESSEE
Agency: Tennessee Student Assistance
    Corporation
Mailing address: Parkway Towers Suite
    1950
404 James Robertson Parkway
Nashville, Tennessee 37243-0820

TEXAS
Agency: Texas Guaranteed Student Loan
    Corporation
Mailing address: P.O. Box 201725
Austin, Texas 78720-1725

UTAH
Agency: Utah Higher Education Assistance
    Authority
Mailing address: P.O. Box 45202
Salt Lake City, Utah 84145-0202

VERMONT
Agency: Vermont Student Assistance
    Corporation
Mailing address: P.O. Box 2000
Winooski, Vermont 05404-2601

VIRGINIA
See ECMC [#]

WASHINGTON
Agency: Northwest Education Loan
    Association (NELA)
Mailing address: 500 Colman Building
811 First Avenue
Seattle, Washington 98104

WEST VIRGINIA
See PHEAA (Pennsylvania)

WISCONSIN
Agency: Great Lakes Higher Education
    Corporation
Mailing address: P.O. Box 7858
Madison, Wisconsin 53707

WYOMING
See USAF*

NOTES:

*USAF = United States Aid Funds, Inc.
Mailing address: P.O. Box 6180
Indianapolis, Indiana 46206-6180

[#]ECMC = Educational Credit Management Corporation (ECMC) (Transitional
Guaranty Agency's new name)
Mailing address: American Bank Building
101 E. 5th Street, Suite 2400
St. Paul, Minnesota 55101

Step 2. Date Stamp. Every garnishment should be date stamped on the day it is received in the payroll department. This begins the audit trail and establishes the garnishment's timeline for processing.

Step 3. Verify. It is the responsibility of the payroll department to ensure that all the garnishments it processes are legal and valid. This means making sure that it is assessed to a current employee of the company, it is from the proper source, it was delivered properly on the proper form, it is completed correctly, and that it is allowed under the applicable laws. As for the legalities, some companies have decided to take this decision from payroll and turn it over to inhouse legal counsel. This is actually not a bad idea. With the complicated rules, regulations, and now case law that surround garnishments, it may be the wave of the future for payroll to work directly with counsel.

- Is it our employee? The payroll department must determine if the employee is currently working for the company by verifying the social security number and name on the garnishment against company payroll records. If the name matches but the social security number does not, that does not mean that the garnishment is invalid. It could be an error in the issuing party's records or in the payroll records. If this occurs, the payroll department needs to contact the issuing party to verify the garnishment is valid. If the garnishment does not belong to any employee on the payroll records or the employee did work for the company but is now terminated, then the payroll department needs to return the garnishment to the issuing party with a letter of explanation.

- Is it from the proper source on the proper form? A tax levy on Form 668-W from the IRS is an example of a proper source on a proper form. If it is for child support, did it come from the child support agency on an Order/Notice for Child Support or is it from an attorney's office? If it is from an attorney, it does not mean the garnishment cannot be accepted and processed. It just means that anything that comes from someone other than the normal issuing party for that type of garnishment and is not on the normal form for that the issuing party needs to be investigated further to make sure the garnishment is legal and valid.

- Is it completed correctly? Is all the proper information provided? If any required information is missing, the payroll department will need to contact the issuing agency to request that a new form either be delivered or faxed.

- Has it been delivered properly? Was it mailed directly to the payroll office or did an employee or someone else just drop it off? Depending on the type of garnishment, either way may be valid, but the payroll department must make sure that however the form was delivered, it constitutes proper delivery.

- Is it allowed under the law? Is this garnishment legal under the governing laws? Where the employee works and lives can determine what garnishments can be processed. For example: Some states do not permit creditor garnishments. If this employee works in such a state, but the employer is located in a state that does allow this type of garnishment, then the employee's work state laws would prevail. Also, are there other, higher priority garnishments ahead of it? These are some of the laws that the payroll department must research to decide if the garnishment is legal and can be processed.

Step 4. Answer Back. Once the garnishment has been determined to be valid, it must be processed through the payroll and the first step after verifying the garnishment is to answer it. Most of the garnishments received today have response forms included in the envelope with the garnishment, for example, the federal tax levy. Keep in mind that the time allotted to respond is usually very limited. Therefore, once the verification is done, the responses should be completed and returned to the issuing party immediately. If no response is included with the garnishment and state or federal laws do not require a response, then payroll can move on to the next step. However, some payroll departments prefer to always include a response. So if no response form is included, use a template created for this purpose. A more in-depth discussion of this type of form is included in Section 1.6(g).

Step 5. Tell the Employee. The employee must always be informed of garnishments that have been received. Most forms, such as the IRS Tax Levy, include parts that must be given to the employee. This required notification usually has a limited time frame as well. In addition to the required notification provided with the garnishment, the payroll department should include its own letter explaining how the garnishment will be handled in the payroll department. Proper wording for this notification is discussed further in Section 1.6(d).

Step 6. Determine the Pecking Order. If the employee has more than one garnishment, then the payroll department needs to determine the pecking order or deduction priorities for the garnishments. Different types of garnishments carry more weight under the laws than other types of garnishments and they must always be deducted before anything else. With one exception, it does not even matter in which order the garnishments were received by the payroll department. This priority order is discussed in more detail in Section 1.6(f). Once the priority order has been established, the payroll department must complete the next step before going further in the processing.

Step 7. Is There Enough Money? With one or more garnishments, the employee may not make enough money to take all the deductions required. Because garnishments are deducted from disposable or net pay (depending on the type of garnishment) and not gross wages, it is possible for the payroll department to "run out of money before running out of garnishments." The payroll department needs to determine if all of the required amounts can be deducted. If they cannot, then the payroll department needs to communicate this to the issuing party or parties. How to do this is discussed in Section 1.6(g).

Step 8. Set It up on the Payroll System. Once the previous conditions have been satisfied, the payroll department can set up the deduction on the payroll system.

Step 9. Set It up in the Payroll Files. After processing into the payroll system, the department needs to set up a file for the garnishment while it is active or store it for record retention when it has been satisfied or has become inactive. Garnishments should not be filed in one big file but each garnishment for each employee should have its own separate manila folder with the employee name, I.D. number, and garnishment type on the outside of the folder. Garnishments should be kept in a separate file drawer from all other payroll information and should never be kept in the employee's personnel or main payroll file. Although there is no "federal or state law that prohibits an employer from making a garnishment known outside of the payroll department, there are strict laws and court cases that prohibit an employee from being "disciplined" for having a garnishment. And the only efficient way to prove that the employee never received any discipline for having the garnishment is to not let anybody other than payroll know of the existence of the garnishment. This includes human resources. If payroll and human resources are common departments, extra care needs to be taken to ensure the employee's privacy. How to keep the garnishment secure in accounts payable is discussed in Section 1.6(e).

Step 10. Setting up the Garnishment. The final step is to set up the garnishment in the tracking system, which is discussed next.

(b) Creating Tracking Spreadsheets

A tracking system outside of the payroll computer system needs to be created and used if the payroll department wants to account for garnishments in an efficient manner. The computer system does not usually track a multiyear garnishment (carried over from year to year) or track when payments were made or the check number. The spreadsheets should be created as follows:

- There should be a spreadsheet for each individual garnishment that keeps a running total of the entire payment history, regardless of calendar years. This spreadsheet should contain the payroll date, the amount of the deduction, the check number and date, and the date the payment was mailed or made if done by EFT. It should have the current balance if the garnishment is a tax levy, creditor garnishment, or child support arrears.
- Reconcile the spreadsheet for the individual payroll. This reconciliation lists the deductions for that particular payroll only.
- Create a master spreadsheet that tracks the total garnishments per payroll and keeps a running month to date, quarter to date, and year to date total. This is used to reconcile the general ledger account(s).

If the staff member has the expertise, the spreadsheets can be created to automatically feed into the master spreadsheet, or individual spreadsheets can be used.

(c) Reconciliation to the Payroll System

Once the spreadsheets are created, the deduction amounts need to be reconciled back to the payroll system. The reason for the cross-references is simple. If the garnishment is paid straight off the payroll system, then if the garnishment deduction is less that the amount ordered on the garnishment, it would be hard for the staff member to know this without reconciling each individual garnishment to itself. If paid from only the paper files, then new garnishments may be missed. The cross reconciling will help make sure that all payments are made properly.

After reconciling the garnishments to the payrolls for the month, the general ledger needs to be reconciled. These spreadsheets will assist with that task.

(d) Notifying the Employee

As discussed in Section 1.6(a), the employee should be notified when a garnishment is received. Most garnishments have a form to notify the employee of the issuance of the garnishment and the payroll department must processes these forms as required. But another notification also needs to be sent to the employee. This one comes from the payroll department itself. It is not required by law, but the efficient payroll department will send it because it cuts down on employee phone calls, communicates all the information to the employee about when and how the deductions will be handled by the payroll department, and reminds the employee that the payroll department does not have the authority to delay, stop, or adjust legally served garnishments.

The notifications should take the form of a memo addressed to the employee. The payroll department should create a template for each type of garnishment that may be received. The template is then completed for each employee when a garnishment is received. The memo is sent along with a copy of the garnishment and the official notification. An example of each type of memo is illustrated in Exhibit 1.10. The memos should contain:

- The type of garnishment received

- On which payroll the deductions will begin

- The amount of the deduction, if known, or reference to the IRS tax levy chart if it should apply, or the percentage used if the garnishment is based on a percentage amount

- Contact information for the deduction amount only

- Disclaimer of the responsibility of the payroll department with regard to imposing the garnishment

When sending information to an employee concerning a garnishment, it should always be sent to the employee's home. This prevents other employees from even guessing what is in the envelope and ensures privacy for the employee.

(e) Paying the Garnishment

The payroll department handles different types of garnishments and each could have a different payment due date. Even the same type of garnishment, such as child support, may have different due dates depending on which state has jurisdiction. To be efficient, the payroll department needs to establish regular, set pay dates for garnishments. Since there could be a chance that a child support payment may be due on the date the

Exhibit **1.10**

Letter Templates for Notifying Employees

Child Support:

To: Insert employee's name
From: The garnishment section of the payroll department
RE: Child Support Order

The payroll department has received a child support order in your name. The order was received on (insert date). As required by law, this order will be processed on the (insert pay day date) payday. A deduction in the amount of (insert amount) will be taken from your wages.

A copy of the child support order and other notification paperwork has been enclosed with this notice.

The payroll department is not responsible for child support orders issued in error or for the deduction of monies for valid child support orders. If you have any questions concerning the amount of the deduction or the starting date of the deduction, please contact the payroll department via e-mail at (insert address here) or via phone at (insert number here). If you have any questions concerning the child support order itself, please contact the issuing party.

The payroll department

Federal Tax Levy:

To: Insert employee's name
From: The garnishment section of the payroll department
RE: Federal Tax Levy

The payroll department has received a federal tax levy in your name. The levy was received on (insert date). As required by law, this levy will be processed on the (insert pay day date) payday. The payroll deduction for tax levies is calculated from a chart supplied by the IRS. A copy of that chart is included with this memo.

A copy of the tax levy and the appropriate notification paperwork also has been enclosed with this notice. Please complete the employee portion as indicated and return it to the payroll department within three days. Failure to return the employer portion will not affect the processing of the tax levy.

The payroll department is not responsible for tax levies issued in error or for the deduction of monies for valid tax levies. If you have any questions concerning the amount of the deduction or the starting date of the deduction, please contact the payroll department via e-mail at (insert address here) or via phone at (insert number here).

If you have any questions concerning the tax levy itself, please contact the Internal Revenue Service.

The payroll department

EXHIBIT **1.10**   *(CONTINUED)*

Letter Templates for Notifying Employees

Creditor Garnishment:

To:	Insert employee's name
From:	The garnishment section of the payroll department
RE:	Creditor Garnishment

The payroll department has received a creditor garnishment in your name. This type of garnishment is issued by the Marshall's Office (or insert appropriate issuing agency) for the collection of an unpaid bill. The garnishment was received on (insert date). As required by law, this order will be processed on the (insert pay day date) payday. A deduction in the amount of (insert amount) will be taken from your wages.

A copy of the garnishment and other notification paperwork has been enclosed with this notice.

The payroll department is not responsible for creditor garnishments issued in error or for the deduction of monies for valid creditor garnishments. If you have any questions concerning the amount of the deduction or the starting date of the deduction, please contact the payroll department via e-mail at (insert address here) or via phone at (insert number here).

If you have any questions concerning the creditor garnishment itself, please contact the issuing party.

The payroll department

---

employee is paid, that is the best day to choose for making garnishment payments. The payroll department should process the payments for garnishments so that the checks will be available for mailing on payday or before. If making electronic payments, these should be transmitted on payday as well.

The most efficient method for producing garnishment payment checks is to request third party checks through the payroll system. However, many payroll departments do not have this option so they request the check through accounts payable. This is normally not a problem except that the accounts payable files are normally not as secure as the payroll department's. To avoid having other department supervisors or anyone else from gaining access to garnishment information, it is best to submit check requests a little differently for garnishment checks than for other checks. For example:

- Any like garnishments going to the same payee should be requested on the same check, if the receiving agency allows it. This prevents any one amount from being traceable. For example, all IRS deductions should be on one check.

- All check requests should be submitted without any identifying information other than what is absolutely necessary. For example, the name of the payee (such as the IRS) should be listed and the amount should be listed, but under "reason for check" it should simply say "garnishment deductions" and the payroll date. Neither the names of the employees involved nor the amounts of the garnishments should be listed. This information should be added to the check stub after the check is returned to the payroll department for mailing (if a list is not included with the check). In addition, no backup should be attached to the check request copy that is processed by accounts payable. Of course, the proof of the deductions needs to be attached to the check request for approval, but this can be transferred back to the payroll copy after signing. This keeps the information secure within the payroll department. To satisfy any internal audits and the like, one more item can be added to the check request: "For backup, see the payroll department."

(f) Handling Multiple Garnishments for One Employee

As discussed in Section 1.6(a), it is possible to have more than one garnishment for an employee. In fact, an employee could have several of one type of garnishment. If the employee has multiple garnishments, it is the responsibility of the payroll department to determine the amount of each deduction according to the limits established in the rules and regulations and according to the priority order. For example, under current regulations, an employer may deduct only 50 percent of disposable pay for child support. The payroll department must be sure to follow the rules for disposable pay and then take up to 50 percent to satisfy the garnishment. If the employee has two child support garnishments, the rules remain the same. The amount to deduct increases, but not the amount the deduction may be taken from. So it is possible that the payroll department may not be able to take the full amount of a garnishment. If this happens, the payroll department must follow the rules for making the deductions. These regulations can be found in the federal Consumer Credit Protection Act and in each state's statutes.

(g) Communicating with the Issuing Party

As previously stated, communication is the key to processing garnishments efficiently. This communication includes keeping the issuing parties of all garnishments informed of any variances in the amount required to be withheld and the amount actually withheld. If the payroll department must deduct less than the required amount, a letter of explanation as to why the shortage occurred should accompany the payment. The payroll department should create a template to use when communicating with the issuing party. The template should state the date the garnishment was received, acknowledgment that it is being processed, the date deductions will begin, the expected first payment date to the issuing party, and the payroll contact information. A sample template is included in Exhibit 1.11.

Other communications that are required by law between the payroll department and the issuing party of a garnishment occur when an employee terminates. It is required by most state laws to inform the issuing agency when an employee terminates if there is an active child support or medical support order in place. Some states supply the form and others just require the information to be submitted. No template is needed for this notice. A simple letter on company letterhead that communicates the required information is sufficient.

Exhibit 1.11

Answer Back Form Template

(ON COMPANY LETTERHEAD)

Date

Place issuing party contact information here

Re: Place garnishment type here

Dear Sir/Madam:

This letter is to confirm that the payroll department of ABC Company has received a (insert type of garnishment here) garnishment for our employee (insert employee full name here), social security number (insert employee's social security number here).

This garnishment was received on (insert date here). It is being processed by my department and the first deduction will be made on our (insert payday here) payday.

If you have any questions, please contact me at (insert contact information here).

Sincerely,

CHAPTER 2

Staffing the Payroll Department

2.1 CREATING A FIRST-RATE PAYROLL DEPARTMENT

Creating a first-rate payroll department is not an easy undertaking. Payroll is a unique career field and department. Few other departments can boast of so many deadlines and penalties if any one of them is missed. But as unattainable as top-notch efficiency may appear, payroll departments must always strive to achieve it.

Of course, before any goal can be met it first must be fully defined. So what exactly is a first-rate payroll department and how does a department know when it has achieved first-rate status? Like physical beauty, it can be in the eye of the beholder. However, all first-rate payroll departments have several traits in common:

- The department is run efficiently with documented procedures and standardized job functions.

- The payroll staff has an excellent mixture of experience and education.

- The payroll staff is constantly kept up to date on the latest changes in regulations and legislation.

- The department utilizes all available means to keep in constant communication with its customers.

- The department is interactive with all other departments and is especially diligent in attending meetings and other functions to represent the payroll department as conscientious and professional.

(a) Is There a Typical Payroll Department?

All first-rate (and even struggling) departments share similar traits or procedures. But is there a typical department? Surprisingly, the answer is yes. Although each company is unique with its own methods and culture, payroll departments all share one thing: they all must follow the same rules and regulations. The company policy may dictate when an employee is paid but it still must fall within the parameters of the law. All payroll departments are subject to the same deadlines and penalties if they are missed.

A typical payroll department has:

- One or more staff members who may or may not have advanced degrees but who all learned payroll the same way—on the job training.

- Constant deadlines to pay employees, deposit taxes, and produce quarterly and year-end reports and forms.

- The constant battle to have the department recognized for the excellent work it has done all year long and not just remembered for the one payroll that went wrong.

- The ability, unlike other departments, to close out the old year while simultaneously running the new year.

(b) Running the Department

If payroll departments are similar by nature, then so is the method for running them. To run a first-rate payroll department, two things are necessary: a master payroll calendar (discussed in Section 8.2) and written procedures that are followed to the letter for each task on the calendar. Of course, things come up daily that deviate from the master calendar and those things will need to be dealt with. But the calendar keeps the department constantly moving in the right direction.

(c) Creating the Payroll Department Dream Team

In a perfect world, some payroll managers feel that a payroll staff consisting entirely of Certified Payroll Professionals (CPP) with 20 years of payroll experiences each would be the dream team for payroll. But would it? Actually, blending that kind of experience with mid-level employees and first-year trainees is most likely to produce a payroll dream team. Extensive experience is always needed, but staff members with less experience are also needed to handle many of the day-to-day tasks that assist the experienced payroll professionals.

When assembling a payroll department, one of the first questions that must be answered is how many staff members are needed for the department. Several factors come into play when trying to determine this number including:

- What is the number of actual employees being paid each payroll?
- What is the number of manual checks that must be processed each payroll cycle?
- What is the number of states or federal EINs that must be processed for taxes?
- What is the number and types of benefits offered to employees? Does payroll handle any of the input?
- Does the payroll department handle the setup of new hires?
- What type of system is used and does it require extra staff due to age or to complexity?
- Is there a customer service counter that must be staffed?
- What is the garnishment workload?
- How is the time captured? Is there a time and attendance system or is time input manual with paper records?

Once the optimal number of staff members has been decided, the desired experience levels and qualifications must be determined. An efficient method for handling this task is to refer back to the payroll calendar and procedures manual. List each job that the department must perform and then start grouping them into like tasks. The necessary experience level will begin to emerge for each of the groupings. It is always best to have a large mix of experience and education so there is room for advancement for those who want it. For example, time record input and basic payroll may be done by an entry level staff member, while the multi-state tax deposits may require greater experience or even a CPP. There is, of course, higher criteria for supervisors and managers. Management experience is needed but payroll managers and supervisors also need hands-on experience in actual payroll procedures.

As the job duties gel into the staffing requirements, each position should be finalized by creating job descriptions. A well written job description clearly defines the essential functions of a job and helps to determine a job's worth in an organization. Job descriptions also form the basis for a sound (read: defensible) wage and salary structure.

But what if the payroll department is already a functioning entity? What if a new payroll department is not being created, but a long-standing department needs to be revamped? The suggestions discussed here can be applied to any payroll department. The only adjustment needed when reconfiguring an existing department is to take the experience of the current staff into consideration when organizing the jobs and tasks.

(d) Writing Procedure Manuals

It is discussed throughout this book and it bears repeating: the efficient payroll department has written procedures for each job or task it performs. Writing procedures for a payroll department is an arduous and time consuming task. But it must be done in order for the department to function at peak efficiency. Written procedures ensure that each task is done completely, accurately, and in the same manner each time it is performed. This enables the payroll department to perform each task correctly and consistently no matter how many times or who performs the duty. This is especially true in large departments, however, even single person departments can benefit from written procedures. In addition, written procedures are helpful in training new or backup personnel. Documenting procedures forces you to look at how each process is performed and helps in streamlining procedures and cleaning up bad habits that may have built up over the years. It also assists new employees and especially new supervisors or managers in assessing and evaluating office procedures in a noncombative way.

So how should a payroll professional write procedures for the department? The basic requirement to writing good, easy to follow, and accurate procedures is to write in plain and simple English and to structure your directions for someone who has absolutely no payroll background. This sounds easy enough, but is actually difficult, as payroll is a very technical field and each task usually involves multiple steps. In addition, the person writing the procedures usually has vast knowledge and experience in payroll and it is sometimes difficult for an experienced person to break the directions down to their most basic level. However, the following suggestions for writing procedures are well tested and work every time—even though at first glance they may sound a bit silly. Keep an open mind and these tips can help the department write accurate and complete procedures. The foundation of these suggestions is simple:

Write the procedures as if they were going to be used by an alien from another planet!

No, this is not a joke. If you can create a "person" in your head and keep that person in mind while writing, it really helps to keep you focused on explaining the procedures— simply and in plain English. Why an alien? Why not just use a current staff member? The reason is that because most payroll professionals don't know any aliens first hand, they will not assume their alien has any knowledge of payroll procedures. However, if they write for someone they know, such as a current staff member or backup person, they may unconsciously tailor their wording to the level of expertise they know that person has. If the person changes, the level of expertise could also change and the procedures may not be as useful. Here is an example of how to set up the "alien" in order to help you clarify your procedures.

Developing the Alien

Let's use a character called Zot from the planet Zygot. Although he is from another planet, he does know the English language. Keeping this in mind, you can, of course, write the procedures in English. However, he does not know slang, payroll terms, IRS or DOL terms, or your company's idioms. So as you write, you cannot use any of these terms without giving a full definition of the items first. Example, your company calls a new hire form the EHF (Employee Hire Form). Everyone in the company knows this term. However, a new person in training may not. That is why you cannot use it in a procedure manual until it has been explained. That is why you keep Zot in mind when writing. He would not know this term. Basically, you cannot assume that the person reading and using the procedures understands anything unless you explain it first. You can see how this can help in writing the procedures. It forces you to keep things in simple and easy terms.

Now, let's give Zot some other characteristics. Let's say he cannot go backward when reading nor can he turn to other pages but he can use a computer and he can read your payroll system and company manuals. How does this affect writing the procedures? Well, it means you cannot take shortcuts by saying things like "refer to page 13 for how to do this part" or "go back to step two." You must write out each part completely every time. However, you do not need to explain how to input to the payroll system or your company policies. You can reference the manuals when needed.

Can you develop Zot in any way? Of course you can. If your payroll department never hires anyone without at least one year of payroll experience, then give that information to Zot when writing the procedures. However, if you frequently hire payroll staff without any payroll experience, then you must always keep Zot's relative lack of experience in mind when writing.

(e) Writing the Procedures

After developing your alien, you need to begin the writing process. But how to get started is always a question. Here are a few more suggestions to assist you in the procedure writing process.

First, what procedures do you need? A good question for sure. You should start the process by making a list of everything you do in the department, no matter how simple or small an item. If it is a task that needs to be performed, it needs a procedure. Keep Zot in mind. Would he know it needed to be done or how to do it if you didn't write the procedure for it? This is your basic starting point. Then check to see if you have any old procedure manuals lying around. These might make a good starting point no matter how old, or perhaps it may be better if you started from scratch, whichever works best for you. Where to start? Just pick one procedure on your list and get started. It does not matter which one. They do not need to be done in processing or any other type of order. That will come later when you put them in your manual.

When writing the procedures, never attempt to write a procedure from scratch while actually performing the procedure during normal working hours. This tends to slow you down while you are trying to work and creates very sloppy procedures. Because your mind is faster than your hand, you may skip steps that you think are minor details or that you do automatically without thinking because you have done them so many times before.

However, never write procedures strictly from memory either. Again, you will no doubt skip steps or leave out critical details that you always remember to do when you are doing it.

Actually, the best way to write procedures is to combine the two methods. First, take a few moments and write down the procedures for the process you want to document. Do this strictly from memory. Put down everything you can remember in the proper order that you remember it. Then the next time you perform the task, take out your procedures and try to use them. Keep Zot in mind during this step. You should have written the procedures for a nonpayroll person, in plain English, with no referrals to any other sources except software or company manuals. Follow the procedures you wrote to the letter. Do not do anything not listed on your procedures. You will see very quickly how many steps you skipped or put down incorrectly and you can make notations on those while you are working. This step will need to be done several times. Remember that writing procedures is not a quick process.

When you are totally satisfied that you have the procedures done correctly and in easy to follow steps, give your procedures to another employee in the payroll department. Let them perform the task using only the procedures you wrote to see if you both agree that they are complete and accurate. If there are problem areas or disputes on how a step is to be performed, make those corrections now. If you are in a multiple person department, do not be surprised if the other person does the procedure slightly differently or in a different order. This is typical of large departments and one of the main reasons for having procedures, to ensure that everyone does the task the same way. However, if you are the sole member of your payroll department, arrange for your backup or your boss to use the procedures. This allows another pair of eyes to make sure that they are accurate and easy to follow.

When you are totally satisfied that the procedures are complete and accurate, give them to a nonpayroll person to read. This will ensure that you have not included any slang or "payrollisms" in the procedures.

Note that writing the procedures is not the end of the process. Now that the written procedures are complete and accurate, it is time to add the final touches. Make sure that you include screen prints for each procedure if they are needed and of course, samples and examples. For example, you are writing the procedures for processing a Form W-4 in your department. When you have the procedures completed, include:

- A copy of the form itself. Yes, employees should know what the form looks like, but please remember Zot.

- Samples. If you are telling the user of the procedures how the form should look when it is completed, then include an example of a completed form.

Next are a few frequently asked questions (FAQs) on procedure writing to tie up any questions you may have.

(f) FAQs Regarding Writing Procedures

Q: Should I start writing procedures using my computer or long hand?

A: This is actually a sticking point in getting started for some people. The basic answer is, do whatever you like best. You can start with paper and pen then switch to computer when you have the first basic draft down. This allows for a lot of scribbling, note making, and starts and stops, which sometimes helps to get the process going. Alternatively, you can start right away using your word processing software. It is up to you.

Q: Should the procedures be numbered in some way?

A: Yes they should. As discussed in the next question, procedures are only useful if they are readily available. You should number your procedures based on some criteria such as processing date, chronological order, or something similar.

Q: Should I put them in a notebook or combine them in some way?

A: Definitely. This is very important. When each procedure is complete, it should be included in a final book on payroll procedures. This "book" can be either paper or electronic, but all procedures should be in one place, in a logical order, and numbered. The book also should have a table of contents.

Q: Should the pages of each procedure be dated?

A: Yes. You should put the date the procedures were originally written and then each subsequent update should be listed. Each page should be dated and updated so the reader knows when that section of the procedure was changed.

Q: How often should I update my procedures?

A: That depends on the procedure. For example, if it concerns forms, then it should be updated whenever the form is. An example of this would be the Form W-4. This form is updated by the IRS every year, so the procedures should be updated as well. This should be done even if it is only to replace the sample form. Another example is processing a supplemental check. Because the supplemental rate may change each year, this procedure would have to be reviewed to ensure that the rates are correct. In general, it is a good idea to review the procedures at least annually.

Q: How long should my procedures be?

A: As long as it takes to explain the procedure in the most basic terms. Remember, word count is not critical. But also remember that longer is not necessarily better.

(g) Technology and Payroll

It is believed that payroll first began in biblical times. Since then the payroll department has followed the growth of technology from recording a transaction on papyrus to quill pens to computers and PCs. The payroll department has always embraced new technology that helps in processing the payroll more efficiently or faster. But there are other ways that modern technology can assist the payroll department besides processing paychecks.

Modern computer software helps in reconciling the payroll by allowing huge spreadsheets to de done and stored electronically. It speeds up the reconciliation process tremendously because the calculations can be done instantly. Spreadsheet software also helps in tracking garnishments, making tax deposits, and monitoring time sheet input. The efficient payroll department requires that all reconciliations and spreadsheets be done electronically. Not only is the speed and efficiency increased, but this also allows for files to be transferred between employees and departments easily and quickly without the original files ever leaving the payroll department. There are also many other types of software available to the payroll department to assist in performing necessary tasks. Word processing is especially important. Spreadsheet software should not be used for sending letters and memos and word processing software should not be used for creating spreadsheets.

But the greatest boost to the payroll department in terms of communicating with its customers is the Internet or, more precisely, e-mail. No longer are hundreds or thousands of notices or fliers printed, folded, and stuffed into the payroll checks. Now the payroll department can send a quick message to the vast majority of the employees instantly. This allows greater communication between payroll and its customers. Also indispensable is the technology of the intranet, which is a private website strictly for the employees of the company to use. This is especially useful for the payroll department. Forms, schedules, calendars, and notices can be posted for immediate access by employees.

New technology is also helping payroll make further strides toward becoming paperless. Forms W-2 may now be delivered to employees electronically and some states are allowing the pay stubs to be distributed electronically if the employee has direct deposit.

(h) Outsourcing

In creating a first-rate payroll department, it may not be efficient to process some tasks in house. In this modern age, technology may be available through a third-party vendor that can handle the task faster and more efficiently. Basically, sometimes it is just better to let someone else do it. This can apply to the entire payroll system or to just a single item, such as pay cards or the employee self service system. Whatever the task, it may be more efficient and cost effective to outsource it. More and more items are available to payroll for outsourcing to payroll processors, including garnishments. So when establishing a dream payroll team, remember that some of the tasks a staff member would do might be accomplished more efficiently through outsourcing.

2.2 MANAGING THE STAFF

There is more to managing an efficient payroll department than knowing the laws, rules, and regulations and keeping the company in compliance. There is the human factor—the staff. The human beings that comprise the payroll department are just as important a component to running an efficient payroll department as the computer system or any procedure manual. Hiring the right person for the job, giving him or her the proper training, and making sure that duties are delegated correctly goes a long way toward creating and maintaining an efficient payroll department.

(a) Hiring a Payroll Professional

Hiring staff members is a basic job function of any department manager. But hiring a staff member to join an already efficiently running payroll department or someone who will help to build one is a difficult balancing act. What should a payroll manager look for or look out for when hiring a payroll professional?

- *Question Payroll Experience.* Of course payroll experience counts if the position is other than entry level, but the payroll manager needs to make sure it is true payroll experience. Many job applicants will list payroll as one of his or her job duties. However, in actuality, all he or she did was help collect and input time cards. If you are looking to fill a time record entry position then that experience may be sufficient. But if the position requires three years of full time payroll experience, then ask more questions to determine if the applicant has the necessary experience. Asking specific questions on the exact nature of the payroll tasks, and time spent on the job devoted exclusively to the payroll function is the best way to determine true payroll experience. This is especially true of applicants who come from smaller companies with combined job duties. Many times the applicant believes that working once or twice a month in payroll is extensive payroll experience because he or she does not know the profession well enough. Questions that require the applicant to explain specific procedures, how they were performed, and how often will help you make this determination.

- *Question Payroll Knowledge.* Unless the applicant has a current CPP designation, it is probably a good bet he or she has never had his or her payroll knowledge questioned or tested. Even if the applicant has worked full time in a payroll department for five years, that does not necessarily equate to five years of payroll knowledge. Payroll is learned on the job. Unlike some other office professions, the applicant did not go to school to gain the knowledge of the basics and then apply that knowledge to build experience in the real world. The prospective employee is only as knowledgeable about payroll as the person who trained him or her. All applicants should need to take a test of his or her payroll knowledge relevant to the position they are seeking. The test should be based on the experience level for the position. This is not the CPP test. Just ten or fifteen questions on general payroll knowledge should be sufficient. Keep in mind that the test must be focused on the exact tasks the applicant would perform. For example, if the position never handles garnishments, then garnishment questions would be excluded. However, if the position is in the tax section of the department, questions on deposit requirements and quarterly tax returns would be relevant. If upward mobility is part of the department's long-term goals, knowledge that would lead to this mobility can be learned later. The test can be easily created from reference guides or other sources. In fact, some payroll manuals include mini tests in each section to help in studying the material and include the answer keys as well. Actually taking the questions from various independent sources can help in alleviating bias in the test questions. Multiple-choice questions are fine. The test can be written or given verbally during the interview. The human resources department can even administer the test.

If the applicant has a current CPP designation, then that clearly demonstrates the applicant's knowledge is sound. The interviewer can assume that the applicant has kept his or her knowledge current through recertification by either retesting or attending the appropriate training programs and seminars. But what about a previous certification? Suppose the applicant had a CPP at one time but has allowed it to expire. In this case, the payroll manager needs to question the reason behind allowing the designation to expire. The CPP is a difficult test and once the payroll professional has achieved the certification, there must be compelling reasons for not keeping it. Did the applicant's previous employer not pay for the training needed to recertify? Did the workload on the previous job not allow enough time for attendance at seminars or training sessions? It is important to find out why the certification was allowed to expire. It could be a red flag regarding the current status of the applicant's payroll knowledge.

- *Question Payroll Education and Training.* How much actual formal education has the applicant had and/or how many training sessions has the applicant attended? This is important information to have when hiring a payroll professional. Experience is obviously important, but attending seminars or training classes on strictly payroll-related topics is also vital. Attending these types of classes demonstrates that the applicant is interested in gaining formal knowledge of the rules and regulations governing the payroll profession. The applicant should be questioned on who presented the class and what topics were covered. Not having this formal training does not necessarily eliminate a potential candidate, but it may mean training may have to be provided later on.

- *Question for Other Skills, Training, and Experience.* Many times when interviewing for a position in the payroll department, the concentration is on the applicant's payroll experience and knowledge. Sometimes other skills and training are ignored or glossed over. Remember that to build or to maintain an efficient payroll department, many different types of skills may be needed. Some of these skills might include customer service training or software expertise. Word processing and spreadsheet software is constantly utilized by the payroll department. Having a staff member who is formally trained in these areas can go a long way toward creating an efficient department.

(b) Training and the Payroll Department

The payroll manager should never assume that a staff member who has ten years of experience does not need training on the basics of any topic. Just because someone has been doing payroll for a number of years does not mean that person has been trained properly or at all. Payroll has traditionally been a learn-as-you-go profession and sometimes staff members learn incorrectly. So before a payroll manager establishes a training program for the staff, he or she needs to take the time to do a training or needs assessment for each staff member. This would include establishing the history of each employee's training both at the current company and in previous positions. With limited training budgets for most payroll departments, a skills or training assessment test will help focus the limited resources where they will do the most good.

How does the payroll manager conduct one of these assessments? By simply testing the employee's payroll knowledge and examining his or her job duties. The employee takes a test on the basics of payroll. If he or she passes this test, then a test on intermediate payroll is given. The tests do not have to be specifically created for this assessment but can be pulled from most payroll manuals. The tests should not include company policy or system specific questions but be on general payroll knowledge for the employee's level of experience and job duties. Employees are tested until they have successfully completed all the answers for the level of job knowledge they must have. Doing these assessments on each employee is time consuming. But if the employee can pass the tests, then it may not be fiscally sound to spend limited funds on training the employee does not need.

Job duties are the second area that should be assessed before setting up a training program for an employee. If the staff member never handles garnishments or does tax reconciliations, then sending that employee to a garnishment class just because he or she does not have that type of knowledge is not efficient staff training.

It is agreed that a proper payroll staff training program is critical to maintaining an efficient payroll department. But what should be included in this training program? The following points list the major areas that should be considered:

- *Basic Payroll.* This training includes the fundamentals of payroll knowledge. The class usually covers the fundamental rules of wage and hour law, and taxation and fringe benefits on both the federal and applicable state level. All payroll staff members need this basic knowledge.

- *Intermediate/Advanced Payroll.* This is for staff members who have reached this level in their job duties and experience. This training includes the more advanced fringe benefits, quarterly returns, and garnishments.

- *Year End.* This training usually covers all the basics of closing out the year and producing the Forms W-2. The knowledge gained in this type of class needs to be updated annually. The class normally covers the current SSA filing requirements and any changes in tax regulations, wage and hour law, or reporting requirements that will occur in the new year. It is common to send at least one of the senior staff members working on year end to the class. This person can then report back to the rest of the staff.

- *Specialty Payroll Task.* For staff members who handle the specialty items or the more complex tasks in the department, specific training in those areas should be given. Topics for this type of training include garnishments, expatriates, or multi-state taxation. These classes usually cover just the one topic and are extremely efficient in teaching the concepts needed in a short period of time. Efficiency is paramount, as the attendees are not forced to sit through hours of non-related information.

- *Payroll Computer System Software.* How to do the basic input and navigate the complexities of report writer programs is the focus of this training. All staff members, including the manager, should have formal training on the payroll system software. The training should be conducted by the software company or the vendor of the outside payroll processing company. However, more often than not, this is not the case. Usually, in order to make the budget, training is the area that is trimmed by the time the final contract is written. What usually happens is one staff member gets the hands-on training and then comes back to train the rest of the staff. This is extremely inefficient. First, it presupposes that the employee understood everything correctly. And second, it assumes the staff member is capable of teaching the information correctly. Even if it is the payroll manager who is receiving the training, it should not be assumed that he or she can effectively transfer it. System training is critical to an efficient payroll department. Not only should each staff member be trained when a new system is installed, but this training should be repeated whenever significant upgrades are performed. In addition, each new staff member should receive first-hand, formal system training and not second-hand training from another staff member. This will help ensure that the bad habits or idiosyncrasies of one staff member are not passed on to the entire department.

- *Software.* Software training is sometimes overlooked because it is not payroll or system specific. But the payroll department uses word processing or spreadsheet software the same as any other department. Formal training on spreadsheet or word processing software can help improve the efficiency of the department by giving the staff member the knowledge to perform essential tasks without trying to figure out how to do them or constantly using the help feature. This training can be done in a class setting or by tutorial.

(c) Delegation of Duties

The proper delegation of duties is a critical part of managing a payroll staff. It is up to the payroll manager to make sure that each employee's job duties are within his or her knowledge and skill set so that the tasks can be done efficiently and within the compliance and deadline parameters. However, the employee must still be given some challenging work to allow for knowledge and job growth. It is indeed a balancing act. Of course, if the payroll department is a "party of one" this delegation is simple. But with two or more employees, this task does take more time and thought. The following points should be considered when deciding on the most efficient delegation of duties for a payroll department:

- *Combined Years of Experience of the Entire Payroll Department.* If the staff is relatively inexperienced in payroll overall, this must be taken into account when delegating job duties. Even though one employee may have ten or fifteen years of experience, if the other staff members have only two or three, this will affect how tasks are distributed.

- *Years of Experience of Each Individual Staff Member.* The experience of a particular staff member must be considered when delegating duties. Staff members who have a number of years of direct payroll experience will expect the more challenging assignments.

- *Depth of Knowledge and Skills of Each Individual Staff Member.* It is important to remember that years of experience do not necessarily equate to job skills or knowledge. An employee who has worked for ten years in the department handling time records input, masterfile input, and customer service may not have the necessary skills and knowledge to now handle garnishments and tax deposits (at least not without further training).

- *Training and Education Background.* How much formal training and education a staff member has can affect the delegation of duties. Although payroll as a profession is not a degree program, there are facets of the job where a college education or professional training courses are very useful. This is especially true in the areas of accounting and reconciliations.

2.3 STAFF MOTIVATION AND MORALE

How many times have you heard it said that "people are our most valuable asset"? Given that the wages of the payroll staff probably consume up to two-thirds of the department's budget, it would seem that properly caring for and retaining each worker makes good business sense and that staff morale would be a high priority. But in the real world, that just is not always the case. However, staff morale has a direct effect on the efficiency of the department. And although it is not always easy managing the department and motivating the staff, for a payroll department to build or maintain its efficiency it must be done.

In addition to the normal problems that most managers face, being the manager of the payroll department entails dealing with a whole different set of concerns when it comes to staff motivation and morale.

(a) Overcoming Payroll Negatives

To increase or maintain efficiency and to assist with staff morale, it is very important that the payroll manager recognizes and accepts that there are negative aspects of working in the payroll department. These negatives, which seem to come with the territory, can affect the staff's morale tremendously. But only by recognizing and analyzing these areas can a payroll manager then learn how to turn the negative aspect into a positive experience. The first thing that must be done is to identify the major "cons" in the payroll department. Turning them into "pros" comes next. Some of the negative payroll aspects are:

- The payroll department is filled with constant deadlines. Examples include time-sheet deadlines, input deadlines, report deadlines, payday deadlines, and manual check deadlines to list but a few. In addition to the department deadlines, there are also the legal and government deadlines to contend with. Tax deposits must be made on time, quarterly and year-end reports, and so on. Of course, the payroll department cannot miss a deadline. Unlike other departments, if payroll is late, the consequences are severe. Penalties and interest are stiff for missing a tax deposit, not to mention what would happen if payroll were actually ever late!

- Another area of negativity in the payroll department is the constant pressure from management and other departments to never make a mistake, to never be late, and to always be able to handle any request.

- The payroll department receives little if any positive feedback from other departments. In fact, payroll usually only hears from another department if they want something. There is an old saying in payroll "if you process 500 checks on payday and make a mistake on one, who do you hear from? The one with the mistake. You never hear from the 499 who had a perfect check."

- Government bureaucracy also causes great negative energy for the payroll department. It can be difficult to keep up with the constantly changing regulations from the IRS, Wage and Hour, and State agencies, to name a few.

- There is a great lack of empathy from other departments in understanding what it takes to produce a payroll. There is very little comprehension on what guidelines the payroll department must follow. How often have you heard this sentiment: "You input the time sheets on Monday and the checks come back on Friday; what do you do in the meantime?"

Once the major negative aspects have been identified, the next step is to look for ways to turn them around to positive experiences and to make the payroll department more efficient in the process. To accomplish this, certain pitfalls need to be avoided:

- *Other People's Schedules.* The payroll manager needs to establish the department's schedule and stick to it. The other departments should respect the payroll department's needs concerning time frames just as the payroll department respects theirs. If time sheets are due on Monday, then they should be submitted on time.

- *Other Departments' Crises.* There is an old saying: "Bad planning on your part does not constitute a crisis on my part." Although the payroll department wants to be as cooperative and helpful as possible, its deadlines need to be respected as well.

(b) Creating Payroll Positives

Now that the negative areas have been identified and the pitfalls pointed out, it is time to examine ways to change this negative energy into a positive force. The following are some simple ways to achieve this end:

- *Deadlines.* It is not possible to completely take all the negativity out of having so many deadlines. Payroll is what it is and that is based entirely on deadlines. But having tools to handle these deadlines can help curtail some of the stress that deadlines cause. The best tool is the payroll master calendar. Knowing which deadlines are coming up and being prepared for them goes a long way toward being able to handle the pressure. But the payroll manager also must be aware that people with certain temperaments can handle the pressure of massive deadlines while others cannot. It is important to hire payroll staff members who have an even temperament and are accustomed to handling deadlines.

- *Delegation.* Delegation is another way to handle deadlines and high pressure. Make sure that the pressure of deadlines is distributed evenly throughout the department. One staff member should not be given all the high pressure deadlines, even if he or she has the most experience or the temperament for it. Even if the payroll department is a party of one, this can still be accomplished by separating and organizing high pressure jobs to be done on different days and at different times.

- *Being Perfect.* To handle the pressure from other departments to be perfect and to never make a mistake is to do the most basic and simple of things—admit everyone in the payroll department, including the manager, is human and fallible and then move on. Mistakes will happen. Errors will occur. Striving for perfection is a noble goal, but beating yourself up for not achieving it does not help in making the department more efficient. Instead, strive to reduce errors by improving input techniques, catch errors before the check is released by running edits, and fix errors immediately without worrying about the blame. This still gives the aura of being perfect without the pressure of it. Should a manager in another department start beating up on the payroll department for making a mistake, admit yes, the department did make a "human" error, fixed it, and has now moved on.

- *Positive Feedback.* To get positive feedback from other departments and from management is a difficult task. However, it is not an impossible one. See the "payroll by walking around" and the "letting the company in on it" techniques listed below. Use these techniques to get noticed! It does take time and effort, but the results are well worth it.

  o *Payroll by Walking Around.* The first thing to do is to get out of the department! The payroll department staff (and especially the manager or supervisor) tends to stay put behind their desks plugging away. But good management of the payroll department demands getting out and going among the department's customers and peers to find out what is going on. The payroll manager cannot find out about glitches in the payroll process, such as constantly misrouted checks (the change of the department notice never reached payroll) or a wrong address (no change submitted), unless someone goes out and asks. Do not wait for them to come to you. By that time there will be hostility and bad feelings. Remember, when asking how the department is doing, ask for positive feedback too! "What are we doing right?" is a valid question. If your department is doing a good job, take the well deserved compliment.

  o *Let the Company in on It.* Payroll information such as current laws, rules, and regulations is not a closely guarded secret. The payroll department staff is not charged with being the keeper of this information. In fact, it is the payroll department's responsibility to keep the rest of the company up on the latest changes as they occur. This will prevent misunderstandings and create goodwill and visibility for payroll. It also goes a long way to establish the credibility of the department, which helps with its image. There are many ways to disseminate this information to the company including putting articles in the company newsletter if there is one, posting articles on the payroll department's intranet website, or even sending a payroll update via blanket e-mail.

- *Make Contacts.* To counteract the negative aspects of governmental bureaucracy that payroll must deal with, the department needs to establish a government liaison list. Compile a list of all local, state, and national agencies that the department must deal with and whenever possible, begin to make contact with someone in that agency. Then when a problem does arise or a question comes up, the payroll staff member can turn to someone reliable. The best place to begin to draw up this list is through professional organization meetings such as the American Payroll Association (APA). The local chapters of the APA have speakers periodically throughout the year from all agencies concerning payroll. This would be an excellent place to begin collecting those business cards.

- *Lack of Empathy.* To handle the lack of empathy from other departments requires action on the payroll department's part. The payroll manager should educate the other managers and departments on the needs of payroll so they can have a better understanding of the department's requirements. He or she should communicate why payroll must follow certain standard procedures. This is best done by attending management meetings and individual meetings, through quality circles, and by using the company newsletter.

(c) Payroll Is Important Too

Payroll managers must do their best to communicate and work with other departments. This topic is discussed many times in this book. However, it is imperative for the payroll manager to remember one thing—payroll is important too! The payroll manager who fails to be in constant communication with his or her staff and to work closely with them to attain common goals actually becomes an obstacle to an efficient department. Removing this obstacle is very simple—communicate and work closely with the department staff. Show the staff they are important. Give them full support and help them achieve the goals of the department as a group as well as grow as individuals. For a reality check on his or her communication and working relationship with the payroll department staff, a payroll manager should ask, "In the last several months, what have I done to:"

- Be accessible (physically and mentally) to employees who would like my attention?
- Be considerate of my staff's needs?
- Provide employees with the training, tools, resources, and feedback required for success?
- Keep employees in the loop?
- Help team members maintain an appropriate balance between their professional and personal lives?
- Demonstrate respect for employees' time and talents, as well as recognizing them as individuals?
- Solicit and listen to staff ideas and concerns?
- Help everyone develop and grow?
- Fairly distribute the workload?

Other tips for giving the payroll staff the recognition and communication they deserve include:

- Make new staff members feel welcome. Create a first-day ritual for all new hires. This could include a senior-level employee showing the new hire around and introducing him or her to all payroll staff as well as other staff members.
- Submit press releases to the local newspapers when new staff members are hired to announce the recent addition to the department. If not the local paper, then at least make the announcement in the company newsletter or on the payroll department's intranet site.
- Announce all changes to staff including promotions or new job assignments of significance. Again, if the local newspaper announcement is permitted this is the best

way to show recognition to the staff and demonstrate their importance.

- Don't assume anything. Find out what the employees want from their jobs and how they want to grow. Then help them structure a career path. Too many managers mistakenly assume that they know what motivates their employees.

- Properly evaluate the performance of all employees and set goals and objectives for the performance of key people. Honest evaluations help employees. Give recognition for employee accomplishments and the tools to grow in the job.

- Communicate the results of the employees' efforts to them. Employees need to feel like they know what is going on in the company and the department and how their work affects both. Are they making a difference?

- Involve the staff in major decisions where possible. At least listen to the input. Often the ones who do the work have the best ideas.

- Put qualified staff members up for any awards or recognition programs offered by the company. Sometimes the payroll department is seldom recognized in these efforts.

- Allow staff members who desire it to represent the department at company functions such as new employee orientations.

- Spend time with the staff. Hold meetings or informal sessions to exchange information and updates.

(d) Departmental Upward Mobility

The payroll staff members need to know that upward mobility is available if they want it. One of the problems with many payroll departments is that some staff members who have nowhere to go soon lose the motivation to maintain efficiency.

The payroll manager must establish a line of succession to a managerial position so that the staff can see that it is possible to work toward that goal. If there is no chain of command between the manager and the staff, this may be a position that could be established to create upward mobility. Upward mobility could also include positions of supervisor or manager outside of the payroll department in crossover positions such as human resources or benefits. It is not the greatest wish of the payroll department to lose a knowledgeable and well trained staff member, but it helps the payroll department keep employees motivated if they know mobility is attainable. Lead positions might also be created. However, it is never advisable to create meaningless positions with worthless titles. Employees are wise to this and it will not be motivational but instead might cause animosity.

2.4 WORKING WITH HUMAN RESOURCES AND OTHER DEPARTMENTS

The payroll department is one of just a handful in the company that closely interacts, almost on a daily basis, with all other departments. In fact, the payroll department does not just work closely with managers or supervisors but with every single employee in the company, not just once in a while, but every single payday. The payroll department not only gives something to every employee—namely, a paycheck—but it needs to get something back as well—a time record, masterfile input, or tax deposit check just to name a few. And all of this must be done in a time frame that allows little room for delays. That is why one of the ultimate goals of a well managed and efficient payroll department is to be able to find a way to work effectively with other departments, especially human resources. Working efficiently means not only providing what the other departments want but also getting from them what the payroll department needs.

(a) Payroll Has Deadlines

The payroll department faces critical deadlines every day. These deadlines include, among others, tax deposits and reports, direct deposits, and garnishment payments. But one of the biggest obstacles the payroll department faces is getting other departments to understand these deadlines, especially human resources. For unlike finance, accounting, human resources, or even the warehouse, when these departments miss a deadline the repercussions are minor compared to what will happen to payroll. For example, what if the accounts payable department misses paying a vendor by one day? Just an oversight. An honest mistake. There are repercussions, of course. The vendor may become angry and refuse to do business with the company. The company may lose a discount. But in all honesty, how often does that really happen? It is more likely that the vendor would be phoned, accounts payable would explain why the payment was a day late, and in all probability, the relationship would be repaired, the discount restored, and so on.

What if the department that was late was not accounts payable but payroll? Suppose the payroll department missed by just one day paying an employee or making a tax deposit. Is it the same thing? Not by any means whatsoever! Could the vendor whose payment was one day late file a complaint with both federal and state government agencies, which in turn could trigger a complete investigation including an audit of the company? Probably not. Is there any possibility that the vendor is unionized and that he or she would file a grievance over the late payment? Probably not. If it were a tax deposit to the IRS that was one day late, would it be easily resolved? Does the vendor have the authority to impose an automatic penalty of 2 percent on the total payment owed? And if the penalty is not paid, does the vendor have the authority to levy the assets of the entire company and the wherewithal to carry out that levy? Probably not. And could that vendor decide to audit the company's entire payment practice, serve the accounts payable department with a court order, review all the records or files pertaining to its payments, then penalize the company for any improprieties the audit uncovered? Probably not. But this is exactly what happens to payroll. And this example is exactly what the payroll professional needs to cite any time another department says, "why are payroll's deadlines any more important than anyone else's?" They are because they are. It is just that simple. It is not the payroll department's choice to have critical deadlines with penalties attached for missing one of them; it is just a fact of business life. A payroll department that firmly establishes this fact will find that it goes a long way toward making working with other departments much smoother and more efficient.

However, human resources, accounts payable, and other departments cannot help payroll meet these deadlines unless they know about them. It is a common mistake made by many payroll professionals to assume that other departments, especially human resources or accounts payable, would know what these deadlines are. After all, not everyone in the company would know when accounts payable is going to do a check run, but everyone certainly knows when payday is! Although that certainly is true, it does not mean they know all the other deadlines associated with payday, or that they relate payday itself with the processing deadlines. And why should they? The other departments have their own deadlines to meet and tasks to perform in order to meet them. This is why it is payroll's responsibility to give clear and concise information about what it needs from these other departments in order to meet its deadlines. It must also make it very clear that getting this information on time is not intended to make life easier for the payroll department or to make its workload easier, but in fact, it is to keep the company in compliance and to avoid penalties, fines, and interest from being assessed against the company. One of the most efficient ways to accomplish this task is to create and distribute calendar memos.

As discussed in Section 8.2, the payroll department should set up a complete processing calendar for each new year. The calendar or parts of it should be distributed to other departments to inform them of processing and other deadlines. But how should this calendar be distributed efficiently? Should the payroll department just print out copies and distribute them? Actually that could work, but it is much more efficient to create a quick memo to let the other departments know what payroll needs. It is important to remember that they have their own work to do and their own schedules to meet. A quick one-page memo containing the due dates has a better chance of being given the necessary attention. Bombarding other departments with a 12-page calendar filled with all the work payroll has to accomplish in a year, and then expecting those departments to highlight what applies to them is just not going to get the desired results. It is true that the purpose of giving the other departments the calendars is to make sure that the deadlines are met to avoid penalties or fines from being assessed against the company, but they are still payroll deadlines and ultimately the payroll department's responsibility. What the payroll department is trying to do is to ask for cooperation and assistance to accomplish its goal of keeping the company in compliance. Showing respect for the other department's valuable time goes a long way toward that. In essence, if the payroll department wants respect for its deadlines and workload, then it must show that respect to others.

The calendar memo should be created and distributed as soon as possible after the department's master calendar for the new year is completed. The memo or memos should definitely be distributed two to three weeks prior to the first deadline listed on the memo.

The memo calendar should be created for any task for which payroll will receive information or input from sources outside of its own staff. These tasks may include:

- Time record submission

- New hire input (if done by another department such as human resources)

- Submission of new hire information if the payroll department is responsible for input

- Masterfile updates such as pay raises or address changes if a department other than payroll is responsible for making these changes

- Submission of masterfile update information if the payroll department is responsible for the input

- Benefit setup if done by a department other than payroll

- Submission of benefit input information if the input is done by payroll

- Due dates when accounts payable must return checks to payroll in order to make garnishment payments or tax deposits

Individual memo calendars do not necessarily need to be done for each task or item. If the memo calendar is going to one department, then all the tasks for that department could be included on one memo. This does save the other department from being swamped with payroll calendars. Again, the memo should be kept to only one or two pages. Distribution of the calendar memo can be in whatever method works best for the department. E-mail, paper memo sent through intercompany mail, or hand delivered is fine. The date and time the memos are delivered is important to record. This will help if there are any future disputes. A sample memo calendar is shown in Exhibit 2.1.

Recipients should not receive this memo unaware. The payroll department should explain to the other departments why the memo calendars are being issued. The head of the department or equivalent should get a quick e-mail or phone call as a courtesy notice. If possible, the memo calendars should be included in any manager meetings. The payroll department should explain to the other departments involved that the memo calendars will increase processing efficiency, save the company money, and prevent noncompliance issues.

(b) Getting the Information Needed

The payroll department runs on information. New hires, Forms W-4, pay raises, and the like all make the department function. Because the receipt of information keeps the department humming, lack of that information could bring it to a screeching halt. That is why for a payroll department to be efficient it must constantly know what information it needs, where it needs to go to get it, and how long it will take to receive it. Almost all of the information the payroll department processes is submitted to them. This includes items such as time records and masterfile

EXHIBIT 2.1

Sample Memo Calendar

TO: Human Resources
FROM: Payroll Department
Date: December 13, 20X4
Re: Payroll processing deadline calendar for 20X5 for the completed input of
             new hire information.

To ensure that the payroll department is able to create a computer system generated payroll check and avoid the costly process of creating manual checks for all new hires, the input of all new hire paperwork must be completed by each date and time shown below for the payroll indicated.

Payday	Input due date and time

Sample: List all pay days for the company and the input dates that the payroll needs.

Thank you very much for your cooperation with this matter. If you have any questions or need to discuss any of the deadlines listed please don't hesitate to call or e-mail me.

changes. However, there will be times when the payroll department will need to go get the information because the other departments may not be aware that the information should go to payroll. It is payroll's responsibility to contact the other departments to inform them that the information is needed. But what is the best way to obtain this information?

Getting information from other departments sometimes takes tenacity and tact. The payroll department needs to request the information with enough force to demonstrate that the information must be furnished promptly, but with enough tact so as to not appear demanding and unreasonable. An efficient method to request this information is the plain and simple memo. By sending a memo the request is in writing, it explains in detail what is needed, and establishes an audit trail of the request if needed. Before the request can be sent out, several things must be done first.

First, the payroll department has to determine what information it actually does need. Basically, whatever information is processed in other departments and not automatically sent to payroll must be requested. This information may affect year end or employees' wages. Some of the areas that payroll may need additional outside information on include:

- Personal use of a company vehicle
- Group term life insurance premiums that are paid on behalf of retired employees
- Relocation or moving expenses
- Educational assistance
- Dependent care payments

Once the determination is made as to what information is needed, payroll must then determine when the information must be received in order to process the information properly. The master calendar should be consulted for this purpose. After that is determined, the next step is to decide what format the information must be in when it is received. Does it need to be an electronic spreadsheet or will a paper copy do? The next step is to determine who has the information and how it needs to be requested. What department handles the information? Can the memo be sent directly to the staff member or should it be sent to the department head? After all these details are worked out, there is only one more thing to determine, but it is an important step. The payroll department must explain *why* it needs the information. The key to asking other departments to take the time to assemble information for the payroll department is to justify the request with the rule, regulation, or company policy that requires the information to be submitted to payroll. Phrases such as "this must be furnished" or "you are required to give" are not sufficient. The actual IRS text (or the wording from the Circular E or other publications may be used rather than the actual code) will go a long way toward making your case.

In creating the memo, remember to keep it short, specify exactly what is needed, and give the exact date the information needs to be returned to payroll. The memo can be e-mailed or sent via paper means. Under no circumstances should this request ever be made by phone. At least one month's notice should be given to the department to assemble the information, if possible. For example, the payroll department needs the accounts payable department to furnish a list of all educational assistance payments that it made for the year. It must be provided in time for processing by the last payroll of the year. If the last payroll of the year is December 31st, and payroll needs time to process the report, then the accounts payable department should receive the notice by November 15th. A sample letter to the accounts payable department requesting all payments for educational assistance is included in Exhibit 2.2.

EXHIBIT 2.2

Sample Memo to Request Information for Payroll from Another Department

To: Accounts payable
From: Payroll
Date: November 19, 20X4
Re: Information request for educational assistance payments

The Internal Revenue Code requires that all payments paid on behalf of any employee for educational assistance be reported in the employee's wages and taxes withheld if the amount exceeds $5,250 per employee per year. I have enclosed a copy of the excerpt from the IRS Publication 15-B below to demonstrate this requirement.

> **"Exclusion from wages.** You can exclude up to $5,250 of educational assistance you provide to an employee under an educational assistance program from the employee's wages each year."

Please review your payment records for the current year and furnish a list of any payments that exceed this amount that have been made to or on behalf of any employee. Please show the employee name, ID number, and the amount. If you prefer, you may include a list of all payments made to all employees, regardless of amounts. Please e-mail this report and send over a paper copy. Please send by December 23, 20X4 for inclusion in the December 31, 20X4 payroll.

Please continue to monitor payments made after the effective date of the report through December 31, 20X4. If any updates to the report are needed, please furnish this update to the payroll department as soon as possible after the payment is made.

If you have any questions, please feel free to contact me.

Thank you very much for your help in this matter.

CHAPTER 3

Management Issues

3.1 CUSTOMER SERVICE

Customer service. This is the new buzzword for the twenty-first century. Making sure customers receive what they need or want in a quick and efficient manner is the basis of good customer service, but is ensuring that a customer is happy with your product relevant to the payroll department? The payroll department's "product" is its paychecks. It is not too hard to convince your "customers" (the employees) to come back time and time again for this product. So, does it matter if the service the employee receives is good? Yes, actually it does, especially when it comes to department efficiency. Giving the payroll staff the proper training and tools to assist the department's customers/employees will aid in handling questions quickly and efficiently. This saves money by conserving staff time at the customer service counter or on the phone. It also creates goodwill for the department, and indeed for the entire company, when its customers are treated politely and in a professional manner. However, the one thing that can adversely affect customer service in the payroll department is whether the employee's request violates any government regulations.

(a) Can Payroll Achieve Customer Service and Compliance?

The biggest impediment to giving excellent customer service in the payroll department is when what the customer wants conflicts with compliance requirements. The first objective for the payroll department is compliance with wage and hours laws and IRS regulations. Many times an employee will want the payroll department to perform a task that is in direct violation of one of these regulations. For example, the payroll department receives a tax levy from the IRS for employee B. The payroll department processes the garnishment properly, including notifying the employee. The employee then requests that the payroll department hold off taking the tax levy for a couple of payrolls to give him time to work things out with the IRS. Of course, payroll would not legally be permitted to do this and must deny the employee's request. Naturally, the employee perceives this as bad customer service. However, the IRS regulations are very clear on what the payroll can and cannot do in this instance, so the payroll department's hands are tied. There is no way to work with the employee on granting his request. Does that mean there is no way to work with the employee? Although the department cannot delay the deduction of the tax levy, it could inform the employee about the IRS voluntary deduction form and could even have that information on hand to give to him. In addition, the payroll department could work with the employee by deducting the money as required, but holding off on sending in the money until the last possible moment in order to give the employee some time and yet still be in compliance.

The previous example basically says it all: Even though payroll must put compliance first, it can still find ways to work with the employee. Communication is the key to this type of customer service. And educating the department's customers on payroll protocols will go a long way toward helping increase customer satisfaction in the department. One of the best ways to provide the desired excellent customer service and to remain in compliance with the law is to let the internal customers in on what the payroll department can and cannot do. World-class customer service is a matter of controlling customer expectations. A simple way to educate the department's customers about payroll policies is to publish written customer service policies and procedures. If the employee knows up front what rules and regulations govern the company and the payroll department, it will be much easier to explain situations where the department cannot grant a request. Payroll department supervisors and superiors should work together to establish written guidelines that will minimize misunderstandings between payroll and its internal customers.

(b) Setting Up a Customer Service Policy for Payroll

Written procedures can help clearly explain that the payroll department will do all it can to accommodate a customer's request, but that the department will not deliberately ignore compliance issues for the sake of a customer's needs or wishes. This can become particularly challenging for the payroll department when its staff member has to tell a customer that it cannot do what he or she wants, which in turn causes conflicts with other departments or even supervisors or direct superiors. This is why setting the policy in advance, getting management to buy into the policy, and publishing it will help alleviate most of these situations.

The first step toward writing the customer service policy is to establish the department's customers. There are basically two types of customers that payroll must serve:

Internal Customers. This list includes the company's employees and:

    a. *Human Resources.* Depending on the company hierarchy, HR could be a boss and a customer. Though it is common for the payroll department to be part of the human resources department, human resources is a customer because it directly receives services from payroll, including benefits, information, and payments. Exchanges between the payroll and human resources departments are vital for both to function effectively.

    b. *Accounting.* Again, depending on the company hierarchy, this department might be a customer and a boss. The essential service here is to input critical data from payroll records into the general ledger.

External Customers. Until recently, most payroll departments would not have defined as their customers the federal, state, and local agencies to which they provide information. Nor would they think of vendors—whom the company pays—as customers. But changes in these relationships illustrate the expanse of payroll services.

    a. *The IRS.* Without a doubt, the IRS is a payroll customer. Even if the payroll department is not responsible for depositing taxes and reconciling quarterly returns, it may have to handle tax levies and determine withholding issues.

    b. *State Tax Agencies.* Similar qualifications for the IRS also apply to the state and local agencies that handle taxation.

    c. *Garnishment Agencies.* Agencies that issue garnishments and notice of withholding, such as child support and creditor garnishments, are also customers of the payroll department. It is common for the department to devote a great deal of energy to handling and maintaining paperwork for these agencies.

    d. *Vendors.* Payroll processing firms are customers even though the payroll department pays them and is their primary customer. Also, the bank where the direct deposits are made, insurance agencies for third-party sick pay, and the administrator of the company's deferred compensation plan are customers with a myriad of information needs that only the payroll department can satisfy.

Once the customers are identified, the next step is to list all requests or questions that could arise from each of the customers. External customers also can have questions or requests, so the procedures do need to include any calls or requests they might make. The final step is to supply the answers to the questions. List the rules or regulations that prevent granting certain requests and give any backup necessary.

When the procedures are complete and approved, they need to be distributed. The company's intranet or the department's website is an excellent place to post the procedures. The policies and procedures should be set forth in the employee handbook as well.

3.2 FRAUD

Fraud prevention is a complicated issue for the efficient payroll department. The department must employ streamlined procedures to promote efficiency but still must keep all the checks and balances in place to prevent fraud by the payroll staff.

Fraud can take on many forms and can occur in the payroll department in many ways. These include:

- Paying phantom employees
- Fraudulent additions to approved time records
- Unauthorized increases in hourly rates
- Bogus payments of commissions, bonuses, or incentives that are added to an employee's normal paycheck
- Deduction reversals that add to an employee's net pay
- Illegal Advanced Earned Income Credit payments
- Child support garnishments that are mailed to a custodial parent but are never deducted from a paycheck

These payments often will be done in small increments so as to not draw attention to the change or amounts. The idea for this type of fraud is to have it last over a long period of time. The employee or employees involved want it to go on for years if possible.

(a) Auditing for Internal Fraud

It is the responsibility of the payroll supervisor or manager to ensure that fraud does not take place in the department. It is one of the few departments where access to and distribution of company funds is the primary duty of the employees. This access can lead to fraud even in the best departments. To be diligent in the fight against fraud, periodic audits should be conducted throughout the department for the sole purpose of detecting fraud. These audits can include:

- *Phantom Employee Audits.* These are discussed in great length in the next section.

- *New Hires.* If payroll inputs new hire paperwork, the input needs to be reviewed to reconcile the information in the system versus the actual paperwork.

- *Pay Raises.* If payroll inputs pay raises or has access to input on this master screen, then all pay raises should be compared to the actual paperwork.

- *Reverse Deductions.* Reversing a deduction is a rare input and any reverse deductions should always be verified immediately.

- *Garnishments.* Garnishment checks should be processed as a third-party check directly from the payroll system if possible. If accounts payable checks are used, then proof of a deduction from the payroll should accompany each check request.

- *Tax Refunds or Adjustments.* The payroll department should avoid refunding taxes to employees. Whenever this is done, an audit should be conducted.

- *Payments Made to Terminated or Deceased Employees.* Payments such as these are sometimes routed to a bank account via direct deposit.

When conducting the audits, the number of time records, new hires, and so on that should be included in the audit depends on the number of employees employed by the company. A good rule of thumb is 10 percent. That number can be expanded if any discrepancies do appear.

The audits should be done in secret and without prior announcement to the staff. However, the procedures for conducting the audits should be clearly spelled out in writing and made a part of the department's procedures manual. These procedures should be made available to all staff members and should explain:

- Why the audits are needed. Their purpose and how they affect the efficiency of the department.

- That these types of audits are standard operating procedures for any efficient payroll department.

- How the audits are conducted. This includes the fact that they are conducted in secret and without prior notification to the staff.
- What tasks are subject to audit.
- The step-by-step procedure for how each audit is performed.
- Who is responsible for calling for an audit.

Payroll managers should consult with the company's internal audit department if one exists, to make sure data analysis is one of the tools he or she uses to review and audit the payroll.

Time records are one aspect of payroll that is particularly susceptible to fraud. Internal controls are the payroll department's first line of defense against time record fraud. Some tips on preventing this type of fraud include:

- Each employee should sign and certify his or her time record and then have it approved by a supervisor or, for key managers at the top of the organization, another designated authority.
- Electronic time record systems should use passwords or other access controls to prevent employees from accessing supervisor or approval fields.
- No one should approve his or her own time record.
- When an employee works in more than one office, management should designate one supervisor at each location to approve the individual's time record prior to certifying it for payment.
- Review managers' overtime requests carefully because policies usually prohibit managers from receiving overtime.
- Some companies have policies that prevent overtime in excess of a certain percentage of the employee's base salary, such as 25 percent, unless specifically approved by management. In these cases, to ensure that employees have obtained the required approvals, the payroll system edit should list as an exception any overtime that exceeds the specified amount.

Paper time records are like a blank check. Almost all payroll fraud for time records occurs after the supervisor has approved the time sheets. How? Employees use the blank lines on the time record to alter the payroll information such as callback, standby, overtime, or even straight time after the time record has been approved by the supervisor. To avoid this type of fraud, managers and supervisors should send all approved time records directly to payroll. They should not be returned to the employee. Also, any unused lines on the time record should be crossed out or the last authorized entry on the document should be highlighted to eliminate unauthorized additions.

Some types of time record fraud can be difficult to detect because the manager and the employee may conspire together to commit the fraud. For example, with today's tight corporate budgets, raises are small and sometimes nonexistent. A manager who means well and has staff retention in mind may give an employee a "raise" by allowing fictitious overtime charges. Less likely but still in the realm of possibilities is the unscrupulous manager who may authorize fictitious overtime and then instruct the employee to kick back a large chunk of the money.

The chances of catching fraudulent time records are greatly enhanced if edit reports are created and reviewed for time record input. These edits list any time records that fall out of the established parameters, for example, any employee who receives more than ten hours of overtime in one workweek. The parameters for the edits should never be discussed or released to anyone outside of the management of the payroll department.

(b) Delegation of Job Duties to Prevent Fraud

It is always best to prevent fraud from happening rather than to discover it later. One of the best ways to do this is to make sure that the duties in the payroll department are properly distributed among the staff. This way, a separation exists for all check producing or input to checks tasks. An efficient method of achieving this goal is to set up a fraud prevention program. The program should then be consulted when delegating duties or establishing procedures in the payroll department. The following points should be considered when establishing a fraud prevention program:

- Any staff member who prepares the payroll should not reconcile the payroll bank account.
- The same employee who sets up new hires in the payroll system should not edit the masterfile input report, process the payroll, or distribute the checks.
- Any employee who calculates manual checks should not be able to approve or sign the same checks.
- Only one employee (payroll manager) should be in charge of check stock or paper and all checks or sheets of paper should be logged out and signed for by the employee producing the checks.
- Any staff member who inputs to the masterfile should not be involved in reviewing the edit reports for his or her own input.
- Any employee who inputs time records or updates the masterfiles should not stuff or deliver the payroll checks.
- Reconciliation of the general ledger accounts should be divided up among the payroll staff. One employee should not be responsible for the reconciliations unless he or she has no input responsibilities. No employee should reconcile the same accounts he or she inputs for or processes.
- Only one employee (with appropriate backup) should be able to transmit or process the payroll. This employee is preferably the manager or someone with no input responsibilities.
- All wire transfers should be approved and processed by a staff member who does not input payroll or who did not input the information or employee in question.

A fraud prevention program lists each duty or task in the payroll department and then flow charts them to their conclusion. It then establishes where a job duty break could or should occur to prevent a single staff member from producing a fraudulent payroll check or committing some other type of fraud. See Exhibit 3.1 for a sample flowchart.

EXHIBIT 3.1

Duties Flow Chart for Fraud Prevention

The following flow chart demonstrates some fraud prevention steps that should be taken during the input of new hire information.

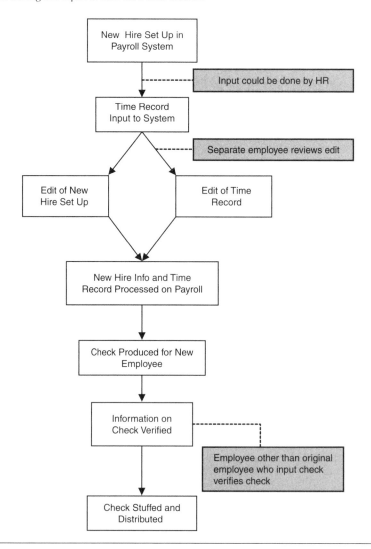

It is difficult to have this type of fraud prevention program in place in smaller departments. Separation of duties is difficult, especially if the department has only one or two employees, but every attempt must be made to do so.

(c) Phantom Employee Audits

Fraud can take many forms in a payroll department but one of the most common methods is known as the phantom employee scam. A fake or phantom employee is "hired" and set up in the payroll system. This phantom employee is then paid normally—no excess hours or overtime to make the employee stand out on an edit report. Usually the payroll staff member works in cahoots with a supervisor of another department. This allows a time record to be submitted that would pass auditing. Once the phantom employee is set up, it is almost impossible to detect and can go on for years. This is especially true in large companies where one extra employee in a large department would be more likely to go undetected. The best method for finding phantom employees or to make sure there are none on the system is to conduct a headcount of employees and compare it to the number payroll checks. This is called a phantom employee check. A team of employees not related to the payroll department passes out the paychecks in person to each employee. The employee must show identification before receiving the paycheck. This confirms that the employee whose name is on the payroll check is available in person. Phantom employee checks cannot be announced in advance. Also, direct deposits must be cancelled for the day of the phantom employee audit. This is because the phantom employee is frequently set up as a salaried employee with payments that flow automatically, via electronic payments, into bank accounts where a paper check does not need to be collected.

Other strategies for flushing out ghost employees require less massive auditing and strategic planning, but still assist in catching or preventing phantom employees. These strategies include looking at:

- *Social Security Number.* Each employee and each payroll record should have a valid social security number. A simple audit test is to use a filter to search for invalid, blank, or duplicate social security numbers.

- *Direct Deposit Numbers.* Search for duplicate bank account numbers for direct deposit. Keep in mind, however, that the company may employ more than one family member and they may have a single bank account.

- *Home Addresses.* Duplicate home addresses need to be verified against new hire paperwork and updates to masterfiles.

- *P.O. Box Addresses.* Search the payroll masterfile for P.O. boxes for home addresses. P.O. boxes are common in rural areas or on rural routes but again, this could help in investigating for phantom employees.

- *Work Location.* Many personnel systems contain information on each employee's work location or address. In some cases, the location is sufficiently detailed to identify the actual workstation or desk of each employee. Matching the payroll data with the work location data will highlight all employees without a valid work location. Additionally, a test for duplicate work locations will identify locations where there is more than one employee.

- *Wage Level.* Where there are clearly defined job classifications with salary levels, a ghost employee may be easily identified if the rate is not appropriate for the classification. (A possible exception might be employees who changed job classifications involuntarily. They may be "salary protected" and paid at their previous classification's rate.)

- *Deductions.* A ghost employee may be receiving a regular paycheck without any of the usual deductions for tax, pension, or health insurance.

- *Vacation or Sick Leave.* Failure to take any time off is a red flag for ghost employees. Match the payroll records with the leave database. These records will identify anyone on the payroll with no recorded vacation or sick leave.

- *Personnel History.* If the records are maintained in the payroll system, the previous work history can be compared. Phantom employees may have no previous employment history, positions, performance evaluations, and so forth. If the information is not maintained in the payroll system, then this audit should be done by hand with paper records.

3.3 DEALING WITH THE INTERNAL REVENUE SERVICE

IRS. Three initials that can send a payroll department screaming into the night. But it does not have to be and actually should not be that way. Compliance with its regulations and correspondence with the agency are simply facts of life for a payroll department. The best way to take the fright out of dealing with the IRS is to be able to handle anything that the agency throws the department's way. In an efficient payroll department, the procedures to handle IRS correspondence and compliance issues should be set up well in advance. To accomplish this, the payroll department must do two things. First, establish procedures on what steps must be taken when and if an IRS notice is ever received. Second, determine which areas of the department could trigger an IRS notice and minimize any potential compliance issues before a notice can be sent.

(a) IRS Notices

But what constitutes an "IRS Notice"? Actually, any communication from the IRS should be treated as a notice and handled immediately. Generally, the first inclination is to procrastinate. But this does not help the matter in the least and can allow penalties and interest to add up. It is also sometimes a habit of payroll departments, who are absolutely sure that all deposits have been made on time, to dismiss IRS Notices because they are positive nothing is wrong. However, when the IRS sends a notice it means that its records and the payroll department's records do not match. The error could very well be on the side of the IRS, but nonetheless, it needs to be handled immediately to correct the situation.

The notices usually come from the IRS Service Centers, are computer-generated, and indicate that a problem exists. This does not mean that the payroll department has made any errors in withholding, depositing, reporting, or the like. It simply means that IRS records show something in the company's account as incorrect and in need of rectifying or that they have adjusted the account and need the payroll department to verify the adjustment. These types of adjustments can include deposits not credited to the account or to the wrong quarter, lost deposits, computer or data entry errors, and so on. The following are the suggested steps to follow when an IRS Notice has been received.

Step 1. Read the notice carefully to determine what exactly the IRS says is wrong and where and when the error has occurred and what they expect the payroll department to do. Right now it is not important to determine who made the error; just pinpoint the discrepancy so the records can be pulled and it can be clearly understood what the IRS is looking for. For example, the IRS notice states that the deposits for the third quarter of 2004 do not balance with the Form 941 for the same period. The IRS states that the deposits are short by $2,184.75. They are requesting payment of this amount plus penalties and interest of $1,137.82. In this case, the third quarter of 2004 reconciliation spreadsheets, Form 941, and deposit records should be pulled.

Step 2. Verify the following:
- All deposits were made on time, in full, and for the correct quarter.
- The Form 941 reflects all deposits made.
- The dates listed for the deposits are correct if a Schedule B was submitted with the Form 941.

Step 3. If an error is discovered, the missing amount should be paid immediately as directed by the IRS Notice. The amount can be deposited and a letter sent to the

IRS informing them that the amount has been paid or a check can be sent with the IRS notice to the address requested. The latter is the better method as it ensures that the IRS will not confuse the deposit with any other quarter or for a different purpose.

Step 4. If no error is discovered in the payroll records, the IRS may have misapplied the payment to the wrong quarter or not applied it to the proper account. Review each deposit to see if the amount missing (not including penalties and interest) matches any deposits exactly. If it does, the IRS has more than likely applied the deposit to the wrong quarter or the wrong account. A letter must be sent to the IRS explaining the error and how to correct it.

Step 5. If no deposit or combination of deposits matches the amount, and all other research does not result in explaining the discrepancy, then the payroll department will need more information before it can determine what happened. The IRS records will have to be compared to the company's records to determine where the error is. Therefore, a letter will have to be sent to the IRS requesting that they send a transcript of all the liabilities and deposits for the company so a determination can be made of where the error has occurred. Do not expect the IRS to make this determination. It is up to the payroll department to find the error, even if it was made by the IRS.

There are two types of letters to the IRS that are discussed above. The first one is the letter to explain why the account is in error and to request a correction to the account and the second one is to request more information from the IRS to determine where the error listed on the notice occurred. The following steps apply to writing both letters:

Step 1. All correspondence with the IRS must be in writing. Never try to resolve IRS notices over the phone until at least one letter has been sent and responded to. A clear record of correspondence is needed if help is requested from the Taxpayer Advocate Office.

Step 2. The letter should be clear, brief, and concise. Do not go into the history of the auditing that has been done, or what measures were taken before writing the letter. State the problem, state the information needed, or state the solution. Keep it to one page or less. To help ensure that the correspondence arrives intact and is complete for the IRS agent, a helpful technique is to type the correspondence right on a copy of the IRS notice itself. Use the back of a copy of the notice as the letterhead for your company if possible. It may not look as neat, but it helps to make sure that the person who opens the envelope does not misplace the attached notice and backup before the letter reaches the agent. This way, all the information about the company and the account are available to the agent. Always restate the company name, address, EIN, and any identifying information in the body of the letter even if the notice is attached. Again, this is helpful to the agent receiving the letter. Always use the bar-coded reply envelope, even if it needs to be attached to a larger envelope to mail. Send the letter by certified mail or overnight signature required to ensure that proof of mailing is available if the need arises.

Step 3. One of the most important things to remember when dealing with the IRS is that the person, yes *person*, reading and handling the company's account is a human being trying to do his or her job. Never write insulting, degrading, demanding, or critical letters. This does not help in getting the problem resolved, which is the whole idea of writing in the first place. Find a better arena to vent any anger toward the government. Courtesy, diplomacy, and tact will go much further. It is also very helpful when applying for help from the Taxpayer Advocate to be able to demonstrate that all correspondence was businesslike, to the point, and most important, polite.

Step 4. Maintain a good audit trail of all the correspondence in case the matter is referred to the Taxpayer Advocate. Keep copies of all notices and the written response to each in chronological order. Keep copies of all supporting documents (e.g., check copies, EFT confirmations, receipts, tax returns, etc.) with the files. Do not rely on having to pull them later from other files.

Step 5. Make sure that the person in the department who is handling the correspondence with the IRS is authorized to do so. It makes the correspondence easier to process by the IRS if the person writing is authorized to receive or give information. Use the power of attorney Form 2848 with the correspondence if the person writing the letter is not a signer of the tax returns.

The following steps need to be included in the letter if the payroll department is requesting additional information from the IRS to resolve the issue in the notice.

Step 1. Ask the IRS to put a freeze on the account in question until the information requested is received. This will halt the accumulation of additional penalties and interest while waiting for the IRS to respond.

Step 2. Explain, very briefly, that the error cannot be determined and request a copy of the account in question for the entire year in question. This will allow review of all quarters and so on, which will assist in auditing the account.

Step 3. Explain that the payroll department is waiting for the information to finish its response to this notice, it cannot determine the error until the information is received and reviewed against company records, and that the matter cannot be resolved until this information is received. This step is important as it puts the responsibility back in the hands of the IRS. This is very useful, especially when the IRS ignores the request, continues to send notices, and the company has to go to the Taxpayer Advocate.

Step 4. If any further notices are received on the same issue before the requested information is received, a copy of the same letter with "Second Request" written in red should be sent back with the new notice. Do not write a new letter as that could trigger a new response on the same issue and will confuse the matter.

Step 5. When the requested information is received, the matter should be dealt with immediately by the payroll department. Penalties and interest will begin again once the information is mailed by the IRS.

The following steps need to be included in the letter if the payroll department is responding to the notice by offering a solution to the problem:

Step 1. The letter should be a restatement of the problem. For example, according to your files, our deposit of May 15th is not shown as being paid.

Step 2. The next step is to state the facts as they have been determined by the payroll department's research, along with the appropriate backup. For example, the deposit of May 15th was made on time. Enclosed is a copy of the EFT confirmation.

Step 3. The final step is to state the solution to the problem. For example, please verify your records and adjust accordingly.

Step 4. Even if no error was made on the side of the payroll department, it is still necessary to request that all penalties and interest be abated. If not requested, the IRS may rescind the penalty but still expect the company to pay the interest on money it never owed in the first place.

If the payroll department has followed these basic instructions and after three attempts has not been able to resolve the problem, it is allowed to use the Taxpayer Advocate Office. However, the department must be able to prove, through written correspondence, that it attempted to resolve the problem through the normal means first. Telephone conversations will not be accepted as proof of this attempt. A sample letter is shown in Exhibit 3.2.

EXHIBIT 3.2

Sample Letter Regarding IRS Notice

The following information was used to create the sample letter to the IRS in this exhibit.

The XYZ Company received an IRS Notice dated January 5, 20X5. It was sent by agent G. Gibbons. The notice states that the company has underdeposited for the third quarter of 20X4 by $2,184.75. According to the IRS records, the company did not make the deposit for July 16, 20X4 as listed on the company's Form 941 Schedule B. The IRS is requesting this payment plus $1,137.82 in penalties and $984.98 in interest. The notice came from the Fresno processing center. The payroll department has checked its records and has determined that this deposit was made. They have the EFT confirmation, which also proves that it was made on time.

XYZ Company
123 Main Street
Anytown, NH
January 7, 20X5

Internal Revenue Service
Fresno Processing Center
Fresno, CA

Dear Sir or Madam:
We have received your Notice dated January 5, 20X5 for the XYZ Company, 123 Main Street, Anytown, NH, EIN 95-1234567, concerning our third quarter 20X4 tax deposits. The notice states that your records show that we are underdeposited by $2,184.75 due to a missing deposit for July 16, 20X4.
We have verified our Form 941 and payroll records and the deposit was in fact made on July 16, 20X4 as stated on our Form 941 Schedule B. Enclosed with this letter please find a copy of the EFT confirmation as proof of the deposit being made on time and in full.
We are requesting that you please correct your records to reflect this deposit and rescind all taxes, penalties, and interest due concerning this account and this matter.
If you have any further questions, you may contact me at:
(insert payroll staff member's contact information here)

Sincerely,

Encl: Copy of IRS Notice Dated January 5, 20X5
Copy of EFT payment confirmation for July 16, 20X4

If the payroll department has attempted to deal with an IRS problem unsuccessfully, it should contact the Taxpayer Advocate. The Taxpayer Advocate independently represents the taxpayer's interests and concerns within the IRS by protecting his or her rights and resolving problems that have not been fixed through normal channels.

While Taxpayer Advocates cannot change the tax law or make a technical tax decision, they can clear up problems that resulted from previous contacts and ensure that the case is given a complete and impartial review.

The personal advocate assigned to your case will listen to the company's point of view and will work with the payroll department to address its concerns. The Taxpayer Advocate is expected to provide:

- A *fresh look* at a new or ongoing problem
- Timely acknowledgment
- The name and phone number of the individual assigned to the case
- Updates on progress
- Time frames for action
- Speedy resolution
- Courteous service

When contacting the Taxpayer Advocate, the following information should be provided:

- Company name, address, and employer identification number
- The name and telephone number of an authorized contact person and the hours he or she can be reached
- The type of tax return and year(s)
- A detailed description of the problem
- Previous attempts to solve the problem and the office that had been contacted
- A description of the hardship the company is facing (if applicable)

The payroll department may contact a Taxpayer Advocate by calling a toll-free number, 1-877-777-4778. Persons who have access to TTY/TDD equipment may call 1-800-829-4059 and ask for Taxpayer Advocate assistance. If the company prefers, it may call, write, or fax the Taxpayer Advocate office in its area. See Pub. 1546, *The Taxpayer Advocate Service of the IRS*, for a list of addresses and fax numbers.

(b) Compliance Issues

There are many facets to the payroll department that could trigger a compliance issue with the IRS and cause an IRS Notice to be issued. Many of these areas will be listed in this section but because they are of such importance, they will be discussed at greater length in other sections. Refer to the section noted if the area is covered more extensively elsewhere. The facets of the payroll department that need to be extensively audited for compliance issues include:

- *Tax Deposits.* Proper payment and reconciliation of taxes is a must for the payroll department. Comparing the payroll itself to the payroll tax deposits is just one area of reconciliation that must be done. See Section 1.5 for an in-depth discussion of how to set up tax deposit schedules and reconciliations. This is usually the number one cause of IRS notices.

- *Tax Returns.* Quarterly tax returns must be reconciled before submission to the IRS. The IRS will compare the return with the deposits received in its computer system. Again, Section 1.5 will discuss how to set up a system to handle this reconciliation each quarter. This is the second most common reason IRS notices are issued.

- *Form W-2.* Although the notice of an out of balance situation for the Form W-2 normally comes from the Social Security Administration, the final notice for penalties and interest for being out of balance comes from the IRS. Reconciliation of the Forms W-2 is a critical compliance issue and is covered thoroughly in Section 7.4.

- *Form W-4 Notices.* This is not a notice that the payroll department has any jurisdiction over. It is a matter between the employee and the IRS. But the payroll department is expected to process the notices and to comply with the information provided. See Section 1.2 for more information.

- *Proper Taxation of Noncash Benefits.* Benefits received by employees in a means other than cash may or may not be taxable. In Section 3.5, this book discusses the need to audit the taxation of noncash benefits.

- *Cash Payments and Cash Benefits.* Many companies are under the impression that if the employee is paid cash or benefits through the accounts payable department that it is somehow nontaxable income. The payroll department needs to consistently work to make sure that any monies being paid to employees are properly taxed. This includes independent contractors. Section 3.5 covers this issue as well.

3.4   HANDLING DEPARTMENT OF LABOR AUDITS

To ensure compliance with the Fair Labor Standard Act (FLSA), the Act authorizes the Wage and Hour Division of the U.S. Department of Labor Employment Standards Administration to investigate for possible violations, inspect an employer's premises, review whatever records are pertinent to FLSA compliance, and question employees to determine whether any violations of the Act have occurred.

(a) The Audit Itself

To enforce the FLSA, the Secretary of Labor may use any of the following measures:

- "Supervise" voluntary settlements under which the employer agrees to pay back wages due employees.

- Sue an employer on behalf of the employees who are due back wages.

- Sue for civil penalties of up to $1,100 per violation in the case of willful or repeated violations.

- Sue in federal court for an injunction preventing the sale, delivery, transportation, or shipment in interstate commerce of goods produced by any employee employed in violation of the law. These are usually called "hot goods."

- Sue for an injunction barring the actual violation of the Act.

The FLSA gives Wage-Hour inspectors broad investigative powers. These include:

- The right to inspect an employer's facilities. Authorized representatives of the Wage-Hour Division generally have the right to enter an employer's premises for the purpose of investigating compliance with wage-hour law.

- The right to review records. Wage-Hour inspectors have the authority to photocopy or transcribe an employer's records. However, all materials must be kept confidential. The representative may inspect only records pertinent to FLSA compliance. Such records fall into two general categories:

   1. Records relating to employee's earnings and hours worked

   2. Records relating to an employee's or employer's coverage under the Act

- The power to subpoena records and to have its subpoena enforced by a federal district court.

- The right to question employees. A Wage-Hour inspector has the authority to interview employees. Such interviews may be conducted in several ways:

   1. On the employer's premises

   2. At the employee's home

   3. Through the use of written questionnaires mailed to employees

The Wage and Hour Division (WHD) is responsible for administering and enforcing a number of federal laws that set basic labor standards, among them:

- The Fair Labor Standards Act

- The Family and Medical Leave Act

- The Migrant and Seasonal Agricultural Worker Protection Act

- The field sanitation standards of the Occupational Safety and Health Act

- The Employee Polygraph Protection Act

- Certain employment standards and worker protections under the Immigration and Nationality Act

- Government contracts prevailing wage statutes such as the Davis-Bacon and related Acts and the McNamara-O'Hara Service Contract Act

- Garnishment provisions of the Consumer Credit Protection Act

An investigator from the WHD may conduct an investigation to determine whether these laws apply to an employer. If the employer is subject to these laws, the investigator will verify that workers are paid and employed properly according to the laws administered, and that youths under age 18 are employed as provided by the child labor provisions. The WHD does not require an investigator to previously announce the scheduling of an investigation, although in many instances the investigator will advise an employer prior to opening the investigation. The investigator has sufficient latitude to initiate unannounced investigations in many cases in order to directly observe normal business operations and develop factual information quickly. An investigator may also visit an employer to provide information about the application of, and compliance with, the labor laws administered by the WHD.

Why is an employer selected for an investigation? The WHD conducts investigations for a number of reasons, all having to do with enforcement of the laws and assuring an employer's compliance. The WHD does not typically disclose the reason for an investigation. Many are initiated by complaints. All complaints are confidential; the name of the worker and the nature of the complaint are not disclosable; even whether a complaint actually exists may not be disclosed. In addition to complaints, the WHD selects certain types of businesses or industries for investigation. The WHD targets low-wage industries, for example, because of high rates of violations or egregious violations, the employment of vulnerable workers, or rapid changes in an industry such as growth or decline. Occasionally, a number of businesses in a specific geographic area will be examined. The objective of targeted investigations is to improve compliance with the laws in those businesses, industries, or localities. Regardless of the particular reason that prompted the investigation, all investigations are conducted in accordance with established policies and procedures.

Investigations may be conducted under any one or more of the laws enforced by the WHD. Most employers are subject to the FLSA, which is the primary federal law of most general applications requiring payment of the minimum wage and overtime premium pay, keeping certain basic payroll and employment records, and limiting the working hours and types of jobs for certain underage youths. The following procedures described for FLSA investigations are generally applicable to WHD investigations under other laws.

Section 11(a) of the FLSA authorizes representatives of the Department of Labor to investigate and gather data concerning wages, hours, and other employment practices; enter and inspect an employer's premises and records; and question employees to determine whether any person has violated any provision of the FLSA.

The WHD investigator will identify himself or herself and present official credentials. The investigator will explain the investigation process and the types of records required during the review.

An investigation consists of the following steps:

Step 1. Examination of records to determine which laws or exemptions apply. These records include, for example, those showing the employer's annual dollar volume of business transactions, involvement in interstate commerce, and work on government contracts. Information from an employer's records will not be revealed to unauthorized persons.

Step 2. Examination of payroll and time records, and taking notes or making transcriptions or photocopies essential to the investigation.

Step 3. Interviews with certain employees in private. The purpose of these interviews is to verify the employer's payroll and time records; to identify workers' particular duties in sufficient detail to decide which exemptions apply, if any; and to confirm that minors are legally employed. Interviews are normally conducted on the employer's premises. In some instances, present and former employees may be interviewed at their homes or by mail or telephone.

Step 4. When all the fact-finding steps have been completed, the investigator will ask to meet with the employer and/or a representative of the firm who has authority to reach decisions and commit the employer to corrective actions if violations have occurred. The employer will be told whether violations have occurred and, if so, what they are and how to correct them. If back wages are owed to employees because of minimum wage or overtime violations, the investigator will request payment of back wages and may ask the employer to compute the amounts due.

Employers may be represented by their accountants or attorneys at any point during this process. When the investigator has advised the employer of his or her findings, the employer or representative may present additional facts for consideration if violations were disclosed.

While every effort is made to resolve the issue of compliance and payment of back wages at an administrative level, the FLSA also provides for the following:

- An employee may file suit to recover back wages, and an equal amount in liquidated damages, plus attorney's fees and court costs.

- The Secretary of Labor may file suit on behalf of employees for back wages and an equal amount in liquidated damages.

- The Secretary may obtain a court injunction to restrain any person from violating the law, including unlawfully withholding proper minimum wage and overtime pay.

- Civil money penalties may be assessed for child labor violations and for repeat and/or willful violations of FLSA's minimum wage or overtime requirements.

Employers who have willfully violated the law may face criminal penalties, including fines and imprisonment. Employees who have filed complaints or provided information during an investigation are protected under the law. They may not be discriminated against or discharged for having done so. If they are, they may file a suit or the Secretary of Labor may file a suit on their behalf for relief, including reinstatement to their jobs and payment of wages lost plus monetary damages.

In the case of the government contracts statutes, contract funds may be withheld for violations under the Walsh-Healey Public Contracts Act, McNamara-O'Hara Service Contract Act, Davis-Bacon and Related Acts, and Contract Work Hours and Safety Standards Act. Administrative hearings or, in some cases, court action may be initiated to recover back pay under these laws. In addition, liquidated damages may be assessed for certain violations. Violators of these laws may also lose their federal contracts and be declared ineligible for future contracts for a specified period.

(b) Payroll's Responsibilities

When faced with a Department of Labor audit, what procedures should the payroll department follow?

- Complete cooperation should always be accorded to the DOL's auditor or administrator. The payroll department should furnish all records and documents requested. The auditor should be given all he or she asks for if it is within the parameters of the scope of an investigation as listed above.

- However, do not give any more than is asked for. Never volunteer more information or more records than is requested.
- Show courtesy and respect to the auditor at all times.
- Inform management as soon as the notification of an audit is received. Management should be involved in all facets of the audit from the beginning to the end.
- Legal counsel can also be included if available. Many companies have staff counsel. This department should be notified by the payroll department of any audits and kept informed of each step.

3.5 COMPLIANCE ISSUES

Keeping the company in compliance with wage and hour laws and taxation regulations is one of the main responsibilities of the payroll department. As discussed in other sections, customer service and efficiency are indeed extremely important. However, it does the payroll department no good if it is the most efficient in getting the employees what they want and need, keeping management happy and making sure the paychecks are on time, if it has violated wage and hour laws or taxation regulations to do it. All this "efficient" department has done is to expose itself and the company to audits and possible fines and penalties. A truly efficient payroll department is one that meets the needs of the employees and management and still is in compliance with all wage and hour laws and taxation regulations.

(a) Internal Audits for Wage and Hour Compliance

How can a payroll manager be sure that the department meets or exceeds all wage and hour compliance issues? The answer is simple, although the execution of the process is complex. Basically, the payroll manager has to conduct an audit for wage and hour compliance internally before any government agency does. He or she must conduct the same kind of thorough procedural audit that an external auditor would do. This audit is not a quick project that can be done in a day, but an overall, department-wide project that may take several weeks or months or even a year to complete, depending on how much time the manager can devote exclusively to this task.

Because the audit should be done on one aspect of the payroll department at a time, there is a starting and stopping point for each task. This makes it easier to complete each phase of the audit, be able to handle other projects, and then return to the next phase. Accuracy, not speed, is the concern for this audit and it can be conducted with the full knowledge of the payroll staff. This is not a secret audit to find fraud or to catch someone doing something wrong. The purpose is to find areas that are out of compliance and fix them before ever having to face an external audit. The payroll staff can be useful in this endeavor.

This type of audit is not to be confused with an external audit conducted by an accounting firm or internal audits. These audits, conducted by an auditor who is not part of the payroll department, are looking for compliance with general accounting practices and company procedures.

The payroll manager should complete the following two critical steps before beginning any internal audit.

1. The person conducting the audit should know all the laws, rules, and regulations concerning the topic being audited. These should be put in writing and include both federal and state regulations. This should not be done from memory but from primary sources (see Section 3.6 for sources). Secondary sources can also be used if the source is comprehensive and includes citations. This can be done prior to each audit for each topic or the entire audit book can be compiled prior to starting the audit. The company policy for each topic should also be included. Many times the federal or state requirements are exceeded by company policy. And, of course, employees can sue if company policy is not followed even if the federal and state requirements are, so specify clear-cut company rules in the audit as well.

2. A comprehensive list of all payroll tasks to be audited should be completed, in writing, prior to beginning the

audit. This serves as a "playlist" of the tasks to be accomplished and helps with assembling the law book discussed in item 1. It also assists in compiling the time frame and work schedule for the audit. A sample list is created in Exhibit 3.3.

EXHIBIT 3.3

List for Wage and Hour Internal Audit

Payroll Topic	Suggested Areas to Question for Audit
Regular rate of pay	• Does the company have any factors that would affect the regular rate of pay such as bonuses, commissions, or shift differential?
	• Do the state and federal regulations match or must payroll allow for a higher state requirement?
	• Can regular rate of pay be calculated by the payroll system? This question has no quick answer. Most payroll systems do not have the capability to calculate regular rate of pay, especially if it crosses over to more than one payroll.
	• If the regular rate of pay cannot be calculated by the computer system, are manual spreadsheets being used?
	• If manual spreadsheets are used to calculate regular rate of pay, are they being done correctly?
	• Are retroactive pay raises being included when calculating regular rate of pay for back overtime due?
	• Does the payroll staff understand the rules concerning regular rate of pay and are they applying them to the payroll processing? This is critical. The company policy and the procedure manuals may state the calculation correctly but the staff may not follow through because they do not understand the concept.
	• Does the company policy meet or exceed the federal and state requirements for regular rate of pay? Does the payroll staff understand the policy?
	• If the employee works more than one job with more than one rate, are weighted averages used?
Overtime	• Does the company policy meet or exceed the federal or state standards for overtime, especially in terms of the hours worked category?
	• If the company is multistate, does the company policy follow each state's requirements if they exceed the federal ones?

EXHIBIT 3.3 *(CONTINUED)*

List for Wage and Hour Internal Audit

- Does the department staff understand how to calculate overtime?
- If paper time records are used, who calculates the overtime hours and are they trained to do so?
- Does the company pay on a semimonthly basis? If so, does the payroll department staff or the employee's supervisor know how to combine workweeks that have been split because the payday occurred midweek? (This is necessary in order to determine if overtime is due to the employee when that workweek is completed by the next payroll.)

Time records
- Do time records follow the proper format to comply with company policy and wage and hour regulations?
- Is time recorded correctly to match state regulations? For example, the state of California requires four time recordings or punches (one in, one out for lunch, one back in from lunch, one out for the night) per day. Just writing in eight hours will not suffice.
- Does the company have a policy regarding the employee signing the time record and is it followed?

Exempt employees
- Although payroll does not usually make the decision as to who is exempt and who is not, it is responsible for paying employees according to those rules. So it is part of the audit to determine if all employees who are paid as exempt employees do indeed qualify for that exemption.
- Are deductions from an exempt employee's pay for such items as vacation, sick leave, or other leaves done correctly under federal and state regulations?
- Does company policy for deductions from exempt employees' salaries comply with federal and state regulations?

Pay stubs
- Does the pay stub comply with the state requirements on which information must be listed?
- If the company is located in more than one state, has each state's requirements been met?
- If the company is using electronic pay stubs, have the state's requirements been met?

EXHIBIT 3.3 *(CONTINUED)*

List for Wage and Hour Internal Audit

Payday	• Is the department paying employees within the parameters of the state's requirements? For example, the state requires that employees be paid within seven days of the close of the payroll, and the payroll closes on Friday. Therefore, the employees must be paid by the following Friday. These requirements are unique to each state and may vary depending on the frequency of the payroll.
	• Is the payroll department aware of and in compliance with all state regulations concerning the disbursement of paychecks? This includes times and place of payments, time off to cash checks, and making sure employees are paid on time even if the checks are mailed.
Direct deposit	• Are employees required to use direct deposit? Is this legal under state and federal requirements?
	• Does the form for signing up for direct deposit include permission from the employee to remove a deposit as well as make a deposit of a payroll check in case the payment is made in error?
Paper checks	• Does the paper check contain all information required by the state?
	• Are paper checks distributed correctly?
Posters and notices	• Are all posters properly displayed?
	• Are all notices given to the employees when needed?
Garnishments	• Are all garnishments properly documented?
	• Are all required notifications to employees and/or agencies being sent?
	• Is the correct interpretation of disposable pay being used for each type of garnishment?
	• Are the correct amounts being deducted under the Consumer Credit Protection Act?
	• Are garnishments started and stopped at the correct times and for the correct amounts?
Other deductions	• If the company has other types of deductions, such as company loans or purchases, are they being deducted correctly and within the parameters of all wage and hour laws?
	• Does the deduction reduce the employee's pay below minimum wage and is this allowed?

EXHIBIT 3.3 *(CONTINUED)*

List for Wage and Hour Internal Audit

Minimum wage	• Does the company comply with the higher of the federal or state minimum wage?
	• If the company is located in more than one state, are all states' minimum wages being considered?
	• Does the company have learners or apprentices? Are they paid minimum wage and does this comply with federal and state minimums?
	• Is a subminimum wage used and does it comply?
	• Is room and board applied against minimum wage and does this comply with federal and state requirements?
Terminated employees	• Does timing of the payment of terminated wages comply with the state's requirements?
	• Does the distribution of final paychecks comply with the state's requirements?
	• Are the deductions from final paychecks in compliance with federal and state requirements?
Tips	• If the employees receive tips, do they properly report them to the payroll department?
	• If a tipped credit is used, does it comply with federal and state requirements?
Record keeping	• Does the payroll department keep all records in the correct format, with all required information, and with adequate security?

(b) Internal Audits for Federal and State Taxation Compliance

In addition to the wage and hour audit discussed above, the payroll manager should also conduct a similar audit for taxation compliance. This is for both federal (e.g., income, social security, Medicare, and unemployment) and the applicable state taxes including unemployment insurance and local taxes. The stakes for being out of compliance with these regulations are higher than for wage and hour law violations. The Internal Revenue Code (IRC) allows for a personal liability for penalties and the tax if a person is found to have willfully failed to withhold the proper taxes. This audit is conducted in the same general way as the wage and hour audit discussed above. The playlist of what is to be audited should be created and the compliance manual assembled. See Exhibit 3.4 for a sample list of audit tasks.

Exhibit 3.4

List for Taxation Internal Audit

Payroll Topic	Suggested Areas to Question for Audit
Taxable wages	• Are the definitions of taxable wages for each tax correct? • Are the wage bases properly used and updated? • Are they reported correctly on all tax reports? This includes the Form 940, which requires the gross total wages first, then the calculation for the taxable wages. This also includes line 2 of the Form 941 for income taxable wages.
Form W-4	• Are exempt forms discontinued each year at the appropriate date? • Are all forms properly completed? (See Section 1.2 for details.) • Have all the required forms been submitted to the IRS and the state?
Form W-2	• Are the forms furnished to the employees properly and on time? • Are the forms furnished to the Social Security Administration (SSA) in the proper format and on time? • Are the forms reconciled to the payroll and the Form 941 before being submitted? • Are duplicate forms issued properly? • Are forms retained for the proper period? • Is the pension plan box marked appropriately?
Form 940	• Is it completed correctly? • Is it submitted on time? • Is it reconciled against the payroll?
Form 941/state equivalent	• Is it completed correctly? • Is it filed on time? • Is it reconciled against the payroll? • Is it reconciled against the Form W-2?

EXHIBIT 3.4 *(CONTINUED)*

List for Taxation Internal Audit	
Form W-5	• Are the forms available as of the first payroll of the year? • Does the computer system calculate the Advanced Earned Income Credit correctly? • Are the Forms W-5 terminated after the final payroll for each year?
Deferred compensation	• Are all deductions done within the legal parameters? • Does the payroll department apply the plan terms to the payroll properly?
Group term life insurance over 50K	• Is it taxed and reported correctly? • Does the employee pay a portion of the premium? Is that taxed correctly? • If the employee pays the entire premium, is it still taxed correctly? • Are the amounts due deducted from final payroll checks? • How is the taxation computed for retired or terminated employees who are still on the plan?
Cafeteria plan	• Is the taxation and reporting handled correctly? • Is dependent care reported separately? This also includes dependent care that may be paid directly from accounts payable and not through the payroll.
Personal use of a company vehicle	• Is the proper paperwork being submitted to payroll? • Is the proper method being used? • Is it taxed correctly?
Auto allowances	• Are they paid through accounts payable instead of payroll? • Is the proper paperwork submitted for the taxation?
Relocation or moving expenses	• Are they paid through payroll or accounts payable? • Are they taxable or nontaxable? • If taxable, are they processed through the payroll? • Are they reported correctly on the Form W-2 even if nontaxable?
Business expense reimbursements	• Is the proper paperwork submitted? • Is it an accountable or nonaccountable plan? • Does it exceed government limits?

EXHIBIT 3.4 *(CONTINUED)*

List for Taxation Internal Audit

Educational assistance	• Is it a bona fide plan?
	• Does it exceed the limits?
	• Is it paid through accounts payable?
Supplemental wages	• Are all wages that should be supplemental wages treated as supplemental?
	• Are separate checks issued and taxed using Form W-4?
	• Is the current rate used?
	• Does the state have a special rate for bonuses?
Part-time employees	• Are part-time employees taxed correctly?
Prizes and awards	• If awarded by another department, are they taxed properly?
Length of service or safety awards	• Are they awarded as cash or tangible property?
	• Is there a ceremony?
	• Are they taxable?
Payments made through accounts payable	• Is the employee being paid through accounts payable for something other than his or her normal duties?
	• Is this being reported to payroll?
Independent contractors	• Have they been verified as independent contractors?
	• Could they be employees?
	• Is the contractor a former employee now being paid through accounts payable?
	• Is the contractor a current employee being paid for another position or duty?
Gift certificates	• Are they taxed correctly?
	• If given out through another department, are they included in payroll?

Again, this audit is comparing the actual practice of taxation in the payroll department to the regulations to detect any out of compliance situations and should not be confused or combined with any other internal or external audit. This audit can take a long time to complete if done thoroughly. As with the wage and hour audit, the results of this audit should be documented. If a practice or procedure is found to be out of compliance, this should be brought to the attention of management if the payroll manager does not have the authority to make the change. It is important to document any determinations made by management, especially if they decide not to make any changes. Again, IRC does allow for penalties to be assessed against the individual who was found to be the one to decide not to withhold the proper taxation.

3.6 RESEARCH NEEDS

The efficient payroll department must always be as up to date as possible with changing rules and regulations. It must also be able to answer any questions from employees or provide the regulations on any payroll subject to management. Fortunately, with twenty-first century technology these tasks are much easier to perform. Why? Because now, instead of having to keep dozens of IRS publications, state employer guides, and forms on the shelf, all the payroll department has to have is Internet access. Yes, the same Internet that allows someone to buy seeds directly from the growers and wine from Australia also allows the payroll department to have almost any rule, regulation, opinion letter, piece of legislation, publication, or form at its fingertips.

(a) Tracking Changing Tax Laws and Regulations

One of the hardest tasks of any profession has been keeping knowledge and skills current. This is especially true for the payroll profession where the rules and regulations are constantly being created, updated, or deleted by various government agencies.

Fortunately, payroll departments can now turn to electronic methods of keeping up to date as well as the traditional paper means. There are numerous newsletters from for-profit information sources that the payroll department can purchase to keep up to date on new rules and changes in regulations. These are issued weekly, biweekly, or monthly. They can be on paper or electronic via e-mail. These newsletters, or reports as they are sometimes called, provide updates but may also include how-to articles to help the payroll professional learn new tricks of the trade to increase efficiency or compliance or even customer service.

Also available from these sources are e-mail weekly alerts that let the recipient know that a bill has just been introduced, a wage base or interest rate announced, or administrative changes to a department have been made. Some of these e-mail alerts can even be accessed for free.

In addition to the for-profit sources, there are many free newsletters or e-mail alerts available. The IRS offers a digital dispatch e-mail newsletter that comes weekly. It also offers an update service. In addition, many states also offer this type of update as well. In addition to the paper newsletters the states send out, it is possible to get the quarterly or monthly newsletter electronically by signing up on the website. For example, to sign up for the IRS newsletter called "Digital Dispatch," just go to the IRS website at www.irs.gov, click on "information for business," then scroll down and click on "Digital Dispatch" and sign up. One of the best things about these types of updates is that they are quick and easy to read and they do not clutter up the payroll department with mounds of paper. In addition, if an item of interest is found, it can be quickly cut and pasted into an e-mail and distributed. In addition, the e-mail can be forwarded to all staff members. Besides furnishing rules and regulations, most government websites have a "hot topic," "news," "press release," or other designated section that gives the site visitor the latest news.

(b) Researching Laws and Regulations

It sometimes seems that at least once a month the payroll department gets a question it can't answer immediately. The payroll staff or manager usually knows the answers to the standard questions—which wages are subject to withholding, the overtime rules, or when Forms W-2 are due—but occasionally the payroll department needs to search for the solution to a more difficult question or problem. Unfortunately, there is no one definitive source to answer all payroll questions in depth. It is not physically possible to house the entire IRS code, wage and hour laws, and other regulations for the federal government and all 50 states in one source, even electronically. However, the payroll department needs to be able to answer these questions quickly and authoritatively in order to remain efficient. To solve this dilemma before being faced with one of these unfamiliar questions, the payroll department should set up procedures outlining the basics of how to research payroll questions. These procedures should be part of the overall procedures for the department and made available to the entire payroll staff. The staff should be trained in how to use the procedures as soon as they are complete.

There are two types of legal sources available to the payroll department to handle researching questions. These are known as primary and secondary sources. These designations are used by the legal world to indicate the status of the sources. The term secondary source indicates that it is not binding in any court. Secondary sources are publications written by knowledgeable individuals that explain the law. They are explanations presented in clearer, more concise language than the primary authority and are intended to clarify complex topics. There are hundreds of secondary sources available to the payroll professional. Examples of secondary sources are:

- *Complete Guide to Federal and State Payroll Compliance* (IOMA, Inc.)

- *Complete Guide to Federal and State Wage and Hour Compliance* (IOMA, Inc.)

- *Payroll Administration Guide* (BNA, Inc.)

The first two books listed are paper manual guides that can be purchased. These are reference manuals to assist in answering questions of both a complex or simple nature. These books are usually updated annually. It is important to keep current copies of these types of books. Having outdated information is worse than not having any information at all. The third source listed is available either electronically (on a CD-ROM) or as a web-based form. It is a massive series of information packed guides that can answer almost any payroll question and includes citations of the laws. Most of the time, these sources are sufficient to answer any question. Secondary authority sources are also helpful in understanding a new topic and the terms related to that issue.

But on some occasions, the person asking the question would like a "definitive source" or the exact law, rule, or regulation—not an interpretation. In this case, the payroll department needs to consult the primary source. (By the way, the secondary sources also come in handy here as well. They can help the researcher to find the exact primary source needed.)

Primary sources include the Internal Revenue Code (IRC), the Department of Labor wage and hour laws, and the state equivalents. They can also include pronouncements by the departments, publications, fact sheets, or related court cases.

As mentioned, when searching for the primary sources, the best place to start is the secondary sources. A secondary article may cite the primary authority, in which case only the original regulation or ruling needs to be located. It may also give the researcher the special terms that he or she needs in order to search for the primary source. For example, the payroll department is given a question about anniversary gifts. These consist of a certificate, a company pin, and a stock award and are presented to the employees for every seven years of service to the company. The payroll department is then asked about taxation of these items and the person asking the question wants to see the IRS code, not the secondary source. Where does the researcher begin? If he or she searched the IRC under "anniversary gifts," nothing would be found. Looking under "gifts" may bring up IRC §102, which tells the researcher that employees cannot exclude the value of gifts received from employers. This might lead the researcher to conclude that all of the gifts being questioned are taxable. However, the secondary authority resource would list this type of gift under "employee achievement awards," which are governed by IRC §274(j). As long as the conditions are met, the tangible property (the certificate and the pin) can be excluded from income, although the stock award must be included in income. The researcher can then take this information and go to the IRS website, link to the IRC, and obtain § 274(j).

If the secondary source does not cite the IRC, the information can still be obtained from the IRS website by doing a search of the appropriate words.

To help the payroll staff conduct research, the departmental procedures should list the sources available for quick reference such as any reference manuals or guides purchased by the company. This listing should include not only the location of the paper books but the name and password to use if the department subscribes to web-based reference guides. In addition, if the department's manuals do not list payroll related websites or the department does not have a reference guide, then all known payroll websites should be listed in the procedures. It is a waste of time for the researcher to have to hunt down the website if someone else in the department already knows where it is. This should be an active list. As a websites change (locations of websites change often) or a new one is located it should be either changed or added to the procedures. This way the list is always as current as possible. Research of payroll related questions is a skill that takes a long time to master. However, the more the payroll staff member practices, the better the skill will become. It is common practice for the manager of the payroll department to research questions but to be truly efficient, the department staff should be able to handle this task as well. Simple research is a good training tool and allows staff members to hone their skills so that employees will be able to handle the more difficult research when it comes up later on. It is also more efficient to have more than one person able to research questions.

(c) Payroll Related Websites

There are literally thousands of websites devoted to the information that payroll needs and uses. It would be impossible to list them all here. In addition, as sites are improved or added, the locations may change so lists can become outdated quickly. Massive lists of all the payroll related sites are also not very efficient. A payroll department that is located in just one state would need a much smaller list than one located in 37 states. Payroll departments are unique and so are the website lists they require. That is why the department should create its own list to use internally. There are, however, just a few websites that should be on all lists. These are the sites, such as the IRS or

DOL, that affect all payroll departments. These sites are, for lack of a better term, link sites. Each site contains a link page that lists other sites that might be of interest to the site visitor. The following is a list of these sites:

- *Internal Revenue Service (www.irs.gov).* This is the IRS website. All forms, pamphlets, and code are available on this site.

- *Federal Department of Labor (www.dol.gov).* This site includes pamphlets, law rulings, and basic wage and hour law information. The site also has an excellent link page to the state wage and hour law websites.

- *Social Security Administration (www.socialsecurity.gov).* This site includes the information on filing Forms W-2 and Totalization agreements.

- *American Payroll Association (www.americanpayroll.org).* This is the site for the professional payroll organization. It has an excellent link page. This link page lists all taxation, wage and hour, worker's compensation, and child support websites.

3.7 SECURITY BASICS

The days of the old time payroll clerk or paymaster sitting behind the lone desk counting out the cash for the pay envelopes and marking everything down in a ledger while wearing a green visor is long gone. Today the payroll professional uses state-of-the-art computer software to produce checks and record transactions. Record keeping is even going paperless, with payroll departments recording time and attendance via computer programs. Employees today can even complete a Form W-4 online and submit it directly to the payroll department via an intranet program without ever touching a paper form.

But one thing that has not changed—in fact, the need for it has increased over the years—is security in the payroll department, the need to keep the records confidential and secure. And in these times, it is also critical to keep the staff secure as well. No longer can that payroll clerk of yesteryear just lock up the ledger in the old safe and go home for the night. The payroll professional must make sure that the computer records are secure, the paper files are confidential, and that the staff is safe before turning out that light at night. A secure payroll department is an efficient payroll department. There are several areas that the payroll department needs to review to ensure that payroll records are secure and that the staff is safe.

- *The Payroll Department.* The duties of each staff member should be reviewed to determine the highest computer access needed. Not all staff members need complete access to all computer files and programs. For example, submitting the payroll itself to the payroll service may only be done by the supervisor or manager of the department. This function could even be limited to only one computer that is kept in the manager's or supervisor's locked office. Or, if a staff member only inputs time cards or Forms W-4 then total access to report writers or to payroll submission would not be necessary. This type of determination and screening can go a long way in keeping the payroll secure. This type of limited access is also helpful in audit trails and internal security. For example, if only certain staff members have access to the check writing program, then this limits the number of people who can write manual checks and helps with the internal security requirements.

- *Human Resources or Benefits Department.* As will be discussed in Chapter 4, access to the payroll system by the human resources or benefits departments is dependent on how the company delegates the input of new hires and benefit deductions. If the computer systems are not integrated and these two departments do not handle any of the input for the payroll system, then they should have read-only access to payroll computer screens. This is critical in the report writing capabilities as well. The HR or benefits department should not be able to produce reports for payroll areas to which they have limited or no access. If the human resources or benefits departments do handle the input for these payroll areas, then of course, full access to the screens will be necessary.

- *IS or IT Department.* Of course programmers need access to internal payroll system software to be able to handle upgrades and software adjustments. But this access should be limited to the software and not allow the employee to make changes to benefits or payroll screens that affect data such as hourly wage or Form W-4 information. Their access should be thoroughly examined to determine just who needs what access to perform their job functions. This judgment should not be made by IT alone but should be discussed in conjunction with the payroll department. Programmers or IT personnel who do not interact with the payroll software but handle other software functions should not have access to the payroll department's information. For example, IS personnel who maintain the websites or e-mail do not need payroll computer access.

- *Employees.* If your company allows employees to access or submit forms and information from and to the payroll department via an intranet system, it is imperative that security be maintained there as well. Employees should have personal identification numbers (PINs) to be able to submit forms or time cards electronically. The policy manual should also include a stiff penalty for divulging that number to fellow employees. Some payroll personnel will need to know the PINs, but the list should be maintained by the computer security personnel, as with all passwords issued by the company.

- *Hard Copy or Paper Files.* Generally, hard or paper copies of payroll records should always be kept locked securely within the payroll department. However, there are a few areas that need special attention:

  - *Off-Site Storage.* If an off-site facility or facilities is used to store the previous year's payroll data, the payroll department needs to make sure that this area is secure as well. Payroll records should still be kept under lock and key with only payroll staff having access. They should never be mixed in with other department's records to "save space and money." It must be remembered that no matter how old the records are, they still contain sensitive payroll data. Better yet, store all records electronically and destroy the paper copies. The government agencies now accept electronically stored data on microfiche or CD-ROM.

○ *Garnishment Records.* Records relating to garnishments need special security even within the payroll department. The garnishments themselves, and the court and other related documents should be kept in a separate locked cabinet within the payroll department. Access to this cabinet should be given only to those payroll staff members who deal directly with garnishments. Other nonpayroll personnel should have no access to these records. Because most federal and state laws limit the actions an employer may take against an employee with a garnishment or garnishments, human resources or the benefit department would have no reason to have access to these files. If possible, even the screens on the payroll system relating to these items should have limited access.

○ *Auditors.* Whether internal or external, the payroll department should have an established policy on what auditors may see or copy in the payroll department. This will prevent misunderstandings later on when an auditor wants to copy and remove information from the department.

○ *Employees.* Generally, there should be no problem with employees seeing their own information within the confines of the payroll department or through the intranet system with appropriate access codes. This assists the employee greatly when checking to see what he or she is claiming on the latest Form W-4 or what benefits the employee currently has. However, proper identification should always be required when an employee requests information in writing or desires copies of information to be printed by the department. The policy should require employees to pick up such information in person and present proper identification. If the payroll department is located off-site, then the information should be sent in confidential envelopes and delivered by the employee's supervisor.

- *Physical Department Security.* The payroll department itself should be secured under lock and key with limited access. An actual physical key or keys can be used, or combination locks with limited code access can be installed. The payroll department should never be located in an open area where nonpayroll personnel can see or overhear the inner workings of the department. Even whispers can be heard if someone is determined enough. All desks and file cabinets should contain locks. Make sure department personnel use those locks, especially during cleaning times or if the department has open access. All computers should be locked or turned off during nonuse hours to prevent hacking or accidental access. Access to the department by nonpayroll personnel should be limited to working hours and always with someone in attendance. For example, there is trouble with the payroll manager's hard drive or computer programs. She is having trouble getting her e-mail to work or has to have some new software installed. Whatever the reason, this should be done when someone is there to accompany the employee who is doing the repair or installation. If the company has set up a customer service area for a combined employee services department or just one for payroll, this should be a secured area and separate from the main payroll processing area. It should not be just the first desk inside the door. Nonpayroll employees should never have access to the main payroll department area. Even managers and supervisors should be excluded.

- *Staff Security.* The safety and security of the payroll staff is of utmost importance in the minds of payroll managers these days. With violence invading the workplace, no one, especially payroll, is safe and secure anymore. There have even been shootings in the workplace over garnishments in the recent past. With this in mind, the following recommendations are made for the security of the payroll staff.

- Doors to the payroll department should be locked at all times with only exit capabilities for fire safety.
- Only payroll staff and limited upper management should have keys or combination access to the department.
- Customer service areas should be adjacent to the payroll department but they should be separate facilities. The employee staffing the facility should have an exit door that is in the opposite direction of where the "customers" enter.
- Nonpayroll employees should never be allowed into the payroll department.
- Panic buttons should be installed in the department in strategic places. These devices are hidden under certain desks and can sound a silent alarm when activated. There should be such precautions in the customer service area and at least two more in the department itself, depending on the size of the department. Possible locations include the manager's office and the desk closest to the door.
- The payroll door should always be a full door and not a French or half door.
- The name of the payroll staff member who handles garnishments should not be known by the general employee population. It is now customary to include employees' extensions on department websites to help employees call the right staff members when they need assistance. But the garnishment number should be the main payroll line or the manager's number or a separate number with voice mail only capabilities. The call can then be transferred or returned. The employee's name should never be used. Even when answering the phone, the employee should use a code name. E-mails concerning garnishments should also

go to a main address or to the manager's address and then be forwarded. Or better yet, have a separate e-mail address that does not include an employee's name. This can be used for back and forth conversations concerning garnishments.

o No employees should be allowed to be abusive or threatening to any payroll staff member. No matter how upset they are or how much "right" they have to be mad about a mistake or perceived error that has been made, no one has the right to hurt or be threatening to a fellow employee. This fact is sometimes overlooked when it comes to payroll. Many employees and employers somehow have the mistaken notion that payroll is a place to vent anger at the company. It is not! And any incident should be reported immediately.

Security of the payroll records, department, and staff is an ongoing concern for all payroll managers and professionals. With proper support and diligence, the payroll department can maintain a high level of security and can actually increase efficiency by working in a secure and organized environment.

CHAPTER 4

Benefits and the Payroll Department

4.1 SHOULD PAYROLL HANDLE THE COMPANY'S BENEFITS?

Most companies do offer benefits to their employees in this day and age. The benefits can range from basic health insurance to complex cafeteria plans and nonqualified stock options. The human resources department or perhaps a subsidiary department, such as the aptly named benefits department, usually handles the setup of benefit programs. This includes completing the paperwork and assisting the employee in making benefit choices. The question that arises is: how actively involved should the payroll department be in handling the company's benefits?

(a) Who Should Input the Employees' Deductions for Benefits?

The company's benefit plans are usually the domain of the human resources department or one of its subsidiaries. Larger companies may even have a separate department devoted exclusively to the creation, setup, and day-to-day operations of the benefit plans.

Whether it is a large company with an entire department created to handle benefits or a small firm with a "party of one" tackling the task, benefits impact the payroll department. The payroll department has had to adapt over the last 30 years to the changing benefits scene. Whereas once it was unusual for a company to offer more than vacation and basic health insurance, today's extremely complex benefits structures require a sophisticated knowledge of IRS and Department of Labor regulations and code. Helping employees sift through the array of benefits and chose the ones that best their needs is definitely the job of the benefits department. Explaining the various nuances of each benefit and the amount of deductions they require is definitely a task the payroll department wants to leave to human resources. But what happens after the employee has made his or her choice?

Imagine the following scenario. The employee has sat through new employee orientation. He or she has read through the massive benefit paperwork and has made all the choices. It is now time to translate those choices into deductions on the employee's benefit screen in the payroll system. This is where benefits impact the payroll department directly. So the question again arises, as it did with new hires: who should do the input? Should the payroll department be responsible for this input because it directly affects the payroll processing? Or should inputting the benefit deductions be the final duty of the human resources or benefits department in order to complete the benefits package for the new employee?

As with new hires, inputting benefits can be a power or control play among departments. However, there is one and only one thing that is most important to consider when deciding whether or not payroll should input employee benefits, and this is efficiency. Is it more efficient for the payroll department to control the input of benefits or not? The answer to this question is the same as for new hires: probably not. At least, not all the time and not with all benefits. For example, there are some company benefits for which payroll does control most of the input, namely leave benefits. The daily tracking of leave benefits, such as sick leave or vacation time, are usually handled by the payroll department via the time records and accruals. The computer system calculates the amount of leave an employee has each time the leave is accrued or taken. The deduction of time is usually accounted for through the time records. However, there are some types of leave that payroll must coordinate with HR to ensure accurate compliance with government regulations or company policy. These include Family and Medical Leave Act (FMLA) related leave, National Guard duty, and jury duty. It should also be clearly spelled out exactly how each leave will be processed and each department's responsibilities. Delays in processing leave benefits can affect the efficient processing of the payroll.

Inputting the deductions for such items as deferred compensation or health insurance is not usually all that needs to be done when entering an employee's benefit choices into the computer system. So if the company has an integrated system shared by human resources and payroll, the input for benefits can be complicated on the human resources side and it is best left for that department to handle. If the systems are separate and do not feed into each other, then it is more efficient for each department to do its own input. No matter who does the input, the problem that generally arises is that of getting the data in on time to meet the payroll processing deadlines.

(b) Benefits and Meeting Payroll Deadlines

One of the problem areas affecting the payroll department in terms of processing the payroll efficiently is receiving all the necessary information on time. Benefit deduction information falls into this category. It really does not matter if the benefits or human resources department does the actual input or it is sent to payroll for input; the situation remains the same. The payroll department must rely on another department to complete its work and send the information over so it can finish processing the payroll. Receiving the information too late to include in the current payroll processing not only makes the current payroll inaccurate (and could result in the need to issue manual checks), but it has a snowball effect. If deductions are missed on this payroll then they will need to be caught up on the next payroll. Because this is not what the employee is expecting to see in his or her paycheck, he or she must be notified. However, then it is possible for the employee to request that a double payment not come out of the next paycheck, because he or she cannot afford that. Instead, the employee would prefer to have the missed deduction spread out over several payroll checks. This, in turn, creates more input plus reconciling nightmares for the department responsible for balancing the benefit payments. This is grossly inefficient but all too often the norm in many companies.

One way to combat this cycle is to set up a strict input/processing calendar for benefit deductions. The payroll department must set up a year-long calendar noting the exact day and time the human resources or benefits department must either have all the benefits input to the system or get the information to the payroll department for processing in order to meet payroll deadlines. These are drop-dead dates, which must be clearly communicated to the other department(s). If this is the first time the payroll department is issuing such a calendar, it is best to convey the information in a face-to-face meeting, if physically possible. Management should also be aware of the importance of this calendar. It must be reiterated that the consequence of missing the processing deadline is not that it creates more work for the payroll department, but that it costs the company more money in staff and processing time. (Always reinforce the bottom line.)

An important aspect of the efficient processing of benefit deductions is its effect on the employees. When errors are made or processing deadlines are missed, the employee's paycheck is greatly affected. If this is a frequent occurrence, it can affect how the employees actually perceive the value of the benefit. So if a company is offering a benefit to the employees to promote retention, improve morale, and so on, processing errors may negate any positive effects of offering the benefit. In addition, no matter who is actually responsible for the missed processing deadline or the input error, it will be perceived by the rest of the company as a payroll error. This is just a fact of life—if it happens on an employee's paycheck, payroll must be responsible. By the way, this perception extends to management as well, which is why it is imperative that the processing calendar be communicated clearly to all involved. Although the first concern of the payroll department is ensuring that the payroll is processed as accurately and efficiently as possible, the plain fact is that the department also must project a capable and professional image or it will lose its credibility. Constant input errors or missed processing dates certainly will not help. Protect the payroll department's bottom line in terms of budget and salaries. Find the most efficient way to input benefit deduction information in a timely manner, and stick to it.

(c) Customer Service and Benefits

The input and processing of the company benefits through the payroll system is one of the standard tasks of the payroll department in conjunction with the human resources department. However, experience has shown that if an employee has a question concerning anything on a paycheck, he or she contacts the payroll department, regardless of which department was responsible for the input. In fact, employees are usually totally unaware of the delegation of duties that is involved in processing payroll. This is why customer service can be difficult for the payroll department when it comes to benefit questions.

Problems can arise when the payroll department is not responsible for the input of benefit deductions to the payroll system. For example, suppose employee A comes to the payroll department and demands to know why his health insurance deduction was doubled to make up for a missed deduction when he made it perfectly clear that he wanted to do it over two payrolls. It will only make matters worse when the payroll staff member is hard pressed for any answer except "I don't know." At this point, it will not help if the payroll staff member tries to explain that the input duties are delegated to human resources and this problem is really their fault—it just sounds like passing the buck. The best time to let employees know which department to contact concerning benefit questions is *before* the question comes up. If the payroll department is not responsible for the handling or input of benefit deductions or the department only inputs the information furnished by another, payroll must let the employees know. One of the most efficient ways to accomplish this is to create a basic contact list for any question an employee may have about his or her paycheck. For example, if you have a question about vacation accruals, contact the payroll department. If the question is regarding the health insurance deduction amount, contact human resources. It is that simple. The contact list should be posted and communicated throughout the normal company channels. Then if an employee does come to the payroll department with a question that falls under another jurisdiction, it becomes easier for the payroll department staff member to clarify the error and whose responsibility it is. Then, of course, he or she should offer to assist the employee by contacting the appropriate department.

4.2   YEAR END AND YEAR BEGINNING ISSUES

The payroll department is one of the few entities in the company that must close out the old year without so much as a day's break before beginning the new year. This makes this period very stressful and difficult. The efficient payroll department must be totally prepared for the new year, including updating all the charts, tables, or databases in the computer system before the new year and having all the benefits accounted for in both the old year and the new year.

(a) Setting Up New Charts and Databases for the New Year

Most computer payroll systems are designed to calculate taxes or deduct benefits using charts, tables, or databases. The system is dependent on these tables and data to calculate accurate payrolls. That is why they must be completely updated for the new year prior to the first payroll run.

The most efficient method to accomplish this is to create a master spreadsheet of all the tables, charts, or databases in the payroll system. This spreadsheet should include the following for each database, table, or chart:

- The name in the computer
- The purpose—what it does
- Instructions on how to access it
- Instructions on how to update it
- Instructions on where to find the information needed to update it

Some of the tables, charts, or databases that may need to be updated include:

- Federal tax charts
- State tax charts
- Benefit charts to reflect various rates for different employees
- Insurance rate tables

The spreadsheet should list the following for each chart, table, or database:

- Whether or not it needs to be updated for the new year—some charts do not change every year, such as state tax charts
- The date by which the information must be obtained in order to complete the update
- Who is responsible for obtaining the update information
- Who is responsible for handling the update
- The date the update was done
- The time the update was done
- Who completed the update

The frequency with which these tables, charts, or databases have to be updated or changed varies depending on what they are programmed for. For example, the federal tax charts will have to be updated every year. However, the state tax tables may not be updated by the state for several years, so the charts currently in the computer system will not need to be changed.

Who makes the changes also varies depending on how the payroll system is maintained or whether the payroll processing is outsourced. Some payroll departments that are processed in house have IT departments that insist all changes be done on a set schedule, be approved by IT in advance, and be carried out through that department. If this is the case, then the payroll department needs to add the date that the IT department must be notified about the required changes to the master spreadsheet. It is also important to include the date that the research and the assembly of the update data must be complete in order to be able to furnish it to the IT department.

Sometimes payroll departments are responsible for this update themselves. If this is the case, then using the spreadsheet will assist in getting this task done efficiently. If the payroll department has its payroll processing outsourced, a combination of the two previous methods usually works best. The vendor generally handles the tax chart updates but the payroll department would need to take care of updating the benefits. Ideally, the master spreadsheet should denote who handles which updates. A sample spreadsheet is provided in Exhibit 4.1.

(b) Creating New Benefits for the New Year

The human resources department or the benefits department work very hard to ensure that the company's employees receive the best benefits the company is willing to offer. It is part of the departments' jobs to do this. It is also part of their jobs to discover new benefits to offer to the employees. Benefits are a great recruiting and retention tool. However, new benefits for the employees usually means new work for the payroll department.

One of the problems with unveiling a new or improved benefit is that it is usually done at the beginning of the new year, the busiest time of the year for payroll. Another problem that arises when human resources or benefits unveils a new benefit is that they like to keep the new benefit a secret until the big announcement. Unfortunately, they keep it a secret from payroll as well. This poses a problem because the benefit may need to be programmed into the payroll system in order to be taken advantage of by the employee. One way to avoid this potential problem is to communicate early and often to human resources/benefits. Make them aware that payroll absolutely needs to be advised of any new benefits being offered. Impress upon them that this notification must occur as soon as possible after the decision is made to offer the new benefit. This applies to any benefit, even ones that will not be offered through the payroll department. Why all benefits?

EXHIBIT **4.1**

Sample Master Spreadsheet for Tables, Charts, and Database Updates

Chart, Table or Database Name	Purpose	Access Instructions	Update Instructions	Where Information Can Be Obtained

Because the payroll department is responsible for the taxation of all benefits, therefore it is up to payroll to determine if taxation and reporting of the new benefit is needed. If it is, then the payroll department will need that extra time to develop a system to collect the data and report and tax the benefit on the payroll system.

A good way to communicate with human resources/benefits on this topic is to send a quick memo at the beginning of the year asking if there are any benefits being considered or discussed for the new year. A follow-up memo should be sent in June or July as a reminder if there was no response to the first memo or the original answer was no. Send one last memo at year end (November) just to confirm there are no new benefits being offered in the coming year that payroll has not been informed about. These memos are quick and simple and do not need to be formal. A sample of each letter is included in Exhibit 4.2. The memos can be sent as e-mails, of course.

(c) Tracking Benefits or Payments for Year-End Taxation

The payroll system is designed to track and accumulate all the data related to each payroll it processes. Then at year end, the system properly sorts this data and produces the Forms W-2. For the entire year the system has calculated the gross wages, the taxable wages, and the amount of benefits and even taxed it all correctly. But there is one thing, one task, the computer system cannot do, no matter how sophisticated the programming or advanced the hardware technology—and that is to track data it is never given. If a benefit or payment is never processed through the payroll system, it cannot be taxed correctly or reported properly. Worse yet, failure to do so could result in penalties, fines, and interest.

But how or why would a benefit or a payment be made to an employee without it being processed through the payroll? Accounts payable and human resources—that is how and why. Throughout the year, the employees are paid for expenses or provided benefits that may be impractical (or impossible, if it is tangible property) to process through payroll. The following list provides some examples:

Exhibit 4.2

Sample Letters for Reminding Human Resources/Benefits to Inform Payroll of Any New Benefits for the New Year

First memo to be sent in the beginning of the new year (January):

To: Human Resources/Benefits
From: Payroll
Subject: New benefits being considered for the upcoming year

This is just a quick memo to request information regarding any new benefits that are being considered during this year for implementation either this year or next year. I would appreciate a heads-up as soon as possible so that the payroll department can plan for any payroll system adjustments that would be needed or research any taxation or reporting issues.

Thanks.

Second memo to be sent in the middle of the year (June/July):

To: Human Resources/Benefits
From: Payroll
Subject: Follow-up memo concerning new benefits being considered for the upcoming year

I just wanted to follow up my last memo concerning new benefits for the upcoming year. Are the human resources or benefits departments planning on offering any new benefits next year? I would appreciate a heads-up as soon as possible so that the payroll department can plan for any payroll system adjustments that would be needed or research any taxation or reporting issues.

Thanks.

Last memo to be sent at the end of the year (November):

To: Human Resources/Benefits
From: Payroll
Subject: New benefits being considered for the upcoming year

I am beginning my preparation for year end and I just wanted to confirm that the company is not going to offer any new benefits for the upcoming year. If we are, I would appreciate a heads-up as soon as possible so that the payroll department can plan for any payroll system adjustments that would be needed or research any taxation or reporting issues.

Thanks.

- Payments:
  - Business expense reimbursements. Employees may be repaid for personal funds spent on behalf of the company, including mileage.

- Educational assistance. These payments may be made directly to the employee to reimburse him or her for a class already completed or a payment may be made directly to the college or university for an upcoming class.
- Auto allowance. The employee may be given a flat dollar amount per month (or other time frame) for the business use of his or her personal vehicle.
- Relocation or moving expenses. The employee either may have payments made to a third party on his or her behalf or may be reimbursed directly for out-of-pocket expenses.
- Club dues. The employee may have golf, country club, or health club dues paid directly on his or her behalf or may be reimbursed directly for the dues.
- Medical expenses. The employee may have out-of-pocket medical expenses reimbursed. This may include annual physicals.
- Dependent care. The employee's dependent care may be paid directly to the provider or the employee may be reimbursed for his or her out-of-pocket expenses.
- Employee referral awards. Employees may be given cash payments for referring other employees.
- Suggestion awards. Employees may be given cash payments for making suggestions to the company that are implemented.

- Benefits:
  - Personal use of a company vehicle. The employee may be given a company owned vehicle to use 24/7. Though it is technically for business use only, if the employee commutes to work in the car, that constitutes personal use.
  - Dependent care. The dependent care may be provided as a benefit in kind on the premises or paid to a third-party provider as a bulk payment instead of per individual.

- ○ Health club memberships. The company may provide health club memberships to all employees and the payment is paid in bulk and not per individual employee.
- ○ Meals. The employer may provide meals to the employees on site or pay in bulk at a local restaurant.
- ○ Length of service and safety awards. These awards may be given to employees to promote retention or safety.
- ○ Free use of the company service. The employees may receive the service the company provides its customers. For example, employees may receive free cable if the company is a cable service provider.
- ○ Cell phones. The company may give the employee a cell phone to use for business and allow personal use.
- ○ Newspapers or magazine subscriptions. The employee may receive such items as the *Wall Street Journal*.
- ○ Christmas or other holiday gift certificates. Employees may be given gift certificates to a local store or supermarket for a holiday.
- ○ Employee recognition awards. The employee may be given rewards for being voted employee of the month, quarter, or year. The rewards may be trips, tangible property, or cash.

These are just some of the examples of payments or benefits that may be given to employees and not processed through the payroll system. The problem is that some of these items may be outright taxable and reportable as wages; others are taxable and reportable only after certain limits have been reached. Also, some are only taxable and reportable if the employee fails to provide proper backup, while still others may be excluded by the tax code outright but still may need to be reported. However, payroll needs to know what payments were made and which benefits were provided in order to make that determination.

An efficient method of accomplishing this is to develop a spreadsheet for tracking nonpayroll items given or paid to employees. Setting up the spreadsheet itself is very simple. But there are two projects that need to be done in order to begin using the spreadsheet:

First, a complete review must be made of all payments distributed in the previous year through accounts payable, either to the employees directly or on their behalf.

Second, a complete review must be made of all benefits offered, either through company policy or by individual agreement, to make sure that all of them have been accounted for.

The payroll department will need the cooperation of the human resources or benefits department as well as accounts payable to be able to compile the list for the spreadsheet. The items listed previously are a good place to start in terms of what to look for. Once the spreadsheet is created, the departments involved have to decide how to track the information so that it is available to payroll at year end. However, it may be better for the employees if the taxable payments or benefits are tracked year round and taxed all year long instead of coming out of the employee's last check of the year, right around the holiday season.

CHAPTER 5

Payroll Systems

5.1   OBJECTIVES OF A COMPUTERIZED PAYROLL SYSTEM

Choosing and implementing a payroll system is a major undertaking for a company, not to mention an expensive one. There is a tremendous amount of staff time as well as money invested in selecting, implementing, and maintaining the payroll system. It is a never ending cycle as well. Once the system implementation is complete, all the bugs are finally worked out, and the system is running smoothly, it is time to begin installing the upgrade.

Very few companies continue to process their payroll without the aid of a computer. Even small companies with only one or two employees can purchase a "payroll system" in boxed software that runs on the owner's PC. But why process payroll on a computer system? Why should a company, especially a small one, take the time, effort, and money to find the software, implement it, learn how to use it, maintain it, and eventually upgrade or improve it? The answer to that question is simple. History and experience have shown that it is more efficient to process payroll on a computer. Why? This is a question that many payroll departments no longer ask or perhaps have never had the chance to ask. Why use a computerized payroll system? What are the objectives of implementing this method? What should a good computerized payroll system do?

In the late 1960s through the 1970s, in-house computer systems and the buildup of payroll processing service bureaus became widespread. Switching from the tedious manual computations and report building to computerized payrolls made sense. It was a time saver and was certainly much more efficient and accurate, even with all the many bugs that had to be worked out. But customization was not really an option in those days. The payroll manager could not say, "I want the payroll system to do X." It was more along the lines of, "this is what the system can do—work around that." With the changeover to PCs in the late 1980s and early 1990s, in-house payroll systems became more customized and software packages began to offer more tools. To remain competitive, the service bureaus began offering more services and more sophisticated systems. Today, with Windows™ and web-based programs and applications available to the payroll manager, the possibilities are virtually unlimited as to what a payroll system is capable of accomplishing. However, even with today's technology, the astute payroll professional still needs to ask the same question as all those years ago—"what is the objective of a computerized payroll system?" An efficient payroll department must understand all the nuances of every facet of the department and this includes the payroll processing software. It is not enough to comprehend the basics of doing the input and producing the checks; the staff must be able to see how everything is tied together. If a deduction is set up, how does this setup relate to taxable wages? If a payment code is created, how should the computer system report it on the Form W-2? This is why it is important to understand what the system is *supposed* to do and compare that to what it actually does do. The job of the efficient payroll department is to make sure the system does what it should when it should.

(a) What Must a Payroll System Have?

To answer this question is to ignore all the fancy bells and whistles of today's technologically advanced computer systems and get back to the basics of processing a payroll. In essence, the objectives of any payroll system, computerized or otherwise, must include (in no particular order):

- *Basic Calculation of Straight Time Following the Appropriate Federal or State Regulations.* The system must be able to calculate this amount based on every state in which the company pays its employees.

- *Calculation of Overtime or Premium Pay According to Federal and the Appropriate State Regulations.* This requirement is difficult to find in a computer system. Overtime or premium pay requires the use of the regular rate of pay in order to perform the calculations. This rate is calculated based on whether or not bonuses or payments are included in the payroll that could trigger the special calculations. Regular rate of pay calculations can be difficult to produce on a computer system because of all the parameters that are needed if the overtime or the payment that triggers the calculations span more than one pay period. These regulations were, of course, created long before the introduction of computers.

- *Calculation of Gross Wages.* This involves being able to include bonuses, additional pays, piecework, commissions, tips, or imputed income amounts.

- *Calculation of Taxable Wages for All Tax Categories Including Federal Income Tax, FICA Taxes, and State Taxes.* This is also includes the requirement to take the amounts for benefits such as deferred compensation or cafeteria plans into account when calculating taxable wages for each tax category. It should also have the capability to allow the payroll department to determine the taxation of each of those benefits, for example, whether or not it is subject to unemployment insurance and the like.

- *Calculation and Deduction of Taxes.* These include the basics of federal income tax, social security, and Medicare taxes, and all applicable state taxes. It should be able to do this based on formulas or percentage rates. It must be able to calculate supplemental taxes. It must also be able to calculate both types of taxation on one check.

- *Calculation of Employer Taxes.* The system should be able to calculate the employer portion of taxes and employer taxes such as unemployment insurance. The rate for use in the calculation should be adjustable to accommodate changes in the rate from year to year.

- *Update Tax Files and Charts.* The ability to update the tax tables and rates annually is essential.

- *Deductions of Benefit Payments.* The system must be able to deduct all benefit payments for all benefit programs offered by the company.

- *Garnishments.* The system must be able to handle all types of garnishment calculations including tax levies, child support, and creditor garnishments. The garnishments may be based on a table or chart and calculated as a flat dollar amount or a percentage of disposable income. The computer must be able to calculate all these types of methods. It must also be able to handle multiple garnishments for a single employee. Multiple garnishments could include more than one of the same type of garnishment for the same employee, for example, three child support garnishments for one employee. The program must be able to handle starting and stopping a garnishment based on either reaching a set date, or upon reaching a limit. The system also must be able to handle a percentage and a flat dollar amount for one garnishment, such as a child support garnishment that requires 25 percent to be deducted for current child support and $50 to be deducted for arrears.

- *Net of Check Calculations.* The system must be able to handle net check calculations.

- *Check Printing, Including Pay Stubs or Statements.* State laws have specific regulations on what must be included on the pay stub or statement. The system must be able to meet these requirements.

- *Direct Deposit.* The system must be able to handle direct deposits. This includes the transfer file and reports.

- *Masterfile.* Of course, the computer system must be capable of setting up and maintaining a masterfile. But masterfile is a broad term which includes:

  ○ Employee information such as name (first name, middle initial, last name) address, phone number, birth date, date of hire, termination date, social security number, employee identification number, and state of employment to mention a few basic ones.

- Form W-4 information including the state equivalents plus allowances for any reciprocal agreements or multistate withholding. It must also allow for exempt status if the employee requests it.
- Form W-5 information.
- Visa information, including the capability to block certain taxes, is required under visa regulations.
- Direct deposit information.

• *Reports.* The system must produce informational reports including:

- Payroll register
- Benefits register
- Tax reports
- Direct deposit reports
- Deduction register

• *Transfer Files.* The system must produce files to transfer information to outside agencies. These include:

- Direct deposits
- Benefits
- New hire reporting

• *Interfaces.* The system must interface with other departments within the company to allow for transfer of information from the payroll system to another department's system. The interfaces include posting to the general ledger and human resources.

• *Report Writer.* The system must be able to write reports on demand to pull the data needed in the format needed.

• *Quarter End Reports.* Information to produce quarter end reports should be furnished by the system.

• *Form W-2 Reconciliation.* The system must allow for the production of the Forms W-2 reconciliation each quarter, at a minimum.

- *Manual Check Input.* It would be optimal if the system could produce the manual checks and input them into the employees' files. But at minimum, the system must allow for input of manually produced checks.

- *Void Checks or Check Reversals.* The capability to allow for the reversal of voided checks is a must.

- *Forms W-2.* The system must be able to produce the Forms W-2 at year end including the magnetic media necessary for filing the forms.

- *Retaining Information.* The payroll information for each employee as well as month to date, quarter to date, and year to date information should not be adjustable nor able to be altered by the system during future processing of items such as manual checks or voided checks.

- *Time Record Input.* The system, of course, must allow for the input of time records. But it must also allow for edits of that input. These edits should contain parameters that are adjustable to meet the company's editing needs.

The criteria just discussed are some of the basic, fundamental tasks that the computer system must be able to perform in order to process the payroll efficiently. The following are "extra" items the payroll system should be able to perform in order to increase that efficiency:

- Be able to calculate regular rate of pay calculations under any conditions. The addition of a time keeping system may be needed to accomplish this task.

- Have the capability to allow for the addition of deduction codes or payment codes.

- Have the capability of calculating manual checks within the system with automatic input into the employees' wage information.

- Be able to produce third-party checks for garnishment deductions.

- Have the capability to produce multiple checks for a single employee.

Knowing what the payroll system can and should do is an important step in establishing and maintaining an efficient payroll department. However, it is also important for the payroll manager to have a comprehensive understanding of how a basic computerized payroll system operates, regardless of whether the department has their own system or relies on an outside vendor or service bureau for their processing needs.

(b) How Does It Work?

First, let us assess the basic system setup and terminology. The first step in computerized payroll processing is to establish a computer file for all employees on the payroll. In computer parlance, a file is a collection of records, and a record is a collection of data elements. Data elements are the specific items of information necessary to identify and pay a particular employee correctly (i.e., Social Security number, name, address, pay rate and frequency, hours worked, etc.).

When a company hires a person to fill a specific job for a negotiated rate of pay, a special set of documents is used to collect the information needed to identify this new employee and to make sure that the employee is paid the agreed-upon amount at the right intervals. These documents are then given to payroll to input to the system. Examples of these documents would be the Form W-4, new-hire paperwork, insurance forms, and so on.

The collection of all the employee records input to the computer's payroll system is the payroll masterfile (or the payroll database). This masterfile is typically stored on some type of magnetic media. Depending on the hardware used, the files will be kept on either magnetic disks or magnetic tapes.

The system user's ability to access and work with the records and data elements on the masterfile requires a key that is defined by the user. In most payroll systems, this key is an employee identification number. The company may use the employee's Social Security number or a separate number. It must be noted here that the use of the Social Security number is now discouraged as an identifier, due to the increasing threat of identity theft. The payroll system will sort the masterfile according to these employee identification numbers and will usually require additional keys to print checks, registers, and reports. Department number, job classification code, employee's last name, and the like can be used as additional identifiers, depending on the outputs and reports you want to generate.

In addition to each employee record that must be established on the masterfile, each group of records reported under a company employer identification number (EIN) should also contain a special set of data elements called a header record. As the name suggests, a header record is a record that heads a group of employee records that you want to access or report under a common identifier. Header records might be company name and address (for W-2 printing), division or department, and so on.

A special coding for pay frequencies for all of the employee records follows the header record. This series of pay frequency "counters" and corresponding period-ending dates help the system keep track of which payrolls are being processed and the company's month-ending, quarter-ending, and year-ending dates. These counters are updated yearly.

Deductions also have special codes indicating which deductions are to be taken from the employee's pay and how often they are to be taken.

Another set of vital records used by a payroll system are the tables for calculating taxes and other deductions. Usually, the system vendor will provide the federal and state income tax tables, FICA tables, and the table of wage limits for state and federal unemployment taxes. However, because each company has its own experience rating for state unemployment insurance, the payroll department will have to make sure that the system tables are updated to reflect the company's state unemployment rates each time a notice of rate change is received.

If the vendor does not supply state and federal tax tables, the payroll department will have to obtain this information from the taxing agency and manually enter the changes to the system tables. No matter where the information comes from, the payroll department must make certain the tables are updated and contain the correct information.

In addition to tax and unemployment tables, many systems contain tables for making employee benefit and other deductions, producing special reports, generating warning and error messages, and other system or user-defined tables deemed necessary for accurate payroll processing. Usually, the more sophisticated the system, the more tables it will contain.

As change documents (Form W-4, new hire paperwork, pay changes, etc.) are received by the payroll department, they must be entered into the payroll masterfile so the system can be updated. The system will accept either a batch file (accepting the changes and holding them until the payroll is run) or permit online processing, which is basically instantaneous access to the masterfile.

Payroll file maintenance must be accomplished prior to the processing of the payroll calculation cycles so that the information used to determine earnings, taxes, and deductions for any given pay period is correct.

Most payroll systems today allow the payroll checks to be processed using the exception method. This method requires inputting of time and wage data only for employees whose pay changes from payroll to payroll. Therefore, it is primarily used for salaried employees whose pay normally does not change each payday. Once a standard salary has been established for these employees on their masterfile records, the system uses this information to pay them the same salary each pay period. Only if the salary changes from the standard (bonuses added, sick pay, vacation, etc.) would additional input be required. Hourly employees, however, usually require the time data to be input each pay cycle. The data must be collected each payroll, formatted into an acceptable transaction, and input to the system.

Computerized payroll processing normally provides printed reports to let the processor know which transactions have been accepted into the processing cycle and which, if any, transactions have been rejected by the system. During file maintenance, for example, the system will reject any transactions that are improperly formatted, coded, or input. These reports are usually referred to as the "file maintenance edit reports." They will include a list of transactions, indicating whether or not they're acceptable and if not, the reason they are being rejected. This tells the processor whether or not a correction needs to be made prior to processing the payroll.

The system should also provide another type of edit report during the pay processing cycle. The format for these reports usually depends on how you batch your input. If time card data is prepared with departmental totals, the system will read these transactions, add them up on a departmental basis, and provide a listing of the transactions, plus the batch total derived by the system. Matching the totals against the batch totals provided by the system report verifies the input and allows any out-of-balance situation to be uncovered quickly.

(c) What Is Available?

Whichever type of computerized system an employer uses, an automated payroll processing procedure typically includes the following steps:

Step 1. Collecting time and attendance.

Step 2. Organizing and entering the data into the payroll system.

Step 3. Maintaining and updating employee data on pay rates, deductions, and other information subject to change in order to ensure accurate calculations.

Step 4. Calculating pay and deductions according to company policies and federal and state rules and regulations.

Step 5. Producing paychecks and other reports based on the data in the system.

Computerized payroll systems generally are divided into two basic categories: in-house systems and those outsourced to service bureaus. Both of these categories offer three levels of sophistication. The first level of system is most suited to small employers with straightforward work schedules. This system has the employer input the data from time cards. The data is then transmitted to the system and paychecks are calculated and printed.

A more developed system uses electronic time clocks to record time and attendance data entered by employees through the use of personal identification codes or badges imprinted with pay codes and other important information. The system automatically calculates hours, pay, and other variables such as pay differential. This speeds up the processing of employee data and reduces input error rates. This system is very useful in workplaces that have complex scheduling or staffing arrangements, several collective bargaining units, shift differential, and so on.

The most advanced system is especially suited for employers who have already installed personal computers or workstations for other reasons. This personal computer-based central time and attendance software system collects data from individual time-recording terminals, which are then processed by a central personal computer.

An in-house system is one that is designed, programmed, and installed on the company's computer. It requires personnel to maintain and update software and hardware.

There are advantages and disadvantages to having the system in-house. These include:

- Advantages:
  - The software programs are usually written by people who are familiar with the company's policies and procedures.
  - The system can be designed to fit existing hardware.
  - The user has a great deal of input as to how the system will perform.
  - Training is easier because company personnel are involved in the programming.
  - Edits are usually built into the system so the user can have as many as needed before the actual update of the masterfile occurs.
  - Timing of the runs is usually at the discretion of the user. Changes and additional input can be made right up to the last minute.

- Disadvantages:
  - The computer is located in-house. While it is convenient, it occupies a great deal of physical space and requires a controlled temperature, special fire prevention precautions, control measures, and security.
  - Downtime does occur and can present problems when the staff is working under strict deadlines.
  - Disaster contingency plans may not be in place.
  - Capacity could become a problem. The number of earnings or deductions fields used for storage of information may become inadequate if sufficient provisions for growth and change are not made at the time the custom program is designed.
  - Changes requested of the programmer may get placed on a schedule and take longer to implement.
  - Changes required due to the addition of new programs, such as a 401k plan, may not occur when other deadlines prevent timely reprogramming.
  - The programmer who originally wrote the program may leave the company.
  - Documentation may become obscure when reprogramming is done over the course of time.
  - Cost may exceed using a service bureau.

A service bureau is a company that markets one or more systems applications. The client purchases the use of both the service bureau's hardware and software. Service bureaus work closely with the user during the planning stages to determine the user's needs, which programming features are available, and what type of customized programming may be needed. Usually the client is charged by the number of items processed. There are advantages and disadvantages to using a service bureau for payroll processing. These include:

- Advantages:
  - Very little downtime observed by the user. If problems occur, most service bureaus have backup computers in other locations that can take over processing the client's payroll.

- Service bureaus have developed standard calculations and reports that fit most companies' needs.
- Custom reports are provided using report writer programs.
- The user incurs no hardware costs other than one or more terminals.
- Direct access can be obtained through a terminal.
- Latest updates are done by the service bureau.
- Company computer and programming staff are freed for use by other personnel.

- Disadvantages:
  - Costs are variable.
  - User control is limited. Last minute changes of input are difficult.
  - Reports and programs may not meet user's needs. Special programs may be required.
  - Response to change requested by user may be slow.
  - Turn-around time may be longer than desired.
  - Running several edits is not practical.

5.2   INTERFACING AND INTEGRATION

The payroll department is responsible for furnishing data to various departments throughout the company. These departments include human resources, finance, accounts payable, and accounting. This information provided includes benefits, taxes withheld, and basically all the journal entries needed to post the payroll to the general ledger. It is extremely important for the payroll system to be interfaced or integrated with the computer systems of other departments in order for the payroll department to operate at peak efficiency.

(a) Interfacing: Working with Other Systems and Other Departments

As mentioned, the payroll department is a key player in providing information to the other departments. This is especially true when it comes to the general ledger. Because payroll costs can exceed 70 to 80 percent of the entire costs of doing business, this information is vital to running the company. And of course, the financial papers could not be produced without it. Before the computerization of the payroll department and the eventual interface between the payroll department and the general ledger, the payroll department was required to write the journal entries that posted or entered the information from the current payroll into the company's general ledger. This task sometimes took days to complete, depending on the complexity of the payroll and the size of the department. Now of course, the computer system interfaces with the general ledger and this information is sent over electronically without payroll having to process the journal entries manually. But this does not mean that the payroll department does not need to understand the interface or what information is being sent.

This is especially true if the system is being upgraded or changed. The payroll manager should include in the departmental procedures the general ledger account information for just this purpose, as well as for training for the payroll department staff. In general terms, the following general ledger accounts relate to payroll. These are merely descriptions of what the account is and may not precisely match the name that is listed in the company's general ledger. It is important to know whether the account balance is a debit or a credit and what type of account it is—asset, expense, or liability—as well as its purpose. This is listed in Exhibit 5.1.

The payroll department must also be aware that the company as a whole does not run on the same time frame as the payroll department. As each payroll passes, the payroll department posts to the general ledger, pays what must be paid including taxes and garnishments, and then moves on to the next payroll. When payrolls are processed is usually only important if it falls at a quarter end or year end. Keep in mind that other departments have different criteria when accounting for the payrolls. The general ledger runs on what is known as an accounting period. This is generally one month long. This means that usually the general ledger is closed at the end of each month. Companies normally run on what is known as the

Exhibit 5.1

Payroll Related Accounts for the General Ledger

Account Description	Purpose
Accrued vacation	Tracking vacation owed but not taken
Accrued wages	Wages owed but not yet paid
Benefits—employer contributions	Amounts paid by the employer for benefits. This is normally divided among the various benefits the employer offers.
Benefits—employee contributions	Amounts deducted from the employee's paycheck and used to pay for benefits. This is normally divided among the employee's various benefits.
Bonuses—accrued	Bonuses owed but not yet paid
Bonuses—paid	Bonuses paid out
Cash	Cash on hand
Commissions—earned	Commission due but not yet paid
Commissions—paid	Commissions paid
Employee Social Security withheld	Social Security deducted from the employee's paycheck but not yet paid
Employee Medicare withheld	Medicare deducted from the employee's paycheck but not yet paid
Employer Social Security	Matching Social Security for the employer portion
Employer Medicare	Matching Medicare for the employer portion
FUTA	Federal Unemployment Tax liability for the employer
Gross wages	Divided among the various accounts for each department or subdivision
Federal income tax withheld	The tax taken out of the employee's paycheck
Net pay	The amount that will eventually be paid out to the employee as net wages and the amount that comes out of the bank account
State unemployment insurance	The amount the employer pays for state unemployment
State income tax withheld	The tax taken out of the employee's paycheck
Local income tax withheld	The tax taken out of the employee's paycheck

matching period. Expenses incurred are matched to the revenues earned. For payroll purposes, this basically means that the salary or wage expenses are recognized when they are earned and not necessarily when they are paid. It is not very common for the payroll department to pay wages through the end of the month on the last payroll processed in that month. There is a lag time between when wages are earned and when they are paid. This has to be accounted for in the general ledger when the accounting period is closed for the month. Under the matching principle, all wages earned through the end of the accounting period must be recognized as expenses regardless of whether or not they were paid out through the payroll. To accomplish this, the general ledger creates what is known as accruals to account for this amount. How accruals are computed depends on the company policy. But the payroll department should understand how the accruals are computed and how they impact the general ledger. This is important in case reversals or questions arise. It should also be remembered that all other payroll accounts are subject to accruals including Social Security and Medicare taxes and vacations.

Besides the general ledger itself, the payroll can be distributed to other departments. In fact, there are many accounting subsystems that interface with the payroll system. It is important for the payroll department to be aware of these subsystems in order to run efficiently. These subsystems include:

- *Accounts Receivable.* This may include employee purchases that are paid through a payroll deduction.
- *Inventory or Cost Accounting.* There could be certain employees whose wages have to be applied to cost accounting or inventory.
- *Accounts Payable.* Payroll deductions for travel advances or credit union deductions may be directed to accounts payable.
- *Benefits Administrator.* The information for employee wages or benefit deductions, such as health insurance or deferred compensation, may be sent directly to the benefit administrator.

(b) Integration—Payroll and Human Resources Working Together

With the advent of computers, the payroll department was one of the first departments to automate. At first, computerized payroll systems took over the enormous task of calculating the payroll checks, which had previously been done by hand. At that time, journal entries, check printing, and reports were not yet an option. Over the decades though, the systems became more sophisticated and began taking over more and more of the manual duties in the payroll department. In order to enable the computerized paycheck calculations, the payroll department also had to computerize its database as well. During this same time, the human resources department also began to automate. This department began to use its computer system to track compensation, benefits, employee relations, and affirmative action. So unlike payroll, which developed a computer system to do calculations, human resources leaned more toward information storage. Because the two departments had different needs and their computer systems evolved separately, stand-alone systems became the norm for both departments.

However, over the past several years, the departments began to realize that integrated systems would be more efficient, as both departments share the same database. The early stand-alone systems that were developed were not made to integrate, so instead, interfaces were developed that allowed the two systems to share information and to talk to each other. But common data entry was not the rule of thumb. Today, service bureaus and software companies offer completely integrated payroll/ human resources systems. So now the question arises, should the company integrate payroll and human resources or not?

There are benefits to having an integrated payroll/human resources system. These include:

- *Elimination of Duplicate Databases and Duplicate Data Entry.* Because databases are shared, the need for redundant data entry is reduced. A new hire needs to be set up only once on the system and both departments may then use the information for their own purposes. This obviously saves data entry time and is much more efficient.

- *Reduced Processing Time.* The need to interface or refresh files is reduced or eliminated.

- *Comparison of Databases Is Eliminated.* There is no longer a need to constantly compare databases to ensure that the data in both files are identical.

- *Need for Resources Is Reduced and This Results in Cost Savings.* Because both departments use the same database, this allows for shared use of the system's resources for tasks such as file or data storage. With only one master file instead of two, storage capacity and memory is freed up for other uses.

- *System Upgrades.* With only a single database, upgrades to the system are more cost effective.

- *Less Money Needed for Technical Support.* If the system is shared, then technical support is concentrated on only one system instead of two.

Just as there are benefits to having an integrated payroll/human resources system, there are also drawbacks. These include:

- *Who Owns the Database?* If the payroll department and the human resources department are not integrated, creating an integrated database may lead to problems and misunderstandings on who owns the information in the database.

- *Inconsistent Definitions and Multiple Uses of the Data.* It is possible that the data needed may not be the same for both departments and this would necessitate extra precautions to make sure that all data is set up in a way that is useful for both departments. For example, the date of hire for an employee in the payroll department is the date of the first day of work for which the employee needs to be paid. Whether the employee is a new hire or a rehire is not relevant for processing the payroll. However, in the human resources department, the hire date is related to benefits. If the employee is a rehire, then two dates may be needed in the system to properly account for all benefits.

- *Timing Differences between the Departments.* One department's use of the database may tie up the system for the other department.

- *Accessing the Data.* It may not be easy to export the data from the system. This may cause people to use report writer programs and restrict the use of the system to all staff members who need it.

Whether or not to integrate the two systems is a question that many companies are facing today. One type of system that companies are researching is the Human Resources Information System (HRIS), which combines both human resources and payroll and allows for other services such as employee service centers. An HRIS is a system of software and supporting computer hardware specifically designed to store and process all HR information. An HRIS combines separate HR systems into a centralized database that performs the majority of HR transactions. HRISs are particularly useful for payroll and benefits administration.

A sophisticated HRIS will simplify transactions, automate administrative tasks, and minimize paperwork. It provides a consolidated database to coordinate self-service technologies. Employee self-services such as intranets, kiosks, and voice response unit systems (VRUs) are dependent on HRIS to be effective. Through system integration, an HRIS will reduce duplication and error while improving access to employee information.

HRISs are steadily becoming a necessary component of HR because of the increasingly global perspective of businesses. The combination of new technology and the subsequent loss of physical boundaries requires comprehensive HR systems that can maintain one database while also incorporating a diversity of additional systems and capabilities.

5.3 SELECTING A COMPUTERIZED PAYROLL SYSTEM

Selecting a computerized payroll system is a major decision for any company to make. The system must calculate the gross pay of the employees in compliance with all federal and state requirements, withhold correct taxes according to the IRS and state rules, deduct benefit amounts, and print checks or do a direct deposit of the net check. It must also comply with court orders for child support and IRS tax levies. The system must provide the management of the company with valid data to make critical business decisions. And if management had its wish, this system would always work perfectly without costly maintenance, never need an update or upgrade, and cost virtually nothing to operate. As most payroll professionals know, the last wish will never happen, but the other tasks are exactly what a good payroll system is supposed to do.

It is a fact of life that as companies grow or change or as time passes, payroll computer systems must be replaced. However, purchasing a payroll system is a major financial decision that cannot be made in haste or without in-depth knowledge of what the department already has or needs or wants. This is why the most efficient way to purchase a new payroll system is by completing a series of steps to determine which system would best suit the current and future needs of the company while staying within budget. These steps include:

Step 1. Set up a project team to oversee the creation of the Request for Proposal (RFP) and the eventual selection of the new payroll system.

Step 2. Analyze what the current system actually does, how it does it, and how long it takes to do it.

Step 3. Compute how much the current system costs to operate.

Step 4. Determine the technical requirements that the new system should have.

Step 5. Analyze what the payroll department currently requires its system to do in order to process the payroll efficiently.

Step 6. Add a wish list for what the payroll department would like the new system to be able to do (and hope for the best).

Step 7. Decide if the new system will be an integrated system combining payroll and human resources, if this is not currently the case.

Step 8. Look to the future and try to determine what the payroll department may need the system to do a few years down the road.

Step 9. Prepare the RFP.

Step 10. Select the system.

Step 11. Implement the system.

(a) Set Up the Project Team

Before the new system can be requested or the needs of the payroll department even be determined, a project team must be set up to handle all the tasks involved in choosing a new payroll system. The team should consist of the payroll staff members chosen for this project, a representative for each end user of the system, technical advisors for the hardware, and a management or finance representative if desired. If the system is to be integrated with human resources in the future or if the current system is an integrated system and this is to continue, then the human resources department will need to choose a staff member for the team as well. These main players will perform the day-to-day duties involved in choosing a new system. However, any department that interfaces with the new payroll system will need to have an ad hoc member on the team when the time comes to determine the interfaces needed. These ad hoc members might include staff members from human resources and/or benefits (if not an integrated system), accounts payable, finance, and of course, general ledger. The technical advisors chosen should be well versed in the areas of payroll and/or human resources.

This team will determine the success of the project. The payroll staff member(s) chosen for the team should be given the time needed to successfully complete the project and should be relieved of other duties when necessary. This member should have knowledge not only of the rules and regulations governing payroll, but of company policy as well. The staff member should be extremely knowledgeable about how the current payroll system works and the inner workings of the department in general.

Invariably, all the stakeholders in this process will want a say in its selection and implementation and this, of course, can lead to conflicts. Because conflicts among project team members can quickly derail the success of enterprise wide systems, the project plan must include mechanisms for problem resolution. Some suggestions follow.

- *Early Intervention Is Key.* The best way to approach conflict resolution is to address the issue head on and work directly with the individuals involved. This will take the tension out of the air and quickly get the project back on track—and on budget. Consider the following further suggestions for keeping the team on track.

- One method of intervention includes having other team members participate in problem resolution with the individuals who are having the disagreement. If the team has an outside implementation consultant, consider having him or her intervene (referee).

- Many conflicts arise because people are set in their ways or want to perpetuate traditional corporate processes or procedures. To help avoid this, team members should be encouraged to "think outside the box" and to challenge old ways of thinking.

- Sometimes there is one individual who is in conflict perpetually. In that case, don't be afraid to substitute someone else.

- *Recommended Procedures.* Avoiding problems in the first place is the most important factor in developing and executing an effective conflict resolution procedure. Having a solid project plan, good project-management skills, and team communication will go a long way toward avoiding conflicts. This will remove much of the uncertainty and ambiguity about goals, objectives, status, roles, and responsibilities that can lead to conflict. Of course, no matter what anyone does, trouble can arise for a variety of reasons. The key to handling a problem is to empower those individuals who are most knowledgeable about it to make a decision and resolve it. This involves setting up a power level for everyone involved in the project. A power level is simply an individual's range of authority with respect to the project; it dictates the problems he or she should deal with. If an individual cannot resolve a particular problem, it should be "kicked upstairs" in the project team hierarchy. However, specific criteria should be set up for this, or the staff may tend to pass the buck to a higher-up whenever something challenging comes along.

- *Establish a "Decision Pecking Order."* The following is a suggested scheme that lays out each individual's authority and the criteria for kicking a problem upstairs. This assumes the following pecking order in terms of the level of project participants: team members (lowest), team leader, project manager, steering committee, and project sponsor (highest):

  - *Team Members.* These individuals are responsible for day-to-day activities or decisions affecting their own work—not the work of others. All of their work and the decisions they make should follow established standards. If an action they will take affects other team members or members of another team, they should confer with their team leader prior to acting.

  - *Team Leader.* This person oversees any activities and decisions involving the team for which he or she is responsible. When a team member's activity will affect other teams or team members, the team leader should intervene to verify that the proposed action will not have a negative impact on the project. When activities and decisions initiated by the team can affect other teams, they should immediately be presented to the project manager so that the team's progress is not delayed.

  - *Project Manager.* This person is responsible for activities and decisions involving other teams or the project as a whole. He or she should not make decisions that involve changes to project direction, scope, or performance (such as dates, resources, budget, etc.). When these types of decisions need to be made, they should be presented to the steering committee.

  - *Steering Committee.* This group resolves any issues that would change the project's charter or budget or have a material impact on the organization. The steering committee should also address those issues that cannot be resolved by the project manager. However, the steering committee should not deal with issues that determine whether or not the project continues (such as overall budgeting, corporate approvals, and corporate priorities). These should be turned over to the project sponsor.

○ *Project Sponsor.* This individual is responsible for approving the initial budget, timelines, resources, scope, priority, and implementation goals. He or she should handle any issues that the steering committee cannot resolve and should interface with management on an ongoing basis.

(b) Analyze What the System Needs to Do

Once the project team is set up, the first task they need to undertake is to thoroughly examine the current payroll system. This review of the current system should be well documented so that it can be used in comparison with the prospective new computer system. When reviewing each area, the team will need to keep several questions in mind:

- Is this task or document needed?
- Why is it needed?
- What purpose does it accomplish?
- Who originated it?
- Who eventually gets to use the information?
- How often is it used or created?

By answering these questions, the team will bring into focus the purpose and use of each payroll form, task, or process that is currently being utilized. This is the first stage in selecting a payroll system and is known as a "needs analysis."

The areas that the team needs to review include:

- Masterfile and all forms used for input into the masterfile, including new hires, address changes, Form W-4, pay raises, and direct deposits
- Time records
- All steps, procedures, or processes used to run the actual payroll
- All edit reports

- Check printing process
- Direct deposit process
- Check distribution
- Tax deposit reports
- All payroll reports
- Interfaces
- Employee histories
- Manual checks
- Voided checks

The approximate labor time required for each process should be included in the needs analysis as well. This will be used later in the costing phase. This review is a critical part of selecting a computer system. It is time consuming, but the payroll department must know exactly how long the current system takes to process these areas in order to compare it to the capabilities of the new system.

Once this review is finished, the next step is to fix a price on the current payroll system. The new payroll systems being examined will then be compared to this cost to determine proper budgeting for the new system and to validate any cost savings. This step is extremely important, especially if the payroll department is considering outsourcing the payroll processing to a service bureau where each individual process may have a cost. This will allow the department to compare apples to apples. If the payroll department is currently using a service bureau, this costing must also be done to compare the new system to the old.

Areas to include in this cost assessment are:

- If using a service bureau:
  - Base price of processing
  - Cost of additional processes or reports
  - Maintenance costs
  - Upgrade costs
  - Technical support
  - Shipping of payrolls
  - Interfaces or outside vendor files

- If the current payroll is done in house:
  - Total cost to process the payroll in terms of computer time, tech support, paper and printing supplies, postage and so on
  - Maintenance of the system
  - Technical support
  - Upgrades

Also included in the costing is the cost of labor, which is the average salary of the payroll staff multiplied by the amount of time needed for each process. This helps in determining the costs of each item as well. The next step is a very technical one.

It is important to determine the technical environment requirements for the new system. The combination of hardware and software that makes up the technical state for an application is called the platform. The project team must determine the following:

- What platform will support the system being purchased?
- Will additional hardware or software be needed to support the new system?
- If additional hardware or software is needed for the new system, what time frame will need to be allocated for acquiring these items?

The next step is to review the current processing requirements. Most of this task was completed when the needs analysis was done. Now what needs to be added are the policy requirements that govern the payroll processing. Some of these items might include:

- How does the company pay its employees? Is there a piecework, commission, or shift differential?
- Is any other data used to compute gross wages?
- Does the system need to use accumulators for use in a later process?
- Does the system need to track restrictions, limits, minimums, or maximums for such items as educational assistance, vacations, benefits, or other deductions?
- Are there different frequencies or schedules of payments?

Again, this list should closely follow company policies.

After documenting the good and the bad of the current system, the project team should be ready to tell the company what the new system must be able to do. When purchasing a new system, existing functions should never be lost. The new system must do everything the old one does and more. And it should do it better, faster, cheaper, and more efficiently.

The last step before creating the request for proposal is to look at the old system and create a "wish list." The wish list should contain features that the old system did not have but the payroll department wishes the new system would. These are items that do not affect the integrity of processing the payroll but would make it more efficient. These might include:

- *Manual Processes.* Is there anything that payroll must now do manually that a new system could automate?

- *Sorting of Information.* Could the information on reports be sorted better for ease of use? The same applies for the masterfile, screens, setups, and so on.

- *Additional Data.* Is there any data that could be added to the computer system that would allow for faster processing or increased information?

- *Reports.* Are there any reports that the department does not get now that would be useful to have?

(c) Prepare the Request for Proposal

Now the project team needs to create the request for proposal (RFP). An RFP is actually the request for a bid from the vendors. Therefore, the team also needs to put together a list of qualified vendors. This list can be compiled from a variety of sources including the current vendor, vendors that the payroll staff may have worked with in other companies, or new vendors discovered through Internet research. The vendors should be of a size and capability to handle the company's needs and wants. There is no limit to the number of vendors that receive the RFP. Actually, the more bids the better.

The RFP should include information about the company and what is required in the new computerized payroll system. Include information such as:

- A complete overview of the company
- How the payroll department is organized and where it falls in the hierarchy of the company
- The particulars of the numbers:
  - Number of EINs
  - Number of states
  - Number of localities
  - Number and type of benefits
  - Number of employees involved
  - Number of payrolls processed and frequency
- Number of unions involved, if applicable
- Type of computer system being used
- Preferred platforms
- Types of applications being explored (integrated or not?)
- Interfaces needed
- The needs that were documented by the project team in the needs analysis
- The due date for the return response and number of copies needed
- Contact person's name and contact information
- Request for pricing breakdowns to be included with the return proposal
- References
- A list of business partners

(d) Select the System

While the project team is waiting for the return of the proposal responses, it should develop a scoring system for these bids. This will allow all the vendors to be graded using the same criteria. There should be a grading formula. When the live presentations are given, the same criteria should be used for each presentation. The finalists should then be chosen.

The next step is to analyze the software packages or services that the finalists have offered:

- Check out the references and find additional ones the vendor did not submit with the proposal.

- Attend demonstrations of the system. Try to do it at an actual company as well as observing the vendor's demonstration model. Work with the models to test screens for ease of use.

- Get explanations of how tasks are accomplished. Compare them to the current system.

- Compare the system to the needs analysis and make sure that all required items and wish-list items are included.

- Check out reports and edits—how do they read?

- Find out about upgrades—what are they planning that will be different than what is being shown now?

- Attend a training class for an hour or so to see how good the training actually is.

- Analyze every cost—do not take the bid at face value.

When all of this has been completed by the project team, the final task is to select the system. The formal proposal outlining which system to select should be submitted to management and then the team should be disbanded.

The best way to remove some of the uncertainty from new payroll system installation and implementation is to negotiate for what is needed and wanted before the contract is signed. In fact, a choice piece of advice from experts is to start negotiating the wish list point by point before the selection of the final vendor is made. Why? Vendors running against one another will be more flexible on terms than one that already has the job. Also, document any promises the vendor makes along the way, especially early on. For example, if a vendor brings up some special feature or customization during the demonstration, be sure to ask, "If we end up going with you, will you throw in that feature?" and write it down in case the vendor gets amnesia when the contract is hammered out.

Here is the experts' best advice for creating a win-win contract. The goal is to negotiate a contract that is in the best interest of the company—not to "pull a fast one" on the future vendor (i.e., the one the payroll department will have to live with through implementation):

- *Use Project Management Methodology.* Treat the negotiating process as its own project with its own team and phases. The process/project should include these five phases: (1) initiation: who will be involved, tasks, and time frame; (2) definition: determine the company's legal requirements with regard to software purchases; (3) evaluation—assessing the fit between the agreement and the company's legal requirements; (4) selection—choosing the contract version; (5) execution—signing the agreement.

- *Put together an Effective Team.* Forming the team to handle the license negotiation requires knowledge of the team's goal and the essential characteristics that make up a winning team.

- *Define "Covered Groups."* Determine which groups the software license covers. Ask: Is it a corporate or a site license? Is it a CPU or a desktop license? Does it include subsidiaries? If there is a merger or acquisition, can the company extend the software to a new company or division? Try to include umbrella language in the agreement to bring in as many groups as possible.

- *Seek a Perpetual Term.* Many companies do not realize that the license term may be fixed for a certain period of years. Negotiate for a perpetual term, as long as the company stays on the maintenance agreement. Most major vendors are on a perpetual term, but take a look beforehand so the company is not surprised.

- *Address Headcount Restrictions.* The prices on some vendor contracts are based on the headcount level in the company. If this is the case, be aware of the headcount number that would trigger a change in the license fee.

Then project the company's headcount over the next five years and negotiate those prices up front.

- *Allow for Source Code Availability.* If the company is not getting the software's source code with the application, what happens if the vendor goes out of business? If the vendor will not deliver the source code with the agreement, set up an escrow arrangement whereby a third-party holds on to the source code so the company can continue to support the system if the vendor goes out of business.

- *See More Training Time.* In general, payroll system contracts specify a certain number of training days that the vendor will provide, but this is negotiable. Negotiating argument: The more training the payroll staff gets, the more the users will know the ins and outs of the software and the less they will have to call the vendor's customer support staff.

- *Get Approval over the Vendor's Staff.* Include a provision that gives the company the right to approve and change whomever the vendor assigns to the installation. After all, what if the chemistry is wrong between one or more of the vendor's team members and the payroll team?

- *Allow for Third-Party Consultants.* Some basic vendor agreements do not allow the company to bring in outside consultants to work on implementation. Doing so constitutes a breach of the agreement. Make sure this provision is changed. Also, the vendor may subcontract some of the implementation work to a third party, so try to include a provision that gives the company the right to approve the subcontractor. If this can't be done, have the vendor agree to notify the payroll manager or implementation team leader if this happens. The company has a right to know if the vendor is bringing in non-vendor personnel to get the company's system up and running.

- *Check for Indemnification.* Make sure the contract includes an indemnification clause to protect the company from software title trouble (i.e., a third party may claim it owns the software and that the company is infringing). The indemnification clause says the vendor will "hold the company harmless" and vigorously defend its title so the company does not have to go to court.

- *Change Payment Timing.* Software payment terms and timing will probably end up somewhere between what the vendor wants and the company's ideal situation. Vendors will ask for 90 to 100 percent of the money up front. Instead, negotiate to spread out these payments over key milestones. Propose a payment schedule of 20 percent on each of these milestones: execution of contract, delivery, successful installation (carefully defined), acceptance, and first production run. Not all of these terms will be accepted, but it is a good place to start.

- *Watch the Maintenance Costs.* Make sure the maintenance costs—which are a set percentage of the software cost—are based on the software's original cost, not on new prices that take effect after the company has acquired the package. Of course, the vendor will balk and say that prices go up. Therefore, use a "CPI cap" approach to limit the annual percentage increase in maintenance to no more than one percentage increase in the consumer price index. The vendor should not increase the maintenance costs more than the rate of inflation.

- *Add a "Most Favored Nation" Clause.* This clause states that the price the vendor gives the company for its product is the most favorable available for the size and profile of your company.

- *Bargain for Documentation.* For printed manuals, the vendor typically gives the company just one set, and if you want more, you have to buy them. Sometimes the payroll department may just want to copy a chapter or a section for distribution within the department, so negotiate this into the agreement. Also, vendors sometimes completely rewrite their documentation and charge the company for it. Experts feel this should be part of maintenance, so it should be discussed up front.

- *Include the RFP in the Contract.* Attach the RFP and the marketing material as supplements to the contract. Experts suggest adding the following language "The vendor agrees the product will operate as described in its response to the RFP and the ways described in the marketing brochures." Be advised that the vendor will not usually readily agree to this. The vendor will maintain that the RFP response was made when the vendor did not yet have enough knowledge of the company. But experts point out that the vendor is legally obligated to follow what they put into the RFP, so the company should pay special attention to the response. What to do? State up front that the RFP will be made part of the contract.

- *Safeguard Your Data.* Provisions need to be included that address what happens to the company's data if the vendor goes out of business. Do this when dealing with hosted Active Server Pages (ASP) solutions because the data rest on servers at the ASP's site. Sometimes the vendor will say that if it goes offline, it will have the company's data available in two weeks in a format of its choice. Make sure that a provision spells out, in this day and age, that the company owns its data and that the ASP has no right to use it in any way, shape, or form.

- *Include Performance Measures.* This applies to ASP-based HR applications. The company needs to address the following performance measures in the contract with the ASP: response time, volume of Internet traffic, service availability (e.g., 24/7), guaranteed uptime, guaranteed bandwidth, reliability of data exchange, and security technologies and actions. Penalty clauses should be included if these measures are not met.

- *Do not Obsess over Price.* If the price of the software is already fair and reasonable, do not haggle over it to get a discount. Instead, agree to the price in exchange for something the payroll department really needs such as extra professional services, more training, greater support, a longer maintenance period, passes to user conferences, or free upgrades. If the company pays for these extras, the cost may be more than the discount the company would have received on the software prices.

- *Use Time as an Ally.* Sometimes the software price becomes a sticking point, and the vendor won't budge. When coming to an impasse with a vendor over price, some experts suggest telling vendor number one that the company will be talking to vendor number two, then stop talking to vendor number one for a couple of days. The vendor, more times than not, will come around to making some changes.

- *Don't Rush.* In today's rapidly deployed software world, the need to get software up and running fast can actually spell trouble. If the team rushes the process, especially the contract stage, it may put the company in a very unsafe position, legally, strategically, functionally, and financially. Do not shortchange the negotiation process just because management wants a system right now.

(e) Implementation

Once the contract has been finalized, work on implementing the new payroll system must begin. The first task is to establish a new team for the implementation. The same staff members can be used for both teams. But the first one should be formally disbanded and the new one created to reestablish boundaries and so forth.

Once the implementation team is established, the members need to be trained on the new system. This includes attending classes and reading the documentation. All team members must become as knowledgeable as possible on the new system. This knowledge will be invaluable in planning all the remaining stages of the implementation.

The next step is to set up the implementation plan. This plan lays out the timeline for each step of the implementation and establishes the goals for the project. This plan must be in writing with specific dates established for each goal. It is extremely critical to remember that once the plan is set, drastic changes to any payroll activity must be avoided. Do not allow changes in paydays or pay periods, and this is certainly not the time to expand the project or to make other changes.

Once the implementation plan is set and approved, the next step is to make a detailed list of tasks that must be completed in order to achieve each goal. The task list should include completion times team members should be assigned to each one. At this time, the requirements for the new system should be documented.

The resources can now be identified. As the implementation progresses, the team members need to begin concentrating on each area of expertise. If there are any areas where expertise is lacking, consultants can be brought in to supplement the project team or to provide knowledge or expertise not available within the company.

As with the previous team, the members of the implementation team will be extremely busy. Every effort must be made to avoid having team members work on implementation and take care of all of their normal responsibilities at the same time. If necessary, temporary help can be hired to cover an employee's normal duties.

All implementation teams need a leader. Someone must manage the project, monitor the timetables, and keep the project on budget and on target. The project manager is a difficult position but a vital one. This team member must have the total support and backing of management. It is sometimes more efficient to hire an outside consultant to tackle this position. This allows the individual to concentrate totally on the implementation project without the distractions of the daily payroll processing. It also brings in experience in conversions that may be lacking in the payroll department or elsewhere.

System design comes next. The actual mechanics of the system must be determined and planned out. This sets down exactly how things will be done within the system. All the functional details, such as calculating earnings, will be decided and implemented. The technical design will de done as well. This includes the work and paper flow, the input of data, and the output. Specifications are also designed at this time. All this information must be thoroughly documented. This documentation will be used for the next phase, development and testing.

In the development phase, each module or unit of the design is delivered using the appropriate software tools. As each unit is developed, it must be tested. Distinct tests are performed for each program or event. For example, each deduction, earning code, or report is tested. To ensure that every module or unit is tested, a test plan should be created. The test plan provides the data for the testing then verifies the results.

If the entire implementation team is convinced that all units have passed testing and are functioning correctly, then the next step is system testing. A system test plan should be created. At this time, other departments may have to be included to test interfaces and so forth. Test data should be created for system testing as it was for unit testing.

Once the system testing has been completed and all team members are convinced the system is performing correctly, then the actual data on the old system needs to be converted over to the new system to begin parallel testing. Before this can be done, the data must be mapped to tell one system where the information goes on the other.

All fields must be verified during the conversion. A conversion plan must be created to complete this verification. If the conversion is accepted, then the final phase of the implementation can begin.

The final phase is the parallel testing. This involves running the old system side by side with the new system using the same data. How long a company parallel tests or how many tests should be run depends on the complexity of the two systems and the data. A parallel test plan should be created to organize the testing and to record the test results.

Finally, conversion to the new system occurs when all parties involved sign off on the parallel testing. The final tasks are to complete the documentation on the conversion and then disband the implementation team.

5.4   DISASTER RECOVERY

After the power outages that affected the Northeast and parts of the Midwest and Canada in 2003, the power shortages on the West Coast during 2002, and the events of 9-11, disaster recovery plans are now a critical part of any company's long-range planning. Those in payroll are acutely aware that any business disruption, natural or manmade, cannot only short-circuit paychecks and third-party transactions, but can also expose the company to penalties and fines for noncompliance in reporting and remitting payroll reports and employment taxes. It is true that when disasters (natural or otherwise) affect a significant portion of the country, the IRS and most states will and do provide tax extensions to employers. However, neither are able to forgive interest for the late deposits or reporting even while abating penalties. So it clearly behooves payroll to do everything it can to ensure that business "goes on as usual" even during disasters.

But how does payroll create a disaster recovery plan (DRP) or improve its existing plan? Basically, the heart of any DRP is organizing the tasks to be executed and thoroughly documenting the procedures for such execution. The first step would be to create an outline of the tasks that need to be done and use this as a guide in creating the detailed procedures.

The tasks listed on the outline are the ones that are considered critical functions of the payroll department. They include:

- Collection of employee data
- Time calculation
- Paycheck calculations
- Information from vendors and third-party benefit providers
- Paycheck printing
- Direct deposit information
- Reports or interfaces with other company departments
- Reports or payments to government agencies including the IRS and child support agencies

Once the tasks are identified and the outline is completed, the next step is to evaluate each process from start to finish. Resources that are absolutely required to complete each function need to be spelled out. Note that this should not be confused with the resources needed to handle the function in the most efficient, cost effective, and time saving method. This is a disaster scenario, and the idea is to cover only the most basic and critical needs until the normal system is back up and running.

Next, "what-if" scenarios need to be created for each of the critical functions on the list. For example, assume submission of time cards by employees has been identified as a critical function. It is normally done via an electronic timekeeping system. A power outage has hit the entire area where payroll is located. The DRP could address this issue by allowing employees not in the affected area to fax paper time sheets to a special emergency fax number. The employees who are located in the affected area could be paid on a standard number of hours with adjustments (such as for overtime) occurring on the following payroll when power is restored. A sample chart of possible critical functions and alternative solutions is provided in Exhibit 5.2.

It is important to examine the critical function at each stage of the payroll process and the significance of a breakdown at that juncture in processing the payroll. It may be possible that some critical functions, though essential for normal processing, may be able to be sidestepped during a disaster.

A DRP must also include hard physical considerations as well as theoretical what-ifs. If the plan calls for the payroll department to be moved to a different location or city, then the office space, computers, backup files, phone lines, phone equipment, and Internet access must be set up and functioning when the plan is approved and not just listed in the plan without actually having a physical place ready. The location information and items such as access codes should be included in the plan as well.

The DRP should also include the human factor. Key personnel need to be identified and trained on the plan so that they may be able to assume each other's duties in the event of an emergency. For payroll, this should include every member of the department. In addition, entire backup teams need to be established. Although backup teams have not traditionally been included in DRPs, the World Trade Center tragedy brought this issue to light when entire recovery teams were

EXHIBIT 5.2

Critical Functions and Alternatives Chart

Critical Function	Alternatives
Time input by employee • Physical access to time clock, time sheet, or electronic time screen • Ability to submit paperwork	• Call in time via special telephone number • Fax time sheet to designated number • Set up preestablished default time sheets
Approver of time records • Access to time cards or time sheets • Access to time reports online	• Able to retrieve time sheets from fax or telephone • Suspend approval until system is operating
Input of hours to system • Data entry by hand from time cards • Input directly to computer system by electronic transfer	• Capability to input at remote site • Establish uniform hours calculation to use until system is reestablished
Calculation of Gross Pay • Done internally by payroll system	• Set up capabilities to calculate payroll manually
Input of information from outside sources • Feed to system from other departments including A/P and human resources. Include advances, relocation, health, and welfare benefits	• Suspend until system is reestablished
Calculation of Payroll • Calculate gross to net of payroll including taxes and deductions	• Establish system to calculate manually
Physical Production of Payroll • Printing of payroll checks • Creation of direct deposit file • Creation of payroll reports	• Establish means to print checks and have check stock on hand • Cancel direct deposit until system is reestablished • Create payroll reports at remote location
Output to External Entities • Tax payments • Garnishment payments • Tax returns and reports • New hire reporting	• If possible, delay until system is operational again but only if postponement results in no fines or penalties • File estimates for taxes until system is operational • Prepare manual reports and returns • Utilize outside vendors to handle until system is operational

killed. For example, the backup team for payroll might be the payroll manager's supervisors (Controller or VP of Finance) or other backup personnel, depending on the size of the department. Those chosen should be employees who are familiar enough with the payroll system to execute the DRP but need not be capable of fully running the department over a long period of time.

To ensure that personnel are available to implement the DRP, communication plans are a critical part of the disaster recovery plan. Emergency meeting places and special emergency phone equipment need to be established and communicated to the teams. This way, companies can quickly identify missing employees and assemble teams.

Disaster recovery plans need to be in effect on a daily basis as well, not just when a disaster strikes. The payroll department should make sure that they:

- Back up systems routinely and that a copy of the backup file is sent to any emergency sites that have been established

- Store primary backup files offsite in a place where they are accessible 24/7 and not in a timed vault

- Have safes that are fireproof and not just "tool resistant"

- Keep a file with offsite backups of all forms the department uses

- Cross-train the payroll department (all functions and all employees for larger companies)

- Establish emergency cabinets with flashlights, extra batteries, a battery operated radio, coins for the vending machines, emergency ration packets, a battery operated clock, one gallon of water for each employee, and a first aid kit

- Have a master list of all voice mail passwords for all employees in the department

- Keep copies of all payroll system and procedure manuals with backup files at the emergency and offsite locations

- Have contact numbers on hard copy files (not in the computer) for each key employee and team member
- Test to make sure that computers and backup files can actually be read and restored
- Keep all information and rations up to date

It takes a lot of time and energy to develop an effective DRP. Fortunately, there are vast resources available on the Internet to assist in writing a plan. Web sites that may be useful in writing a plan include:

- Association of Records Managers and Administrators: www.arma.org
- Business Continuity Institute: www.thebci.org
- Disaster Preparedness and Emergency Response Association: www.disasters.org
- International Disaster Recovery Association: www.idra.com
- International Association of Emergency Managers: www.iaem.com/index.php
- National Association of Contingency Planners: www.acp-international.com

5.5 EMPLOYEE SELF-SERVICE SYSTEMS

One of the latest hot topics for payroll departments is self-service systems for employees. The main reason is simple. Companies are feeling the pressure from top management to cut costs. This is especially true for the payroll department, which is expected to apply modern technology to cut labor costs. But what exactly are employee self-service systems and how can they help the payroll department become more efficient?

Employee self-service systems use the Human Resources Information System (HRIS) to automate many of the labor intensive and time consuming tasks that payroll currently handles for employees. These tasks can include obtaining copies of pay stubs for loans, implementing address changes, updating Forms W-4, setting up or changing direct deposits, and changing benefits. With a self-service system, employees are responsible for inputting the required changes or information themselves. Using their own computers, employees access the system and input the desired changes or new items. These changes are then transferred to the payroll system and reflected in the masterfile.

Self-service is now the trend, it is that simple. Work that the human resources or payroll departments once did is now rapidly shifting to line managers and employees, even in smaller companies. But what are some of the secrets to making self-service work? If the payroll department is thinking of implementing self-service technology, the following tips can make the application of this process a win-win situation for both the employees and the payroll department:

- *Run the Numbers.* Many departments, including payroll at companies large and small, are increasingly being asked to justify purchases. CEOs and CFOs want to know how self-service will affect employee satisfaction and productivity. How does it reduce overhead and administration? How does it help employees and managers make better decisions? The best way to justify the corporate investment in self-service—and nail down the commitment at the top—is to prepare a Return on Investment (ROI) analysis that shows the level of investment and the resulting savings. When the numbers are crunched, it is surprising what is discovered.

- *Assess Readiness.* Do not automatically assume that the company or the department is ready for employee self-service. Resistance to the technology can come from within the department itself. Some payroll staff simply won't want to relinquish control of data to employees.

- *Do not Call It Self-Service.* This term implies that the payroll department is pushing its work on employees. Instead, it can be referred to as the electronic notification system or something similar. This communicates to the employees that this is the method that will now be used to notify the payroll and human resources departments when employees would like to make a change. To further increase user acceptance, the process could be designed so that it is relatively invisible. For example, now, instead of picking up the phone, sending in paperwork, or e-mailing the payroll and human resources departments of a change of address, the employee simply types in his or her new address on the self service system—and that action becomes the actual change of address in the system. Presented this way, employees perceive that no extra work is involved, as they would have had to notify the departments anyway.

- *Expect to Use Multiple Third-Party Vendors.* Unfortunately, there is no one-stop shopping for self-service applications. Even the best system on the market may not have everything the payroll department wants or needs. The best solution is to use the best of breed approach, piecing together modular self-service applications from third-party vendors to complete the desired setup.

- *Choose an Integrated System.* An integrated system interfaces with the payroll department's other systems and can line up with external systems. It brings several advantages including lower investment, easier and faster implementation, flexibility of administration and customization, minimal need for IT resources, and less need for outside consultants. Because the system is linked, rekeying of data is unnecessary. A single point of data entry also means better data integrity.

- *Do not Customize too Much.* Try to use as much of the vanilla version of the software as possible. Otherwise, upgrades can be very expensive. However it should look and feel like the rest of the department's applications. This is a matter of configuration as opposed to customization. Customization should occur after the users have had a chance to provide feedback as to what they need. Never underestimate the ability of the users to navigate the system as it comes out of the box.

- *Make Sure It Is Easy to Use.* Ease of use should be high on the list of considerations when selecting and implementing a self-service application. Portals have become extremely important in payroll self-service because they tie everything together in an easy-to-use, personalized screen. The self-service portal should have all necessary data and allow for transactions that make employees want to stay there and use the features.

- *Personalize It.* Personalization is the key to self-service. Data that is specific to individuals should be right in front of them as part of the self-service application. For example, a sales person should be able to look at his or her incentive compensation data to see how he or she is doing. Other employees should be able to check the amount of vacation time they have available.

- *Review Manual Processes before Converting to Self-Service.* Before automating a process, make sure all of the steps and approvals are in place and it has been thoroughly reviewed. A key concept of self-service is to push down decision-making authority and responsibility in order to streamline various tasks.

- *Require Only One Password.* Implement single authentication for users. Employees should only have to log in once with one password to access everything. If employees need to know more than one password, then they are less likely to use the system. If outside vendors are used to provide software and access for the system, they should provide a "pass through" that allows access without signing on separately to their site.

- *Mount a Marketing Campaign.* Get employees and managers involved with a communications campaign. Conference calls, newsletters, logos, posters, password cards, even paper clips with the name of the site can be used to get the word out and encourage employees to use it.

- *Guide Employees through the New System until They Are Comfortable with It.* When an employee calls the payroll department with a question, it should be answered but "let me show you how to find it yourself" can be added to let the employee know about the site. This can really make a big difference.

- *Collect Feedback.* Once the system is up and running, ask employees and managers for their opinions about the application. Ask which features the employees like and what they would want to add. An easy way to collect this feedback is to add a short, three or four question survey for the users to complete when they exit the application. The questions should ask about ease of use and what changes should be made. Once the employee does the survey, it is not repeated on the same employee.

- *Track the Success.* Once the system is up and running, monitor its use. Track the number of hits, the number of one-time users, the average time spent in the application, and the most popular pages. These statistics can then be used to compare the actual ROI to what was estimated.

As discussed previously, creating the right ROI is critical and can make or break the approval for a self-service application. Here is a good overview of how to approach an ROI analysis for a self-service application:

- *Estimate the Current Costs.* Itemize and break down all payroll processes such as salary changes, new hires, benefits elections, and so on that will fall under the self-service initiative. Then estimate the cost of the current processes, as well as their frequency. Make sure to include the following cost factors: labor and materials, task time and elapsed time, and the number of steps and hand-offs the process requires. Do not forget printing, mailing, or distribution costs.

- *Estimate Self-Service Costs and Savings.* For each process listed, compare the current costs to the self-service costs. The difference is the "process savings" from self-service. This figure multiplied by the frequency of the action gives the total savings.

  - Example: Charlie's Gardening Supply processes an average of 1,000 salary changes each year. The current manual process costs $44.57 for each change but only $18.26 when automated via self-service. The per-transaction savings of $26.41 translates into annual total savings of $26,410 ($26.41 x 1,000 transactions per year). Soft benefits such as employee satisfaction, reduced turnover, faster decision making, and higher productivity need to be factored in as well.

- *Add up the Investment.* The investment in self-service technology consists of two components: upfront costs and recurring costs. Upfront costs include those associated with software license fees, hardware, customization/development, integration with core HRIS, installation, implementation and training, consulting services, employee marketing/training, and process redesign. Recurring costs include those for hosting, software leasing/usage fees, ongoing consulting services, annual maintenance, and customization. Of course, the cost will depend on whether the system is built in house or bought off the rack. Also, the way the system is deployed (such as hosted versus non-hosted, outsourced, etc.) will affect the investment. To help estimate the cost, look to the vendor or seek out the experiences of fellow payroll professionals at similar companies.

- *Calculate the ROI.* Take the total savings and costs developed in the previous steps and calculate the ROI, relating savings to investment over the project's life. See Exhibit 5.3 for an example.

Exhibit 5.3

ROI for Charlie's Gardening Supply

Charlie's Gardening Supply examines the costs and savings (in thousands of dollars) of its self-service initiative over a five-year time frame:

	Year 1	Year 2	Year 3	Year 4	Year 5
Costs	$300	$50	$50	$50	$50
Savings	$200	$200	$200	$200	$200

CHAPTER 6

Paying Employees

6.1 PAPER CHECKS ARE STILL AN OPTION

The total elimination of paper checks could result in savings of up to $100 per employee per year, depending on the pay frequency of the company. Having all the employees on direct deposit or pay cards could free up these costs and allow them to be allocated to other needs or wants. And these are just the printing costs. This figure does not include the additional cost burdens of replacing lost or damaged paper checks. It does not include the cost of having to have a staff member reconcile the payroll bank account and for storage of the check copies to comply with record retention requirements. It certainly does not include the cost of processing abandoned or returned checks under the various state requirements for abandoned wages. So why do employers still continue to offer paper payroll checks? Basically, it is because they are required to do so by law and custom.

Although direct deposit has been around since the 1970s and pay cards are the latest addition to the payroll technology arsenal, many employees still cling to the notion that paper checks are safer and that a paycheck in the hand is the only sure way to be paid. They believe this, and nothing you say or do is going to change their minds. So what can the efficient payroll department do to lessen the burden of producing paper checks?

(a) Handling and Processing Paper Payroll Checks

There are several areas that the payroll department can examine to ensure that the most efficient methods are being used. These include:

- Printing
- Stuffing
- Delivering

Printing of the Payroll Checks. If the checks are printed in house, the payroll department must make sure that the printers used are high speed laser printers with a maximum paper capacity. If the checks are processed by an outside vendor, then negotiating for the best price when the contracts are signed or renewed will help save costs.

Stuffing of the Payroll Checks.   Paper checks require staff time and effort to stuff into the envelopes and this is a laborious task at best. Still, it is surprising how many companies still view this as a manual task, especially if the checks are printed in house. Investing in a check-stuffing machine or even in checks that are self-enveloped will go a long way toward increasing efficiency for in-house check processing.

Delivery of Paychecks.   Most companies still deliver paper checks by hand. The checks are delivered by payroll staff members for small companies and usually by supervisors or managers for larger ones. The payroll department must sort and package the checks into the various departments and disburse them. If the company has multiple sites, this could include addressing the envelopes for mailing and applying postage. There is no real way to streamline this process or to make it more efficient. It is time consuming and labor intensive. However, some time can be saved by having pre-printed labels for mailing and up-to-date mailing lists.

Some companies are resorting to mailing the employee's paycheck if he or she refuses to change to direct deposit. It is believed that this adds incentive for the employee to make the change and it probably does, but it could also open the company up to lawsuits and wage and hour violations if the checks are not received on time due to the U.S. Postal Service. The law requires that employees be paid on payday, not that the check be in the mail, so this endeavor to save the company time and money by getting the employees to switch to direct deposit may end up costing the company more in fines and penalties for violations of wage and hour law.

(b) Replacing Lost Checks

Replacing lost payroll checks is also a time consuming task for the payroll department, but for employees who are still receiving paper checks, the only way to replace a check that has been damaged or lost is to print out another paper check. To make this easier, the procedures for replacing checks should be written and included with the payroll department's overall procedure manual.

Included in this procedure should be the requirement that an employee who is requesting replacement of a lost, stolen, or damaged paper payroll check must complete a request for replacement form. A sample form is included in Exhibit 6.1. Once the employee has requested the replacement, the payroll department needs to determine if the check has cleared the bank and if not, whether a stop payment should be issued. The employee should submit a damaged check with the request for replacement form. If a stop payment is issued, the procedures should establish whether or not the employee must pay for the bank charges (if any) for placing the stop payment. This is more than likely a management decision and it should be given to payroll in writing to include in the procedures manual. If a stop payment has to be issued, the procedures and the request for replacement check form both should state how long the employee must wait before the new check will be issued. This time frame should be determined with help from legal counsel and in accordance with local wage payment laws.

(c) Bank Account Reconciliations

The bank account reconciliations for the payroll bank accounts should not be done by anyone on the payroll staff or by the payroll manager or supervisor. This is strictly for internal

Exhibit 6.1

Request to Replace Lost, Stolen, or Damaged Paper Payroll Check

The following is a suggestion for a sample authorization form for the employee to sign when requesting a replacement payroll check. Before using this sample, the payroll department should have it cleared by its own legal counsel for compliance with state laws.

Request for Replacement of Lost, Stolen, or Damaged Paper Payroll Check

I am requesting a replacement for the paper payroll check listed below. Please process this request as soon as possible, but I understand that it could take up to (insert number of days for bank clearance of payroll checks) days to receive the replacement check. This is to allow time for the payroll department to verify whether the old check has been cleared through the bank account. I also understand that if a stop payment is needed, I may be charged the bank service fee for this stop payment. I also agree that I received the original payroll check on time and that the stop payment and replacement do not affect the payment of wages under federal or state law.

Replacement Check Information:

Employee Name: _____

Employee ID Number: _____

Employee Social Security Number: _____

Payroll date of check to be replaced: _____

Check number of check to be replaced: _____

Amount of check to be replaced: _____

Date of this request: _____

Reason for replacement: _____

_____

_____

_____

Signature of employee requesting replacement check

safeguards and controls. The reconciliations should be done by someone on the finance or accounting staff.

However, communication between the person who reconciles the bank account and the payroll manager or staff is crucial. Checks that have not been cashed or have not at least cleared the bank account may be abandoned wages (this is not necessarily so, but it could be). Therefore, they must be processed as discussed in the next section. However, before it gets to that point, payroll can do several things to verify that the wages are abandoned and they can be done in a more efficient manner and with less stress than waiting until the last minute before the wages have to be reported. These tasks include:

- Creating a spreadsheet to track all uncashed payroll checks by employee name, check number, and what attempts to contact the employee have been made. Also included should be the date the checks become payable to the state.

- Calling or e-mailing the current employee to whom the check belongs to find out why it has not been cashed.

- Writing or e-mailing a terminated employee to find out if the check was received and why it was not cashed.

Payroll needs to know that a check remains uncashed as soon as possible in order to be able to attempt to contact the employee. Therefore, the bank account reconciliation staff member should prepare a list of any checks that have not cleared the bank after three consecutive bank reconciliations. This list should then be given to payroll so that they can begin contacting the employees. The list should contain the check number and the check amount. After each bank reconciliation, a new list should be compiled but no editing should be done. In other words, if a check was included on last month's list and it still has not cleared the bank, then it should appear on this month's list again. This is the only way that payroll can determine if the checks previously listed as uncashed have since been cashed. This also creates less work for the staff member creating the list. He or she does not have to go back and compare previous reports.

(d) Reporting Abandoned Wages

One of the many tasks that falls under the payroll department's scope of authority is reporting unclaimed wages to the state. In addition to abandoned wages, payroll may also have to report other unclaimed employee property such as gift certificates, savings bonds bought through payroll deductions, or company stock. This reporting is not optional. All 50 states have unclaimed property laws that require companies to remit all unclaimed funds to the state. In these cash-strapped times, most states are struggling to find revenue wherever they can and abandoned property is a good place to start. California, New York, and Massachusetts are reportedly the most aggressive when it comes to recouping abandoned funds.

The majority of states have deadlines in the fall for annual compliance. But because the "deemed abandoned" date varies from state to state, the most efficient method for monitoring these rules is to have a spreadsheet to track the deadlines for each state. This information could be added to the spreadsheet discussed under "Bank Account Reconciliations" in the previous section.

Penalties for noncompliance are pretty severe and many cash-poor states have auditors looking for employers, so payroll departments are advised to create a best practices procedure as soon as possible. The following points comprise the four best practice goals regarding unclaimed property, including wages. Specifically:

Minimize the amount of unclaimed property reported to the states.

Recover property that is not really unclaimed property.

Avoid penalties and interest.

Be prepared for a state audit.

To achieve these goals, payroll department should:

- Establish procedures for the department on how to handle unclaimed wages.
- Improve existing controls over the issuance of paper checks.
- Decide who will handle the escheat (abandoned wages) function.

In establishing these procedures, the payroll department should keep several points in mind:

- The most efficient way to control the tracking of abandoned wages is to use the spreadsheet created for tracking uncashed checks.

- Uncashed checks should be reviewed and processed at least once per month to prevent abandoned wages in the first place.

- In payroll, unclaimed property is typically the last paycheck of a departing employee. If the employee is moving, there is a good chance the check could get lost, especially if it is delayed for some reason. Diligent companies continue to try to find a correct address if the letter sent to the employee about the uncashed check is returned. There are several brands of software available that supply phone books nationwide and there are Internet sites that can help track down addresses. Again, the best way to process abandoned wages is not to have any. The more uncashed or unclaimed checks that can be ferreted out and returned to their rightful owners, the less checks to be reported to the state.

- Internal searches. Sometimes an uncashed check is caused by an internal mistake and not because it is abandoned. Before beginning any communication with an employee or reporting wages as abandoned, the payroll department should do an internal search to make sure that the check was not mishandled or voided improperly.

6.2   DIRECT DEPOSIT

Direct deposit of wages is extremely popular among employers and employees alike. More and more employers are establishing direct deposit programs under which the net check is deposited directly into an employee's personal checking or savings account. Some direct deposit programs only allow deposits to employee accounts at the financial institution where the employer maintains its payroll account. This is known as an "Intra Bank" option. However, the majority of direct deposit programs make use of a nationwide network of automated clearinghouses (ACHs) that enables the employer to make payroll deposits into accounts maintained by employees at almost any financial institution in the country. By some accounts, currently, 50 percent of the U.S. workforce and over 300,000 companies use direct deposit. With benefits to both the employer and the employees alike, a direct deposit program is clearly the most efficient way to pay employees.

In order to set up an efficient direct deposit program, it is important to understand what direct deposit is and how it works. Direct deposit is an application of the system known as Electronic Funds Transfer (EFT). This is a system by which commercial payments are made electronically instead of using paper instruments such as checks or drafts. Electronic Funds Transfers use a special set of computer-generated records recorded on a magnetic tape or transmitted electronically to transfer funds between accounts. A paperless entry, like a check, orders financial institutions to make payment of a specific dollar amount.

The direct deposit process begins when an employee authorizes the employer to credit his or her bank account each payday. Under a direct deposit program, an employer must collect employees' account numbers for personal savings or checking accounts, as well as bank transit numbers for the employees' financial institutions. (For more on how to collect this information, see Section 6.2[b].) The payment process begins two days prior to the actual payday. On that day, the employer sends the direct deposit file or tape to the bank where it maintains its payroll account. The company may have the choice of delivering the payroll data on a magnetic computer tape, a computer disk, or by electronic means such as a file transfer or an e-mail attachment. This bank is called the originating depository financial institution (ODFI).

The ODFI sets a cut-off time by which the employer must submit its direct deposit file (e.g., 2 P.M., two business days prior to the effective date of the payroll). For example, if the company's payday is Friday, the bank will need the payroll data no later than 2 P.M. Wednesday afternoon. This bank extracts any entries for its own accounts that employees have there and sets them aside ("warehouses" them) for payday. It then sends the remaining information to the regional Automated Clearing House (ACH). It prepares the remaining entries by assigning a special 14-digit tracing number to each transaction. The first eight digits consist of the ODFI's own transit routing number, while the last six digits are assigned in an ascending sequence. The non-ODFI transactions are then transmitted to a regional ACH.

On the second day, the entries are processed across the ACH network to each employee's financial institution. A regional ACH will route entries either directly to an employee's financial institution or to another ACH, in cases where the employee's financial institution is located in a different region. The key to this process is the use of standardized American Bankers Association transit routing numbers. This is the "address" of each financial institution.

By the third day, the payday or payroll effective date, the entries have arrived at the employees' financial institutions (called Receiving Depository Financial Institutions or RDFI) and are posted to the employees' accounts. On payday, the employee receives an information statement instead of a paycheck. Some financial institutions, for their own convenience, credit the funds into accounts when the advance notice is received on the day before payday, even though the bank itself has not been credited. Other banks use a computerized accounting process called "memo posting." This process provides notice to tellers and automated teller machines (ATMs) that the direct deposit is in a customer's account, even though it technically won't be entered to the account until late payday afternoon. Using memo posting, a bank is able to delay crediting accounts until they themselves have received the funds. The bank's customers enjoy free access to their funds all day payday without having to wait for the bank's accounting system to update balance information (post) at the end of the business day.

Direct deposit programs are subject to several sets of rules and statutes. At the federal level, Federal Reserve Board Regulation E (Title 12, Code of Federal Regulations, Part 205) generally sets forth the consumer protection rights and requirements that apply to electronic funds transfer. Additionally, direct deposit plans are subject to two requirements imposed by the

Electronic Funds Transfer Act (P.L. 95-630; 15 USC 1693e, 1693k). These provisions are:

- *Section 907.* Employers must have advance written consent to transfer funds from an employee's account. In other words, to take back a deposit made in error.

- *Section 913.* An employer may not require an employee to establish an account for receipt of electronic funds transfer at any particular financial institution as a condition of employment.

Most states have adopted rules or positions concerning the electronic transfer of payroll funds directly to employee accounts. A number of states have incorporated their rules concerning direct deposit directly into their labor codes; others maintain an official position as a guideline, and still other state governments have no law or regulation. Employers that are unsure about how state law may affect their direct deposit program may contact the National Automated Clearing House Association (NACHA), or seek legal counsel.

(a) Establishing a Direct Deposit Program

If the payroll department has never had a direct deposit program, then the following steps will be beneficial in setting up a program. If the department has had an established direct deposit program for years, this may be a good time to evaluate the program to make sure it is being run as efficiently as possible.

Step 1. The first step in setting up a direct deposit program is to do a needs assessment. In other words, will any of the employees sign up for the program? If the employer finds a willingness for enough employees to use the program, then they should go on to step two. It is helpful with the needs assessment, especially with management, to outline the advantages and disadvantages of a direct deposit program. A list of these is included in Exhibit 6.2.

Well-conceived employee communications are also critical to the successful implementation of a

EXHIBIT 6.2

Advantages and Disadvantages of Direct Deposit Programs

Advantages of Direct Deposit

Benefits for the employer include:

- Cost Savings—According to the National Automated Clearing House Association, an employer may pay 10 to 23 cents less per payment using direct deposit compared to the cost of issuing paychecks.
- Value as an employee benefit—Direct deposit may be perceived as an extra employee benefit, yet it is inexpensive to the employer.
- Security—Problems of lost or stolen checks are eliminated.
- Streamlining of payroll functions—Less time is spent on account reconciliation.

Benefits for the employee include:

- Convenience—The employee can make fewer trips to the bank and there is less waiting in long lines to deposit paychecks.
- Interest earnings—For employees with interest-bearing accounts, direct deposit puts their pay to work earning interest more quickly than if they had to deposit their paycheck at the bank.
- Availability during absences—Employees out sick or on vacation on payday still have access to their pay as soon as it is deposited.

Disadvantages of Direct Deposit

Despite its many advantages, direct deposit also has a number of disadvantages that you should consider before implementing a program. Among these disadvantages are:

- Employers must constantly update the masterfile of information on direct deposit participants to make sure that terminated employees are not paid in error. This is one reason why companies with high turnover rates may find direct deposit too administratively burdensome.
- It is not totally paperless. Employers still must process employee authorization forms and prepare the nonnegotiable pay information statements that employees receive in lieu of their paychecks.
- Direct deposit transfers cannot be easily reversed when errors are made.
- The employer loses the "float" on payroll funds—i. e., interest earnings for the period between when a check is issued and when it actually is cleared by the employee's bank.
- Payroll processing windows may be shortened because of the minimum two-day processing time required for a direct deposit. Scheduling for holidays becomes even more complicated because of the shortened processing period.
- The ODFI charges for direct deposit service. This reduces the savings an employer may expect from developing a direct deposit plan. Depending on the agreement, most ODFIs will charge a nominal setup or startup fee, a monthly maintenance or tape fee, and a fee per debit/credit (with a minimum number per month required). In addition, there is normally a separate schedule of fees for miscellaneous transactions such as returns or stop payments.
- Some state laws require the employer to absorb bank service charges that the employee may incur as a result of the direct deposit program.

■   205   ■

direct deposit program. Although most employees will immediately recognize the benefits of direct deposit, others are likely to be unfamiliar with or distrusting of the concept of electronic funds transfer and may resist giving up their paychecks. If reevaluating a current program, the manager has to look at the number of employees who are using direct deposit and examine why some employees are still not signing up. What is keeping them from going to direct deposit? Employers may be able to convince some of the holdouts to use direct deposit through communications that demystify the direct deposit process and give testimony to its reliability.

Communications should emphasize:

• Direct deposit offers employees more security than receiving a paper check, because seldom, if ever, do direct deposit transactions go astray. However, lost, stolen, or destroyed paper checks are a common occurrence.

• The direct deposit process uses a prenotification procedure to double-check account information before any of the employee's pay is actually transferred electronically.

Pay envelope stuffers may be a great method for communicating information about direct deposit. For example, a paycheck stuffer emphasizing the convenience of direct deposit may hit home with some employees as they prepare to rush off to the bank to deposit their pay. Other methods employers have used to communicate their programs include posters, videotapes, and special employee workshops. Your bank may be able to provide your company with samples of questionnaires, marketing aids, and sign-up forms.

Step 2. Creating the new hardware and software. To get a direct deposit initiative off the ground, the employer must set up the mechanics of the program with their in-house programming department or a service bureau. They must also contact a bank (either their own bank or shop around for a new one) to set the electronic funds transfer in place. After determining whether direct deposit is available through their current payroll system, employers should speak with several financial institutions and look for the direct deposit service that best fits their company's needs. Here are six areas that may be used to evaluate the choice of banks:

Experience. How long has the bank been involved in electronic direct deposit of payroll checks? Does it or the staff have the required expertise to assist in training the payroll staff and implementing a direct deposit program as well as processing the files through the ACH?

Involvement. Does the bank offer to get involved with helping set up the new program? Will the bank's staff help the payroll department market the new benefit to the employees? Do they offer samples of forms and promotional literature for the payroll department to use?

Flexibility. Can the bank offer the payroll department choices in tape formats, delivery media, deadlines, reports, and so forth?

Service. Does the bank have a reputation for quality, attention to detail, and service?

Sophistication. Is the bank keeping pace with industry developments in computerization and software enhancements?

Price. Are the bank's charges for this service reasonable and competitive with other financial institutions?

There are other factors not related to payroll in choosing a bank, although some choices may not be available due to the company's relationship with its financial institution. But evaluating experience, involvement, flexibility, service, sophistication, and price will help the payroll department to decide on a bank or decide whether using more than one bank is an option. If the payroll department has no choice because the bank has been chosen for them by management, then these factors will assist the department in getting the most out of its relationship with the bank.

Step 3. With the hardware and software tested and in place, the employer must now get the employees to sign up for the program. This should be done through the employee authorization form, as discussed next, in Section 6.2(b).

Step 4. After receiving the employee authorizations, the employer must go through the prenotation or prenote process, which will be discussed in detail later.

Step 5. If all employees prenote with no problems, the employer can begin sending actual deposits through the system.

To ensure a successful setup for the direct deposit program, a checklist for the implementation should be created. A sample checklist is shown in Exhibit 6.3.

(b) Setting Up an Employee for Direct Deposit

An employer must obtain an employee's written authorization before direct deposit of the employee's paycheck can begin. The authorization agreement should also give the employer permission not only to credit the account but to debit the employee's account as well. This is necessary for the payroll department to be able to call back or reverse a deposit made in error. A sample reverse form is contained in Exhibit 6.4.

The employer must keep a copy of the authorization on file for at least two years following revocation by the employee or the employee's termination. The employer, upon request, must present a copy of an employee's authorization to an ODFI or RDFI. While the banks that receive direct deposits retain this right, in practice, this is rarely, if ever, done.

EXHIBIT 6.3

Direct Deposit Implementation Checklist

Whether setting up a direct deposit program for the first time or reevaluating the current plan for ways to increase efficiency, the following checklist will be very helpful.

Internal planning and communication

- Determine whether employees will be offered direct deposit to a single account or multiple accounts. If multiple accounts, how many will be offered?
- Designate the internal direct deposit contact personnel.
- Determine the cutoff dates for the initial employee signup if this is a new program, or for subsequent signups if this is a promotion to encourage new signups.
- Develop a promotional memo or brochure to announce the program if it is new. Send a brochure to new employees to encourage signup.
- Develop the authorization forms, if this is a new program. If reevaluating the program, examine the forms to make sure they conform to standards.

Educating the employees

- For new programs or signup drives, hold meetings to explain the benefits of direct deposit and distribute promotional literature and authorization forms.
- Post bulletin board announcements and promote the program in the company newsletter and on the company intranet site.
- Encourage new employees to sign up by including information in new hire packets.
- Insert stuffers with payroll checks to encourage direct deposit.

Processing concerns

- If a new program, determine the method for the file creation and transmission. If reevaluating the current program, determine if the current transmission method is sufficient.
- Set up the schedule for processing the direct deposit. Announce to employees when setups, changes, or stops are due to payroll in order to be processed with the current payroll. This should be done each year, not just at program inception.
- If setting up the program for the first time, authorizations should be collected and processed together. Once established, direct deposit setups, changes, or stops should be processed each payroll.
- Set up prenote procedures for all authorizations.

It is essential to validate the bank transit and account numbers provided by employees in order to avoid problems in setting up the direct deposit. Therefore, employees should be asked to submit a blank voided check (for checking accounts) or a voided deposit slip (for savings accounts) with their direct

EXHIBIT 6.4

Authorization Agreement for Direct Deposit of Net Wages

Company Name Here
Authorization Agreement for Direct Deposit of Net Wages

I, _____ am an active employee
of (insert company name here). I would like to participate in the automatic direct
deposit program. I have attached a voided check to identify the financial institution
and account number in which I would like to have my funds deposited.

I authorize the payroll department of (insert company name here) to deposit the net pay
shown on my payroll check directly into my:

Checking ☐   Savings ☐

in the financial institution shown on the attached voided check. NOTE: If requesting
direct deposit into a credit union, money market fund, or other accounts sponsored by
investment firms, please contact the financial institution directly for the appropriate
ACH routing number. The routing number on the voided check cannot be used for
these financial institutions.

I also agree to allow the payroll department of (insert company name here) to reverse
any excess deposits or deposits made in error. This may be done by making a debit
directly from my account. I understand that if a debit is made, I will be notified by the
payroll department.

This direct deposit will be automatic and will continue on each payday until I order the
direct deposit to be stopped. This order will be in writing only and on the appropriate
form to be supplied by the payroll department. Upon termination of my employment,
the direct deposit will be automatically stopped prior to processing of my final check.

If changes occur to my bank account number or I change banks, I am responsible for
immediately notifying the payroll department in writing. The (insert company name)
payroll department is not responsible for any delays in deposits if this notification is not
received in time for the current payroll.

Please attach voided check or savings deposit slip here

Signature:_____Date: _____

deposit authorization. The ACH system recommends voided
checks in lieu of deposit slips for checking accounts to ensure
that the proper account numbers are recorded.

The bank transit and account numbers needed to prepare
entries for direct deposit transactions usually are encoded in
machine readable ink beginning at the lower left hand corner
of the check or deposit slip. The first group of up to nine digits
is the bank transit number. It is usually separated from the

other numbers by a colon. The account number is the second group of digits. The third and final group of digits is the check sequence number, which is unnecessary for setting up a direct deposit file and can thus be ignored. Actually, the payroll department must be careful not to accidentally combine the check sequence number with the employee's account number, as this could result in the rejection of a transaction when it enters the ACH network.

Another potential problem in the authorization stage is obtaining account information for credit union accounts, money market accounts, and other accounts sponsored by investment firms. The account information on the checks and deposit slips for such accounts is more than likely to be invalid for ACH transactions. If an employee wishes to arrange direct deposit to this type of account, the payroll department staff member should instruct them to contact their credit union or investment company for a transit and account number that will be valid for ACH transactions. This is a common occurrence and most credit unions and investment firms often will have special direct deposit information forms prepared for employees to submit to their employer. Often this is not a problem with direct deposits to an employer credit union as they usually are handled outside the ACH network.

To create the information needed for the processing of direct deposits, the payroll department must add the information from the employees' direct deposit authorization forms to a special masterfile maintained on the payroll system. Accuracy is critical and data should be audited carefully. The masterfile serves as the basis for the file of direct deposit entries that are submitted each pay period to the financial institution. To ensure that the entries are not erroneous, the masterfile must be updated each payroll to reflect employee terminations and any other changes in bank transit or account numbers due to bank mergers and acquisitions. The payroll department must generally rely on employees to report changes in bank information.

Several days prior to payday, the payroll department will use the payroll system to download data from the masterfile and generate a file of entries for direct deposit transactions.

This direct deposit file must conform to specifications established by the National Automated Clearing House Association so that it can be transmitted through the ACH network.

Prenotification is a process by which the accuracy of transaction data (e.g., employee name, bank transit number, account number, etc.) may be tested before actual dollar transactions take place. As of September 1996, this has been an option for the employer. If the payroll department chooses to use this process, it will need to prepare a special prenote entry for each new direct deposit authorization received from the employees. The prenotification record must be transmitted at least 10 to 15 business days in advance of the first actual dollar transaction. However, because no other method exists for verifying the data on the masterfile with the information on ACH's files, it is extremely efficient to always prenote all direct deposits one full payroll or more before actual dollars are transmitted.

Prenotification entries are included in the batch of other direct deposit entries the department sends to its ODFI, and basically contain the same data fields as other direct deposit entries except that the prenote entry authorizes a transaction of zero dollars and zero cents. Prenote entries that cannot be processed by an ACH or RFDI, are generally returned to the payroll department within six banking days.

When the prenotification record is processed successfully (i.e., it is not returned within six banking days) the payroll department simply updates its files of direct deposit transactions to authorize deposit of actual dollar amounts on subsequent paydays. However, where a prenotification record is returned because it cannot be processed, the payroll department generally must enlist the help of the employee to verify the accuracy of the information provided on his or her direct deposit authorization form. Of course, this is only done after verifying that data entry errors were not made when adding the information to the masterfile. After any invalid information has been corrected, the file is resubmitted for prenotification. It must be pointed out that prenotification is not a completely foolproof system. Sometimes invalid prenotes may not be returned on a timely basis.

New prenote entries must be issued whenever any of the following items change:

- Employee's account number
- Receiving institution's transit routing numbers
- Employer's identification number

New prenotes must be issued at least six banking days prior to sending the first actual dollar transactions under the new account, transit, or identification number. As mentioned earlier, note that changes to bank transit routing numbers frequently arise as a result of bank mergers and acquisitions. This prenote process generally takes one to two payroll periods to complete.

In some instances, the employee may want to set up a direct deposit for less than the net check or to have part of his or her check sent to one account while a separate direct deposit goes to a savings account or another account. If the payroll system is capable of multiple direct deposits, then the payroll department must also set up procedures to handle requests such as these. The easiest and most efficient way to process these types of direct deposits is to create a multiple deposit form. The employee would complete this form by specifying where set amounts of money should be deposited.

(c) Changing an Existing Direct Deposit

Occasionally, an employee will need to change his or her existing direct deposit information. He or she may need to increase or decrease the amount of a direct deposit deduction, change bank account numbers, or even change banks. The payroll department needs to set up strict procedures to make sure that these changes are handled quickly and efficiently. The payroll department has a form to set up a direct deposit for the net check, however, this same form should *not* be used for all direct deposit set ups or for changes. It is much more efficient to have one form for each type of task. This way, the employee will not accidentally mark the wrong item or request the wrong thing. So first a form to set up, change, or cancel a direct deposit deduction should be created and available. Then if the employee wants to change the amount of the deduction or the bank account or cancel the deduction, this can be used for that purpose. However, employees should never be allowed to change a direct deposit for net pay. The employee should instead cancel the first direct deposit and then set up a new one. A sample of the change form for direct deposits is shown in Exhibit 6.5.

EXHIBIT 6.5

Authorization Agreement for Direct Deposit of a Payroll Deducation Amount

Company Name Here
Authorization Agreement for Direct Deposit of a Payroll Deduction Amount

I, _____ am an active employee of (insert company name here). I would like to participate in the automatic direct deposit program. I have attached a voided check to identify the financial institution and account number in which I would like to have my funds deposited.

I authorize the payroll department of (insert company name here) to deduct from my payroll check and deposit the amount of $_____directly into my:

Checking ☐   Savings ☐

in the financial institution shown on the attached voided check or deposit slip. NOTE: If requesting direct deposit into a credit union, money market fund, or other accounts sponsored by investment firms, please contact the financial institution directly for the appropriate ACH routing number. The routing number on the voided check cannot be used for these financial institutions.

I also agree to allow the payroll department of (insert company name here) to reverse any excess deposits or deposits made in error. This may be done by making a debit directly from my account. I understand that if a debit is made, I will be notified by the payroll department.

This direct deposit will be automatic and will continue on each payday until I order the direct deposit to be changed or stopped. This order will be in writing only and on the appropriate form to be supplied by the payroll department. Upon termination of my employment, the direct deposit will be automatically stopped prior to processing of my final check.

If changes occur to my bank account number or I change banks, I am responsible for immediately notifying the payroll department in writing. The (insert company name) payroll department is not responsible for any delays in deposits if this notification is not received in time for the current payroll.

Please attach voided check or savings deposit slip here

Signature:_____Date: _____

(d) Stopping a Direct Deposit

If an employee needs to change bank account number within the same bank or switch to a new bank, he or she should stop the current direct deposit in effect and set up a new direct deposit of net check. This is the cleanest and most efficient way to make sure that the monies go to the right place. The form to stop a direct deposit should be separate from the set up form in order to avoid confusion. A sample stop form is shown in Exhibit 6.6. If the employee wants to stop a direct deposit

---

EXHIBIT 6.6

To Stop or Adjust Amount of Direct Deposits

Company Name Here
To Stop or Adjust Amount of Direct Deposits

I, _____ am an active employee of (insert company name here) and am participating in the direct deposit program. I would like to make the following change(s) in my direct deposit effective with the next available payroll:

Please check the appropriate box(es) below to cancel your direct deposit:

☐ Please cancel the current direct deposit of my net wages.

☐ Please cancel my current direct deposit deduction in the amount of $_____.
    This deposit is made to _____ (please insert the name
    of the financial institution where the direct deposit is made).

Please complete the information below to change the amount of a direct deposit deduction. All information must be furnished in order for the payroll department to complete the processing of this request.

Current deduction being taken for direct deposit: $_____
The deduction is made to: _____
(please insert the name of the financial institution)

Please change the current deduction listed above to: $_____

This form is to be used for stopping a net pay direct deposit or changing or stopping deductions already established ONLY. If you would like to set up a direct deposit, please use our "Authorization Agreement for Direct Deposit of Net Wages" or our "Authorization Agreement for the Direct Deposit of a Payroll Deduction Amount."

Signature:_____Date: _____

---

deduction, then the direct deposit deduction form should be used. But again, if the employee is changing bank account numbers or banks, the old direct deposit needs to be stopped and a new direct deposit set up; this means the employee must furnish another voided check.

(e) Recalling a Direct Deposit

One of the most pressing concerns for payroll departments when it comes to direct deposit is how to efficiently recall a payroll check that has been issued in error or for the wrong amount. Whatever the reason for wanting to recover the payroll item, the method of recovery will usually depend on the timing of the notice to the company's originating financial institution. If the problem is discovered before the financial institution has transmitted the payroll to the ACH system, the payroll department has the greatest and most control over recovery. A phone call to the bank requesting that they delete any problem transactions is simple and straightforward. As a standard practice, the financial institution will ask that the deletions be confirmed in writing. They, of course, will execute the verbal instructions immediately. To handle the recalls efficiently, the payroll department should have on hand a prepared standard form to use for all deletions. A sample form is shown in Exhibit 6.7. Complete procedures for recalling an item should be confirmed with the bank when the program is first established. If this was not done at program inception, the payroll manager should discuss these procedures with the bank now and add them to the payroll procedures as soon as possible.

If the problem is discovered after the payroll items have been released into the ACH system but before they have posted to the employee's account, this information should be relayed to the company's financial institution as soon as possible. The bank, in turn, will contact the receiving institution and request that the item be returned. Again, written confirmation will be requested by both financial institutions and should follow as soon as possible after the verbal request is made. The receiving financial institution will often set the payroll item aside awaiting the written confirmation from the requesting financial insti-

EXHIBIT 6.7

Sample Form for Recalling a Direct Deposit

This form is to be used when a direct deposit must be recalled. Please complete all lines in part 1 and submit for approval before recalling the direct deposit. Please complete part 2 while recalling the direct deposit. Be sure to sign and date where indicated.

Part 1 Approval to recall direct deposit

Payroll Date: _____

Direct Deposit Process Date: _____

Employee Name: _____

Identification Number: _____

Reason for Recall: _____

_____

_____

_____

Requested by: _____Date: _____

Approval Signature: _____Date: _____

Date and Time Recall Completed: _____

Confirmation of the Recall: _____

Signature: _____

tution. Banks should accept faxes as proof of written request. In some cases, e-mail may be acceptable as well.

If the problem is discovered after the payroll item is posted to the receiving account, there may be a problem because legal ownership of the funds in question has changed. Recovery is now much more difficult. This type of recovery is known as a reversal and must be specifically preauthorized by the owner of the account. This is why it is important that the original employee authorization form contain a statement allowing for a debit of the account in case of erroneous postings.

Although retrieving posted transactions is possible, it must be expected that varying and sometimes lengthy delays will occur in the return process. Returns are usually converted to paper and returned back through the banking system as exception items. In the best case scenario, a return may be credited to the corporate account within a few days. However, delays of two to three weeks are not uncommon. The company's financial institution should be following through on the company's behalf in prompting and following through on the timely return of funds.

(f) Electronic Pay Stubs

Eliminating paper pay stubs could result in a savings of $50 to $100 per employee per year, depending on pay frequency, according to recent data from the National Automated Clearing House Association (NACHA). So what prevents more payroll departments from taking advantage of this potential savings? Employee access, state laws, and limited resources are the reasons most often cited by payroll professionals for not implementing an electronic pay stub program. But these reasons are outdated—they were the same reasons for not implementing a direct deposit program in the 1970s and early 1980s, and now direct deposit is the means of payment for over 50 percent of the working population. So in the future, once people begin to warm to the idea, electronic pay stubs could take a bigger share of the ways that employers provide pay stubs to their employees.

First things first—before even thinking of implementing an electronic pay stub program, it must be investigated. The first thing the payroll professional should research is the legal aspects or legal hurdles that may be involved.

Legal Battles. Because providing a pay stub remains a state requirement, employers must review individual state statutes and applicable labor agency interpretations of the governing statutes. The states mainly fall into four categories—no requirement, access based, access and print capabilities, and consent. See Exhibit 6.8 for a breakdown by state.

EXHIBIT 6.8

State Mandate Breakdown for Electronic Pay Stubs

No Requirement	Access Requirements	Access and Print Capability Requirements	Consent Requirements
Arkansas	Alabama	California	Delaware
Florida	Alaska	Colorado	Massachusetts
Iowa	Arizona	Connecticut	Oregon
Louisiana	Georgia	Hawaii	Wisconsin
Mississippi	Idaho	Minnesota	Wyoming
Nebraska	Illinois	New Mexico	
South Dakota	Indiana	North Carolina	
Tennessee	Kansas	Texas	
Virginia	Kentucky	Vermont	
	Maine		
	Maryland		
	Michigan		
	Missouri		
	Montana		
	Nevada		
	New Hampshire		
	New Jersey		
	New York		
	North Dakota		
	Ohio		
	Oklahoma		
	Pennsylvania		
	Rhode Island		
	South Carolina		
	Utah		
	Washington		
	West Virginia		

Note: State mandated requirements are constantly changing in this area as labor departments are being asked to give rulings or the state legislatures are addressing the issue.

Descriptions of the aforementioned four categories are as follows:

- *No Requirement.* These states do not require employers to provide statements detailing an employee's pay information. If employers in these states elect to provide pay stubs to employees, they can do so in electronic format. Florida, for example, has no statute or regulation requiring employers to deliver pay stubs to their employees.

- *Access.* These states require employers to "furnish," "give," or "provide" a statement that details an employee's pay information but they don't require that the pay statement be in writing or on paper. Consequently, a reasonable interpretation of the law suggests employers can comply with the pay stub requirements in these states by furnishing an electronic pay stub. Missouri, for example, requires employers to provide the information but does not specify whether it must be in writing or in any particular method. The employer's obligation is to make sure that the employees have reasonable access to their electronic pay stubs, which might mean setting up kiosks, workstations, or Internet access.

- *Access and Print Capabilities.* These states require employers to provide a written or printed statement that details an employee's pay information. They do not require pay statements to be delivered with the checks or in some other specific medium. A reasonable interpretation of the law in these states would be that an employer can comply by furnishing an electronic pay stub that employees can print. Employees must have both access to the e-pay stubs and the capability of printing them. For example, California's labor commission has issued a specific letter spelling out the criteria and specifications for this printing and access requirement.

- *Consent.* States in this category have a requirement as to how they must deliver the pay stub—either in the pay envelope as a detachable portion of the check itself, or as a separate piece of paper. Under this restriction, employees must consent to receive pay stubs electronically. The state of Wisconsin is an example in this category. Its statute states: "An employer shall state clearly on the employee's pay check, pay envelope, or paper accompanying the wage payment the amount of and reason for each deduction from the wages due or earned by the employee...." Where the statute prescribes a specific method of delivery, such as on the paycheck or pay envelope, electronic deliveries require employee consent. The employees also must be able to opt out of the program and to receive their pay stubs on paper again.

6.3 PAYCARDS

The role of paying workers for their labors is as old as recorded history. From the beginning, payroll has followed in the wake of technology and sometimes even been in the forefront. In ancient Greece, workers were paid in salt or in kind (the term salary is derived from the Greek word for salt). When civilization went to coins of the realm, payroll went right along. In fact, cash was the most popular way to pay employees right up until the 1970s.

In the 1950s, the payroll check was ushered in and began to become the dominant method of paying wages. Almost everyone in payroll has a story about how they themselves have paid employees with cash envelopes or they know someone who used to be paid that way.

The next leap in technology and innovation occurred when direct deposit was born in 1974. This is when the National Automated Clearing House Association (NACHA) was founded. Although available as early as 1974, it was not until the 1990s that direct deposit of payroll checks really caught on with employees. By 1999 the statistics were as follows:

- 50 percent of U.S. employees are on direct deposit
- 100 percent of Japanese employees are on direct deposit
- 90 percent of European employees are on direct deposit

Then in 2001, the latest technology in paying employee wages was introduced—the payroll debit card.

(a) What Are Paycards?

There are different terms used to describe the payroll debit card, including paycards stored value debit cards, and payroll debit cards. Some cards even go by the trade name issued by the card vendor. These terms all mean basically the same thing; paycards are a method of paying the employee by a plastic card that has the value of the net wages.

There are two types of cards: stored value cards and host-based stored value cards. In addition, the host-based stored value cards are broken down into two types: branded and non-branded cards.

Stored Value Cards.   Stored value cards are similar to the pre-paid phone cards or the store gift cards that are popular today. The funds are loaded directly onto the card by the employer. The advantage to the card is immediate issuing for the employer, however, if the card is lost or stolen, it cannot be replaced unless the funds are reissued.

Host-Based Stored Value Cards.   The payroll debit card is by definition a host-based stored value card. Value is associated with the card and this value is stored and authorized centrally on a host computer system versus on the physical card. The card is linked to a virtual account that manages the card's debits and credits in real time. The debit paycard is linked directly to the electronic deposit of the employee's net pay.

Branded Cards.   Branded paycards are cards that carry either a VISA® or MasterCard® logo. The card functions just like a VISA or MasterCard® debit card and is accepted anywhere a VISA® or MasterCard® is accepted. The card only requires the signature of the cardholder to authorize the purchase of goods or services. A personal identification number (PIN) can also be issued that must be used in conjunction with the card in order to perform balance inquiries or withdraw funds at ATMs. The PIN can also be required when using the card for Point of Sale (POS) purchases.

Some of the advantages of branded cards include:

- Because they carry the VISA® or MasterCard® logo, they are accepted everywhere that honors these cards.
- The cards are very easy for the employee to identify with and can make the implementation of the paycard program easier, due to name recognition.

Some of the disadvantages of branded cards include:

- The card must be personalized. This means it can take from seven to ten days to get the card to the employee.
- Because not all merchants use the automated system, the account can be overdrawn by delayed transactions.
- The first payroll and the transfer payroll may experience logistical problems, like nonfunctional accounts or cards, when transferring the employee from paper to the card.
- If the card is lost or stolen, it has to be reissued and must be personalized again.

Non-Branded Cards. This type of card carries the mark or marks of one or more of the major POS and ATM networks and functions just like a debit or ATM card. The employee uses the card to make purchases or to withdraw funds at participating networks such as STAR®, Pulse®, Cirrus®, or Plus®. The card requires a PIN, which must be used for all transactions.

Some of the advantages of the non-branded cards include:

- Instant issue of the cards, as they are not personalized. Payroll or another on-site department can keep them on hand for distribution.
- 100 percent of the transactions are online, so there is no chance of overdrafts.
- The card is FDIC insured.

Some of the disadvantages of the non-branded cards include:

- Not all merchants have the hardware or software to accept PIN-based debit transactions.
- Paper processing is still required to start the account.

(b) Paying with Paycards

Whenever an employer pays an employee, there are legal requirements that must be met. What these requirements are depends largely on the state in which the company operates. The employer's paycard questions may include:

- Can paycards be made mandatory?
- What is considered timely payment in the state?
- What method of payment does the state allow?
- Does the state have any requirements for escheatment?
- Does the state have a "without discount" requirement when cashing payroll checks or when an employee is paid?
- Does the state have pay stub requirements that must be met?

Most of the regulations on these issues are already in place in most states. However, because payroll debit cards are a new technology, some of the legal issues are still being worked out. The following question and answer format will examine the general requirements for each of these issues and where payroll professionals will need to research to make sure any paycard program is in compliance in each state where it will be implemented.

Can paycards be made mandatory? Unlike when direct deposit first began, with paycards payroll professionals have some basis to work from. When researching this question, they can refer to the direct deposit requirements that most states already have in place. If a state allows mandatory direct deposit, then the current thinking is that it will allow mandatory payroll debit cards. Keep in mind, though, that there are no court cases or rulings yet in this area.

What is considered timely payment in the state? Many states have strict windows on the payment of termination pay (such as California, which requires immediate payment). So if the employer is covered under such state regulations, the paycard program must allow for immediate payments and have enough flexibility to keep the employer in compliance.

What method of payment does the state allow? Does the state allow debit cards as payment of wages? So far Virginia has given approval to using the payroll debit card, but Vermont has passed legislation that prohibits the use of the cards instead of direct deposit or paychecks. More states will have to deal with this issue as the program becomes more popular with employers. As of the publication of this book, if the state has not addressed the issue, then the standard legal advice is to follow the requirements of direct deposit. If the state allows direct deposit of wages, then it should allow the use of payroll debit cards.

Does the state have any requirements for escheatment? In other words, when using payroll debit cards, what is considered abandonment of wages (escheat) and what is the employer's responsibility? This depends on the type of card used. If using the stored value cards, then the responsibility falls on the employer. If using the host-based stored value cards, then the responsibility falls on the financial institution.

Does the state have a "without discount" requirement when cashing payroll checks or when an employee is paid? Many states require the payment of wages to be "cash, check, [or] negotiable instrument, payable upon demand, without discount, at some place in the state…" This is where the payroll department must be careful when choosing a paycard program. If the card requires fees for each use by the employee, this could be a compliance issue. However, if the card permits the first use after each payroll to be free, this may satisfy some states. Payroll must research this carefully before signing with any vendors.

Does the state have pay stub requirements that must be met? Many states have requirements that a pay stub or statement be issued with each paycheck. Paycard vendors may offer an electronic monthly statement or pay stub. In tough states like California, this would not be in compliance with state regulations. Before trying to go completely paperless when implementing a paycard program, the payroll department needs to verify if electronic statements are allowed or if paper pay stubs still must be issued.

(c) Using Both Direct Deposit and Paycards

Most of the employees currently on direct deposit probably would not switch to paycards. They have a bank account and like the ease of direct deposit. But as statistics show that as of 1999, only 50 percent of employees in the United States are on direct deposit, then the question must be asked: Why aren't the other 50 percent taking advantage of direct deposit? Perhaps it could be cultural differences, or a general distrust of banks, or that some employees do not want to maintain a bank account because the fees are too high for the little banking they do. Also, there may be some employees who, for whatever reason, are unable to get bank accounts. Instituting a paycard program can benefit all these employees as well as those who are currently on direct deposit.

The employer can reap benefits by implementing a paycard program. Some of these include:

- Combined with a direct deposit program, can make the payment of wages virtually paperless
- Benefit for human resources to use in recruitment
- Cost savings of paycards, direct deposit, and plain paper pay stubs as opposed to processing paper check stock
- Can reduce or eliminate check fraud
- Can reduce or eliminate escheat issues
- Reduces or eliminates employees' need to take time from work to cash checks
- Reduces or eliminates lost checks

There are employee benefits as well. These include:

- Ease of use
- 24/7 access to funds via ATM system
- Automatic bill paying options may be available
- May be able to regain credit worthy status if currently unbanked

(d) Choosing a Paycard Vendor

After the decision to implement a paycard program has been reached, it is time to begin the search for a vendor. But where to start? The following suggestions may be helpful in the search for a paycard vendor:

- Make sure all the legal issues are resolved and that a list of requirements has been created to ensure that the vendor can meet all demands for your program.
- Conduct an employee poll to determine the scope of the need for the program. Payroll needs to know if 10 or 1,000 employees will be using the system before selecting the vendor.
- Decide what type of card the company will offer— branded or non-branded.

Searching for a vendor should include:

- If the payroll is already outsourced, start with the current payroll processor. Many service providers are offering this service to their clients.
- Check with the current bank used by the company.
- Research paycard vendors on the web.
- Ask other payroll professionals in local professional organizations for suggestions and references.

When selecting a paycard vendor, be sure to:

- Check the fee structure.
  - Employer costs may include the cost of the card, the cost of processing each payroll, the cost of processing one-time payments such as terminations and new hires, and extra bells and whistles such as bill paying.
  - Employee costs may include the transactions at ATM and POS networks and extra services such as monthly statements.
- Check the various compliance issues. The vendor must be able to comply with all the regulations in all the states where the company is located.

- Check the technical and system requirements. Make sure that your payroll system and the vendor are compatible and they can meet your processing needs.

- Check for training of the payroll staff. Will the vendor train the payroll department on the software, procedures, and so forth?

- Is training available for the employees? Does the vendor offer training for the employees? Remember, some employees will not know how to use an ATM or POS machine.

- Are marketing tools available? Does the vendor offer marketing tools for the payroll department to distribute to the employees? This is very helpful in selling the program and in getting management on board.

(e) Implementing a Paycard Program

After the search for the vendor has been completed, the implementation of the program can begin. The following are some of the factors that the payroll professional will need to consider when implementing the paycard program:

- What is the scope of the program? If it involves a large number of employees or numerous geographical locations, the payroll department may want to roll out the new program in sections. This should be decided beforehand.

- Marketing the program to the employees should begin immediately. No matter how great the vendor and the program, the payroll department must get employees to use it.

- Employee training should be available as soon as the marketing begins. The employees will need to know how to access their "cash" on the first try, the first payday the program is in effect.

CHAPTER 7

Year End

7.1 START YEAR END OFF WITH A MEMO

Each year, the Internal Revenue Service requires employers to notify any employees who have claimed exempt status on their Form W-4 that the form will expire on December 31 and that they must submit a new one to the employer by February 15 of the following year. The memo is supposed to be sent to the employees in the beginning of December to give them time to submit the new form. As a result, the payroll department has an excellent opportunity to use this memo to also inform employees of upcoming year-end events and let them know what to expect in the new year in terms of tax rates and such.

(a) How to Address Year-End Issues with Your Customers

Because this communication heavy memo is issued in December of each year and covers items occurring in January, it has taken on a nickname, "The State of the Payroll Address." The memo should be no more than two pages, allowing readers to scan it quickly. Full sentences are not required; bullet points are very effective. If the memo is covering updated tax information, it should list the new rates or wages bases but without charts or graphs. These should be made available to the employees either in the payroll department or through the department's intranet system.

(b) What to Include in the Year-End Memo

Each payroll department must decide this for itself. It depends on the aim of the memo, which may include: to provide an informational year-end update; to convince employees to convert to electronic Form W-2 for the first time; and to convey customer service items such as phone numbers and department hours, among other possibilities. The following is a list of items that should be considered when developing the first draft of the memo:

- Social Security wage base and rate for the upcoming year. The math should be done to show the maximum the employee could pay if reaching the limit.

- A reminder that the taxes resume again if limits were reached in the current year. This is always a common question for the first payroll of a new year.

- Medicare wage base and rate for the upcoming year. Though this is usually not expected to change from year to year, employees can benefit from a reminder of the rate and that it has no limit.

- State taxes that affect the employee directly. For example, if the payroll has employees in California, include the State Disability Insurance (SDI) taxes that are taken directly from the employee's paycheck. Again, include the taxes the employee pays, but not new tax charts or graphs. Mention that they are available by request.

- The date the Form W-2 will be mailed. Although the payroll department may be able to process the forms and mail them by January 15 or January 20, it is advisable to state the final required date (January 31) in the memo; this way the department can be sure of meeting the deadline as promised.

- The date by which employees can request a duplicate Form W-2. A payroll department may pick any date it considers is best for the department. The first form must be mailed by January 31 but duplicate requests must be done "within a reasonable amount of time" according to the IRS. February 10 is an excellent date to choose for issuing duplicate forms. This date allows time for any forms to be forwarded and so on.

- Along with the date to request the duplicate Form W-2, include the procedures for requesting the form. If procedures do not exist, this is an excellent time to create them. See Section 7.5 on handling duplicate Form W-2 requests for sample procedures.

- Social Security card number and name should match. The memo is a good place to remind employees that their name and number must match. Though many departments issue a separate reminder for this and another regarding the address for the Form W-2, it is a good idea to add it here as well. Also, a reminder on the IRS's tough stance on filing Form 1040 with names that do not match those on the Social Security card could reinforce your point.

- Address verification. This cannot be requested often enough.

- The item that provoked the memo in the first place; a reminder that the Form W-4 expires if the employee claims exempt and ignores the requirements for submitting a new form. This item should not be listed first, though, because employees for whom it is inapplicable tend not to read the rest of the memo.

- A reminder that the Form W-5 expires at year end.

- A list of payroll holidays, time card submission dates, payroll contact numbers, websites, and so on. This could be sent in a separate memo or on this one, depending on available space.

(c) Distribution of the Year-End Memo

The year-end memo can be distributed in any number of ways:

- Send it through the company e-mail system. This is a quick and cost-effective way to reach most employees.

- Post a copy on payroll's website on the company's intranet system.

- Post hard copies around the company in areas where employees meet, as not all employees within a company may have access to e-mail.

- Include it as a payroll stuffer. Although payroll departments do not think highly of this method, it is an effective way to ensure that all employees receive a copy if paper pay stubs are used.

- If the company is small, sending the memo to each department or employee individually may be practical.

- Include the memo in the company newsletter.

A sample year-end State of the Payroll Address memo is shown in Exhibit 7.1.

EXHIBIT 7.1

State of the Payroll Address Sample Memo

---

1. Social Security tax for (insert year):
   - Wage base:
   - Rate:
   - Maximum deduction: (show the entire mathematical equation)
   - This tax resumes with the first payroll in (insert year) if you reached the limit this year. This will cause a change in the net of your payroll check from the last one in (insert year) to the first one in (insert year).

2. Medicare tax for (insert year):
   - Wage base:
   - Rate:

3. State Taxation:
   - List all taxes for states applicable to employees. If multistate, a separate memo may be sent.

4. Form W-2:
   - The Form W-2 for (insert year) will be mailed to your home (or other method as applicable) by January 31, (insert year).

5. Electronic Form W-2: If you would like to receive your Form W-2 electronically, please contact the payroll department by (insert date here).

Exhibit 7.1   *(CONTINUED)*

State of the Payroll Address Sample Memo

6. Requesting duplicate Form W-2:
   - Available after (insert date)
   - Use form available on the payroll website: (insert site address)
   - Form is also available in the payroll department (state where)
   - We will accept e-mail requests as well. Please send to: (insert where)
   - Please fax requests to: (insert fax number)
   - All duplicate request forms will be processed as soon as possible after receipt. Please allow (insert your time frame here) for the request to be processed.
   - Please specify on form if you would like the duplicate form mailed or picked up.

7. Social Security card and payroll name match:
   - The name on your Social Security card and the Form W-2 must match in the following manner: first name, middle initial, last name. An example: If Mary Ann Jones is on the Social Security card, then the Form W-2 must read Mary A. Jones
   - If you are currently using a name that does not match your Social Security card due to marriage, divorce, citizenship change, or for any other reason, you need to obtain a new card with your correct name from the Social Security Administration. This can be done by mailing Form SS-5, available on the Social Security Administration website at www.socialsecurity.gov.
   - To correct your name on the payroll, please contact (insert contact name and information).

8. Address verification: Your Form W-2 will be mailed to your home address. Please verify this information by checking your payroll check stub or by using the web application. Please correct any errors as soon as possible before December 31. After that date, for Form W-2 purposes, you may only e-mail the correct address to the payroll department at (insert e-mail address).

9. Form W-4 for (insert correct year): If you were claiming exempt from federal withholding on your Form W-4 for (insert year), this form expires on January 1, (insert year). You have a grace period until February 15, (insert year) to submit a new form to payroll. If the new form is not received by that date, the IRS regulations require payroll to change your allowances to "zero" and your filing status to "Single" until a new form is received. Forms may be obtained (give locations).

10. The Form W-5 for calendar year (insert year) expires on December 31. If you are requesting Earned Income Credit payments in advance through the payroll department, you will need to complete a new form for the calendar year (insert year).

11. The (insert year) Holiday schedule, payroll schedule, and forms submission calendars are now available (insert locations).

12. New IRS publications are now available. (List the publications carried and where they can be obtained.)

7.2   PLANNING AND SURVIVING YEAR END

Planning for and surviving year end has always been a very high priority for the payroll department, especially in this day and age of smaller departments but more responsibility. The reporting requirements have only increased over the years and the penalties for making mistakes have increased as well. Year end can become even more complex for companies who have taxable and nontaxable fringe benefits such as relocation benefits and company vehicles. What to report and what to tax can become confusing, especially when expatriates or company officers are involved.

An efficient payroll department should take this hectic time in stride. Preparations for year end should be occurring all year long so that year end itself is just the culmination of the department's work. But to ensure a successful year end, three words must be kept in mind at all times: planning, organizing, and verifying. The small tasks and details are what can bog down a payroll department during this time. Items overlooked until the last minute can cause the Forms W-2 to be rerun or glitches in the processing schedule. These snags can wreak havoc with the year-end schedule and also with the current year payroll. Remember, a team cannot get to the Super Bowl by winning only the last game of the season; they have to win all season long. So it is with year end. The efficient payroll department cannot expect a successful year end without that long winning year, and a winning year starts with a game plan—the payroll calendar.

As discussed in depth in Section 8.2 and as a reminder here, the key to having an efficient payroll department is in the payroll master calendar. This one item will help the department meet deadlines, keep the company in compliance with the various laws, finish workloads, and keep the department organized and running smoothly. Implementing the calendar should be done as close to the beginning of the year as possible. Using the tax years 2004 and 2005 as an example, the ideal situation would be to have the 2005 calendar ready in December 2004, because the payroll department must remember that year end for 2005 starts January 1, 2005. As the department is closing out 2004, it must also begin 2005, including updating tax tables and benefit calculations. This calendar will also assist the department in prioritizing the year-end tasks and in helping to set up the sequencing and timing of this critical workload. Ideally, with all due dates set forth in the beginning, the department can assess which items need to be handled and in what order, so as to be able to meet all the upcoming deadlines.

Once the planning is done, the second important task is organizing. Organizing the department staff is critical during year end. The department needs to avoid duplication of work, all the while ensuring that nothing falls through the cracks. Work calendars (daily and weekly) or to-do lists will help ensure that all items on the department's payroll calendar are being handled on schedule and by only one person. Note also that only one person should create the to-do lists from the master calendar for all employees working on year end.

Before year-end tasks can even begin, the payroll department needs to form a year-end committee. This committee is going to be charged with making sure that all departments involved in providing information or services to the payroll department are aware that they have a responsibility to assist in year end, what is expected of them, and when it is expected. Asking fellow managers or other departments to be on the committee should be done well in advance of the first meeting. This should take place in September or October to allow for planning and scheduling. If resistance is met, the payroll department may need to get higher management involved.

The basics for forming a year-end committee are as follows:

- Include key members from payroll, tax, data processing, accounts payable, finance, and human resources. Any company department that may furnish information or devote time to the process of year end should have a representative. The payroll department may have to think outside the box here. Who handles the company vehicles? If taxation of personal use of a company vehicle is involved in year end, does the manager in charge of the company's fleet need to be at the meetings to make sure payroll knows who has what vehicle and so on?

- Meet as often as necessary but do not waste time in meetings instead of getting tasks accomplished. A complete list of the meeting times and dates should be created before the first meeting and then distributed to the committee members. Then, strictly adhere to this schedule.
- Keep detailed minutes of each meeting and distribute them to each committee member after each meeting.
- Before meeting for the first time, payroll should conduct a review of the problem areas from the last year end. Nothing is worse than encountering the same problems year in and year out. These problem areas should be identified for this year and resolved or minimized at the first meeting.
- Create a schedule of all tasks to be completed with beginning and completion due dates. Assign a committee member to each task. Distribute an updated log to each committee member to ensure that everyone is aware of the tasks and who is responsible for them. As each task is reported as completed or is confirmed as completed because the payroll department has received the required information, the task should be marked as completed and a new task list distributed.
- All changes made should be documented for use in future year ends.
- This committee should be formed and begin meeting early in the fourth quarter, no later than November.

Delegation is extremely important for year end. Departments need to make sure that all the players and departments are active participants. Not all year end jobs are payroll related. Case in point: Forms 1099. Though the forms may be handled by accounts payable, payroll must make sure that any Forms 1099 for deceased employees have been properly prepared.

There is another problem that can arise at year end. Many companies use the calendar year as their fiscal year end. This may create double the year-end workload for the payroll department as well as affect the cooperation it can expect from other departments. Remember, the other departments are involved in their own year-end duties. Communication is key in this type of situation. It must be clearly communicated to management, as well as to the other departments, that if the payroll department must choose between processing for fiscal year end and the payroll year end, the payroll year end must prevail. The easiest and most efficient way to explain why this must be is simple—give management a list of all the penalties that could be assessed if payroll misses its year-end deadline by even one day, not to mention the anger and employee morale problems that would occur if the Forms W-2 were not distributed on time. Each payroll department will need to determine and prioritize the internal organization requirements concerning the closing of company financial records if the calendar year end and fiscal year end coincide.

The payroll department must always simultaneously run the new year while closing out the old one, so tasks will definitely overlap between the two years. The efficient payroll department will be able to switch back and forth between the two years with ease.

To assist in the transition from the old year to the new year, the following points should be taken into consideration:

- If the payroll system is in house, coordinate a meeting with the technical department to nail down the implementation of all new tax updates (if this is their responsibility). Otherwise, set up a schedule to have the updates done by a payroll department staff member. If the payroll system is outsourced, make sure that the vendor has provided a timetable to the payroll department on when the updates will be completed.

- Coordinate with the human resources department for all holidays that will be observed in the new year and plan payroll processing accordingly. This should be done as soon as possible to ensure that the information is taken into consideration when establishing the new payroll master calendar.

- Coordinate with the outside service bureau or in-house programmers and computer operators for the new year's processing schedule. This should be done as soon as possible to assist in drafting the new payroll master calendar.

- Before distributing the first paychecks of the new year:
  - Manually verify the employee taxes of selected individuals. Pull a random sample of employees. Make sure that all departments or types of employees are included in the sample. In addition to these employees, pull one or two employees who reached taxable wage bases in the previous year for Social Security and state or local taxes. Taxes that should be verified include federal and state income tax, Social Security and Medicare percentages, local taxes, and especially any taxes for which a wage base was reached in the previous year. This is to make sure that the taxes have been calculated correctly.
  - Verify the taxes on the employer side as well. Audit the social security, Medicare, federal unemployment and state unemployment wage limits (if available), and employer tax percentage rates for such taxes as SUI. This is a critical task. There is nothing more inefficient than having to adjust a report for the entire year or to adjust the payroll system manually because the wrong SUI tax rate was used to calculate the taxes on the first payroll of the year.

Reconciling the payroll department's data is crucial to year end. All federal and state payroll reports, tax returns, tax deposits, and information statements such as the Form W-2 are interrelated and must be reconciled with each other. The information contained on these records must agree, otherwise, errors will cause an out-of-balance condition. In addition, if the totals do not reconcile, the IRS and/or Social Security Administration will require an explanation and/or a correction of these differences. This could result in a penalty or fine in some cases. To ensure that all returns and reports are in balance, payroll professionals should perform the following reconciliations during the year and then the final reconciliations for year end. The technical steps to handling these types of reconciliations and sample spreadsheets can be found in Sections 1.5 and 7.4:

- Current Pay Period Reconciliation
  - Add current payroll to each previous payroll
  - Balance the month-to-date, quarter-to-date, and year-to-date information. Include gross to net, FICA, FUTA, FIT, SIT, SUI, and local taxable wages.
- Tax Deposit Reconciliation
  - Should be done prior to each tax deposit or payment
  - Should be done monthly as well
- Quarterly Reconciliations
  - Should be done prior to the last deposit of the quarter
  - A preliminary 941 report should be done prior to the last deposit of the quarter
  - A reconciliation of the 941 forms compared to the Form W-2 totals to date should be done each quarter
- Annual Reconciliation
  - Should be done prior to the last deposit of the year
  - Reconciliation of all four quarter 941 forms should be done against the Form W-2
  - Reconciliation of all tax deposits against payroll records should be done
- Year End Reconciliation
  - All four quarter Forms 941 should be reconciled to the Form W-2 totals prior to closing the payroll

It is recommended that reconciliations be done after each payroll, at each quarter end, and then annually. However, if the payroll department does perform some reconciliations annually, remember that all corrections should be discovered prior to issuing the Form W-2 to prevent additional work for the department. However, if an error is discovered after the Forms W-2 have been processed and distributed, a Form W-2c can be issued. However, any corrections done with the Form W-2c do require corrections to Forms 941 and state reports. Also keep in mind that all the steps listed here should also be done for each state in which the company is located.

One big thing that can cause reconciliation problems at year end is the manual check. Each manual check written during the year must be accounted for by year end in order to verify that all checks have been input. Even though most payroll systems now process the check directly through the payroll system and the employee's wages and so forth are updated automatically when the check is written, this is not necessarily true for the voided or reversed checks that may have been created when the new check was issued. One of the major causes of issuance of Forms W-2c is the incorrect processing of manual checks or the failure to void and reverse checks. To avoid a year-end problem, the payroll department should reconcile manual and voided checks a minimum of quarterly. This would include keeping a log of all voided checks as well as the manual check log for all checks issued.

The payroll department must verify that it not only has input and reconciled its own processing but that it has received all the information necessary to close the year from other departments, such as accounts payable and human resources. Items such as relocation, car allowances, personal use of a company vehicle, taxable benefits received, or bonus payments must be included before the final payroll is run for the year. This means that the payroll department needs to begin collecting this data as early as December in order to ensure processing time.

(a) How to Cope with Year-End Stress

The beginning of the new year foreshadows the fast and furious pace at which the payroll manager will operate year round. It seems like there is never enough time to get the Forms W-2 printed, Forms 1099 mailed, and the regular payroll processed. So how do payroll managers make the best of this vexing situation? By planning ahead and managing time, payroll managers can cope with the stress that comes with year end.

Time is a non-reproducible resource, but everyone is given the same amount. When problems seem overwhelming or the payroll manager is facing an incredible number of demands, he or she may feel out of control and overburdened by work. When the stress of year end is added to this, overtime is often unavoidable. But veteran payroll professionals admit that working long hours does not always result in increased productivity or effectiveness. What is the best advice for surviving this stressful time? It is simple. Create a to-do list. Time-conscious payroll managers swear by this simple yet powerful tool for organizing themselves and reducing stress. According to time management consultants, a to-do list consolidates all of the tasks that need to be done and allows the list maker to prioritize those tasks in the order of importance.

Further advice from time management experts includes:

- Write down the tasks to be tackled. If they are large, break them down into individual components. If these tasks still seem large, break them down again. Continue in this manner until everything to be accomplished is on the list.

- When the list is complete, prioritize each task from A (very important) to F (unimportant). If too many tasks have a high priority, review the list again and reevaluate the importance of each task. Then rewrite the list from A to F.

A prioritized to-do list is fundamentally important to work efficiently. Using a to-do list will also ensure that:

- All necessary tasks are carried out

- The most important jobs are carried out first and time is not wasted on trivial matters

- Stress is reduced by assigning a lower priority to a number of unimportant jobs

Similar to a to-do list is the daily or weekly template, which summarizes routine daily or weekly tasks. For example, M–F 9 to 9:30, read e-mail; Tuesday: 3:00 to 3:30, staff meeting. Time management experts also differentiate between effectiveness and efficiency. The former is doing the right thing and the latter is doing something right. The primary goal here is to be effective. Although this manual is about being efficient, with time management, especially at year end, being effective will lead to the entire department being run efficiently. Time is perishable. It cannot be stored or saved for another day. To be effective, time must be used immediately or it is gone.

Time wasters must be eliminated. Even with a prioritized to-do list, it requires diligence to work through the list. The list should be checked often and time wasters eliminated. Many payroll professionals single out e-mail, voicemail, snail mail, and meetings as perennial time wasters during the hectic year end. Following are some proven solutions to handling these items during this stressful time:

- *Responding to Voicemail.* Payroll managers rarely have secretaries or administrative assistants to field phone calls. Voicemail is now every professional's assistant. However, it must be used wisely. This means updating the outgoing message frequently. Some suggestions from time-conscious payroll managers are:
  - Change the outgoing message when lying low to work on year end. If the manager is running Forms W-2 or is otherwise tied up with processing, let the caller know that it will be awhile before the call will be returned.
  - Change the outgoing message when out of the office. If out at year end meetings or working off site, tell the callers. For example, "I will be out of the office between 10:00 and 12:00 noon."
  - Request that callers indicate the best time to return their call. This minimizes the chances of playing phone tag during this hectic time. Also, set aside blocks of time to answer voicemail. Better yet, because payroll may be tied up during normal business hours, ask the caller to e-mail his or her request during this busy time.

- *Reading E-Mails.* Some payroll managers use e-mail to respond to voicemail and schedule time just to read messages. While it is preferable to answer each e-mail before reading the next, sometimes a read receipt and a promised date to respond will suffice during year end. Otherwise, answer all e-mails immediately. The best advice regarding all mail, not just e-mail: open it, respond to it, file it, delete it, and close it. Do not handle it more than once. Other time saving tips for managing e-mail include:
  - Use the subject line to get the reader's attention and to indicate that the mail is not spam.

○ Use the first paragraph to tell the reader what you want.

○ Use deadlines to motivate the reader.

○ Use simple words and short sentences to minimize grammar mistakes.

○ Use the right tone to get the results desired.

○ Answer all questions contained in the original e-mail and try to anticipate new questions the response might elicit.

• *Reading Snail Mail.* Some payroll managers view this as downtime. A reprieve. A respite from the hectic time of year end. Sorting through magazines, newsletter, updates, reports, and letters can be relaxing because the sender is not demanding immediate action. To help with time management, act on simple requests immediately or forward them to the person most qualified to respond. The same rule applies to snail mail—do not handle the same piece of correspondence more than once.

• *Attending Meetings.* With management's help, it must be clearly conveyed to all departments that the payroll manager must concentrate all efforts on processing year end during January, and attendance at meetings will be limited to those related to this endeavor. The payroll manager should connect with another employee who attended the meeting. This person can give the manager the agenda and keep him or her updated on the results of the meeting.

Time management and stress management are cousins. Thus, it is not surprising that payroll managers who control time control stress.

7.3 CHECKLISTS

Payroll has evolved into a complex, multifaceted process over the years. This is especially true at its most hectic period—year end. At this time of the year, not only are there dozens of major and minor tasks that must be performed to close out the old year correctly, but it is also the beginning of a new year, and that too must be handled.

(a) Why Have Checklists?

Sometimes the easiest way to make sure that everything is completed is also the most simple: make a checklist and use it. Listing the tasks that need be done for a successful year end and year beginning, the forms that need to be ordered, the letters or memos that need to go out to employees, and the reconciliations that need to be completed helps keep everything organized and on the right track.

(b) What to Include on the Lists

But what should be included on the checklists? Every task should be listed no matter how small or seemingly trivial. The purpose of the lists is to ensure that all tasks are accomplished and to take the pressure off for remembering what needs to be done. The checklists should be broken down into three categories: year end, Form W-2, and year beginning. This will ensure that the lists are manageable and will help with organizing when each item can and must be completed.

Year End. Before the payroll department can begin the new year, it must complete the old one. Making sure that all year-end items have been completed is essential. Following is a sample checklist that can assist a payroll department in creating its own list to use at year end to ensure that nothing gets left undone. Of course, the list needs to be customized to reflect company-specific items.

Do the State of the Payroll memo by December 1. This memo will include the plea for address updates from the employees.

Set up a system for collecting employee address changes. This could include an intranet site, fax number, e-mail address, or dedicated phone line.

Update all addresses as they are received.

Set up a year-end committee as discussed in Section 7.2.

Make a list or update last year's list of all fringe benefits offered by the company that are not paid through the payroll department but are taxable or reportable on the Form W-2. These may include car allowances, moving expenses, educational assistance, or dependent care payments. Verify with the appropriate department that the information, if not already received by payroll, will be available for processing by the final payroll of the year.

Verify by the last payroll run that all information requested in the previous item was received and has been input into the system.

Do all necessary spreadsheets or calculations to determine taxable wages for fringe benefits that need to be input to the payroll system for taxation or reporting. The most common type of fringe benefit in this category is the personal use of a company vehicle. Mileage logs and odometer readings may need to be collected in order to make these calculations.

Verify pension plan requirements for all employees. If the company has a retirement plan (including a 401k, 403(b), etc.), the retirement plan box on the Form W-2 must be marked for all employees as required by IRS regulations. Depending on what type or types of plans the company offers, the box could be marked differently for different employees. The payroll department needs to verify whether they have a retirement plan, what type of plan it is, and the requirements for marking the box prior to year end. Rules for making the determination on marking the box are included in the instructions for the Form W-2. Marking the box is listed under the Form W-2 checklist.

Create a year-end printing schedule for the IT department or confirm the schedule with the outside payroll vendor.

If one does not already exist, create checklist for all tax forms that will be received or needed for year end. This includes all federal and state quarterly returns, federal and state annual returns, magnetic media filing forms, and so on.

If needed, order Forms W-2.

Verify that all manual checks or voids, and especially reversals, have been properly processed.

After the last payroll of the year, deactivate all Forms W-5 for the year.

After the last payroll of the year, close out all manual check files and logs.

After the last payroll of the year, close out all timesheet files.

After last payroll of the year, close out all spreadsheet files for the year. These might include tax files, garnishment files, and so on.

Make sure that after final payroll processing for the year, all files have been located and are in one place and have been closed out to prepare for Form W-2 reconciliation and processing.

Obtain the company holiday schedule for the new year to assist in creating the payroll calendar for the new year.

Form W-2. After the final payroll for the year has been processed, the processing of the Forms W-2 can begin. To have a successful year end, it is crucial to make sure that everything is balanced, reconciled, and completed before processing the Forms W-2. Having to do more than one W-2 run because of missing or out-of-balance situations is costly and time consuming. The following sample checklist might help in making sure all items are taken care of before calling for the W-2 run:

The previous checklist discussed determining the individual requirements for the retirement plan box. Now it will be necessary to physically verify that the box is marked correctly for each employee. Consult the payroll vendor or systems person to determine how this will be handled.

Reconcile Form W-2 to Form 941 for the fourth quarter. It is preferred that the Form W-2 wages and so forth be reconciled on a quarterly basis to the Form 941. By reconciling quarterly, any errors are discovered in a timely manner and can be corrected prior to the hectic time of year end.

Reconcile Form W-2 wages and so forth with all states for fourth quarter. Again, it is preferable to reconcile wages quarterly rather than waiting to do the whole year at one time at year end.

If quarterly reconciliations were not accomplished, reconcile Form W-2 totals to all four quarterly totals for both the federal and the state forms. W-2s should not be processed until this reconciliation has been completed.

Reconcile the Form W-2 to itself. Have any limits been exceeded? Do state and federal wages reconcile? Are all benefits being recorded in box 12 correctly? Are dependent care benefits recorded in box 10? Are state wages being recorded in the correct boxes?

Year Beginning.   It is sometimes hard to remember in the flurry that year end is also the beginning of a new year. And of course, things need to be done to make sure that the new year gets off to good start. The following is a suggested checklist to help in organizing the new year:

Set up the new year payroll processing calendar. This actually must be done in the old year even though it is a new year item. Outside vendor services usually require that this be done within a certain time frame prior to year end.

Set up the new submission calendar for payroll. This calendar informs the employees when items such as Forms W-4 and the like must be given to payroll in order to be processed.

Verify that all new wage bases for taxes are in place before running the first payroll of the year. Even if an outside service is used, this should be done.

Verify all wage bases and deductions after the first payroll is run. Pull test employees' files to make sure taxes are calculating correctly, garnishments are functioning correctly, and that all benefits are being deducted properly.

Prior to first payroll run, verify that all SUI rates for the new year are in the system to ensure that tax liabilities are calculated correctly from the first payroll of the year.

Prior to the first payroll run, make sure that the new year Form W-4 is available for all employees.

Prior to the first payroll run, make sure that the new year Form W-5 is available for all eligible employees.

To get the payroll department ready for the new year:

Download or order new forms for the new year. When ordering the new Form W-4, do not forget the state equivalents.

Download or order new publications such as the Circular E and State Tax Books for the new year.

Set up the new year tax files.

Set up manual check logs for the new year.

If the company has personal use of company vehicles, distribute new mileage logs for the new year. Take odometer readings if needed.

Order new reference guides or books.

Update all infrastructures. This includes the department websites and bulletin boards (computer and physical) with the new year's information such as wage bases, payroll processing calendars, and pay dates.

Create new spreadsheets for the new year.

Create new time-sheet files for the new year.

Create new report binders or CD holders for the new year.

Make sure that all payroll processing procedures are updated with new rates or procedures for any changes in the coming year.

In February, make sure that all expired Form W-4s are reset at S-0 (Single-Zero) if a new form has not been received.

(c) Delegation of Duties on the Lists

If the payroll department is a party of one, the delegation of duties is pretty simple. But if it is a larger company with more than one payroll employee, the duties need to be broken up to ensure that everyone is involved in year end and year beginning. This helps employees buy into the process and feel connected to this hectic time of year. It is also advisable that the employee who handles a particular task all during the year not handle the reconciliation of that task at year end. This additional set of eyes helps to ensure that no mistakes or processing errors are occurring that could disrupt year end. It also assists in auditing for year end.

7.4 RECONCILIATION OF THE PAYROLL AT YEAR END

The efficient payroll department has been reconciling the payroll all year. After every payroll, the wage and tax totals are posted to the reconciling spreadsheet and the computed totals are reconciled against the computer totals. At the end of each quarter, the Form 941 is reconciled against the payroll totals using this same spreadsheet. The Forms 941 have been totaled each quarter and reconciled against the Forms W-2 edit report. Now the final reconciliations need to be done to close out the payroll. These reconciliations are:

- Forms W-2 against the payroll records
- Forms 941 against the payroll records
- Forms W-2 against the Forms 941

(a) Reconciliation of Form W-2 to Payroll Records

Using the spreadsheets that have been created to conduct the payroll processing reconciliation (discussed in earlier sections) the following year-to-date totals on the payroll should be compared to the Forms W-2 totals:

Payroll Totals	Compared to:	Box on the Form W-2
Federal taxable wages		1—Wages, tips, other compensation
Federal income tax withheld		2—Federal income tax withheld
Social Security taxable wages		3—Social Security wages
Social Security tax withheld		4—Social Security tax withheld
Taxable Medicare wages and tips		5—Medicare wages and tips
Medicare taxes withheld		6—Medicare tax withheld
Advanced earned income credits paid through the payroll		9—Advanced EIC payment
Dependent care benefits deducted from the employees payroll or paid through accounts payable		10—Dependent care benefits

In addition to these totals, there are other boxes that must be verified before the Forms W-2 can be processed. These include box 12, which shows listings for benefits as required by the IRS. These should be reviewed against the payroll records to make sure that the benefits have been recorded correctly.

A very important box that must be reviewed is box 13. This box is for reporting whether or not the employee is covered by a retirement plan. It is critical that this box be marked correctly. The definition of retirement plan can be found in the instructions for the Form W-2 on the IRS website. Penalties can be assessed if this box is mismarked.

The same reconciliation that is done for the federal wages should also be done for the state wages. A separate reconciliation should be done for each state.

One more critical reconciliation should be done before processing the Forms W-2—cross-check the names. As discussed in previous chapters, the name on the Social Security card and the name on the Form W-2 must match according to SSA protocol. A final match verification should be done prior to year end.

(b) Reconciliation of Form 941 to the Payroll Records

The following reconciliation of the total of all four Forms 941 should be done at year end prior to processing the Forms W-2 and closing the payroll. Compare the Forms 941 totals to the year-to-date totals on the payroll reconciliation spreadsheet for the following lines on the Forms 941:

Payroll Totals	Compare to:	Line on Forms 941
Federal taxable wages		2—Total wages and tips, plus other compensation
Federal income tax withheld		3—Total income tax withheld from wages, tips, and sick pay
Social Security taxable wages		6a—Taxable Social Security wages
Social Security tax withheld		6b
Taxable Medicare wages and tips		7a—Taxable Medicare wages and tips
Medicare taxes withheld		7b
Advanced earned income credits paid through the payroll		12

Of course, there will be minute (fractions of cents) differences for Social Security withheld and Medicare withheld so line 9, "fractions of cents," must be taken into account when reconciling.

(c) Reconciliation of the Form 941 to Form W-2

The following final reconciliations should be done between the Forms 941 and the Forms W-2 before processing the final run of the Forms W-2:

Line on Forms 941	Compare to:	Boxes on Forms W-2
2—Total wages and tips, plus other compensation		1—Wages, tips, other compensation
3—Total income tax withheld from wages, tips, and sick pay		2—Federal income tax withheld
6a—Taxable Social Security wages		3—Social Security wages
6b		4—Social security tax withheld
7a—Taxable Medicare wages and tips		5—Medicare wages and tips
7b		6—Medicare tax withheld
12		9—Advanced EIC payment

See Exhibit 7.6 on page 265 for a demonstration of this reconciliation.

7.5 FORM W-2

The final task that every payroll department must perform for each calendar year is to produce the Form W-2 for each and every employee it paid that year. Whether it is a long-time employee who is still working for the company or someone who worked one day for three hours and then quit, all employees need to receive a Form W-2. This section will discuss distributing and correcting the Form W-2. The reconciliation of the form was discussed in the previous section.

(a) Distribution to Employees

The Form W-2 is a six-part form. The payroll department must furnish copies B, C, and 2 to the employee by January 31 of each year following the calendar tax year on which the form is based.

The furnished requirement is met if the form is properly addressed and mailed on or before the due date. If it is the company's procedure to distribute the Form W-2 to each employee in person, then the form must be in the employee's hand on or before the due date. It is not sufficient to simply have the form delivered to the worksite by the due date. For example, suppose the company has 20 stores located throughout the state. The policy is to have each store manager distribute the Form W-2 to each department manager, who then distributes the form to each employee. It is not good enough that the Form W-2 be at the store on or before the due date; it must be distributed to the employee by then.

If employment ends before December 31 of the current tax year, the payroll department may furnish the required copies of the Form W-2 any time after employment ends but still no later than January 31. However, if the employee requests his or her Form W-2, the payroll department is required to give that employee the completed copies within 30 days of the request or within 30 days of the final wage payment, whichever is later.

In very rare circumstances, the IRS will grant an extension of the distribution date. An example of a viable reason for an extension is a declaration of a federal disaster area, in the place where the employer is located, on or near the due date of the form. The payroll department may apply for this extension by sending a letter to:

IRS-Martinsburg Computing Center
Information Reporting Program
Attn: Extension of Time Coordinator
240 Murall Drive
Kearneysville, WV 25430

The letter must be mailed on or before the due date for furnishing Forms W-2 to the employees. The letter must include:

- The company name and address

- The employer identification number
- Type of return
- A statement that the company is requesting an extension to furnish Forms W-2 to employees
- Reason for delay
- Appropriate signature

The Forms W-2 must be retained for four years plus the current tax year for a total of five years minimum. However, it is common practice for payroll departments to keep the Forms W-2 indefinitly, especially with today's technology. This retention requirement also applies to Forms W-2 that are returned as undeliverable. Even though the returned forms are duplicates of the employer's copy, which is already retained by the payroll department, keeping the undeliverable forms will provide proof of mailing of the original form if the issue ever arises. Under no circumstances should the undeliverable Forms W-2 be sent to the SSA.

The payroll department has several options as to the type of Form W-2 to furnish to the employees. They may be the official IRS form, an acceptable substitute form that complies with IRS regulations, or in an electronic format.

- Official IRS form. This speaks for itself; it is the actual IRS form printed and distributed by the agency. Most payroll systems are capable of using this method.

- Acceptable substitute form. Some payroll systems use a facsimile of the IRS's official form. They might print the form with a laser printer, for example. This is totally acceptable, as long as the substitute form complies with specificiations in Pub. 1141, "General Rules and Specificiations for Substitute Forms W-2 and W-3."

- Electronic payee statement. If the payroll department obtains the employee's consent, it may be able to furnish the employee's form electronically. The consent must be in electronic format. The due date remains the same and the payroll department must notify the employee where and when the forms have been posted. This method is gaining popularity as most payroll departments with outside vendors are being given this paperless option. This is an extremely efficient method for disbursing the forms as it does not rely on a mailing address, which reduces the chance of lost or mishandled forms.

(b) Distribution to the Social Security Administration

Copy A of the Forms W-2 or the equivalent magnetic media file is due to the Social Security Administration by the last day in February following the close of the previous tax calendar year. For example, the Forms W-2 for tax calendar year 2004 are due to the SSA by February 28, 2005. If this date falls on a Saturday or Sunday, the due date is the next business day. If it is a leap year, the forms will be due on February 29 (if it is not a Saturday or a Sunday). This due date is extended for electronic filers. If the Forms W-2 are submitted to the SSA electronically (this does not include magnetic media) the due date is extended to March 31.

It is possible to request an automatic extension of time to file Forms W-2 to the SSA by sending Form 8809, "Request for Extension of Time to File Information Returns," to the address shown on the form. The request for the extension must be made before the due date of the Forms W-2. The payroll department will then have an additional 30 days to file the forms. This extension does not affect the due date to the employees. They still must receive their forms by January 31. This extension is usually requested by payroll departments who have run into problems producing the magnetic media or who are trying to submit electronically for the first time.

There are three methods of submitting Forms W-2 to the Social Security Administration: paper forms, magnetic media, and electronic filing. A small employer with fewer than 250 total forms to submit may use any of these methods. Larger companies with more than 250 individual Forms W-2 corresponding to one employer identification number must use only the magnetic media or electronic methods. Descriptions of the three methods of submitting the Forms W-2 are as follows:

1. Paper forms. If the company has fewer than 250 individual Forms W-2, they may be submitted using the Copy A of the six-

part paper form. That is the only copy that may be submitted. The forms should be in alphabetical order by last name or numerical order by the employee's Social Security number. The forms should not be folded and should be mailed in a flat envelope. A completed Form W-3 must accompany the Forms W-2. If there is a large number of Forms W-2 to be mailed, the SSA allows the forms to be sent in separate envelopes provided they are clearly marked as such. This is generally not advisable. Packages have been separated and lost when mailed this way. The most efficient way to mail the forms is to bundle them altogether and ship them overnight with a signature required. Either the U.S. Postal Service or an approved overnight shipper may now be used.

2. Magnetic media. If the company has 250 or more Forms W-2 to file with the SSA, it must do so using either magnetic media or electronically unless a waiver is received. The magnetic media reporting specifications are in the SSA's MMREF-1 publication. This publication can be downloaded by accessing the Social Security's website at www.socialsecurity.gov. The reporting instructions for magnetic media differ from the paper copies in some areas. The Form 6559 must accompany the submission. This method of submission is not just for large employers. Small employers are encouraged to file using magnetic or electronic media as well.

3. Electronic filing. The Social Security Administration has set up a system on its website for payroll departments to submit Forms W-2 electronically. The system also allows the input, printing, and saving of up to 20 forms. This is especially helpful for very small employers. Both services are conducted through the Business Services Online (BSO). The BSO is a suite of Internet services for businesses and employers who exchange information with the SSA. To become a BSO user, all the payroll department needs to do is to register. Initially, there may be some issues with learning the software or with compatibility of files. However, all the information and instructions are contained on the SSA's website. Filing Forms W-2 electronically is an efficient method. This service also has the ability to check for errors prior to submission to help prevent future error notices.

(c) Correction of Errors

No matter how hard the payroll department works or how efficient or diligent it is, an error will occasionally occur on a Form W-2. When this happens, there are two ways to correct the form. Which one the department chooses depends on whether or not the Form W-2 has already been submitted to the SSA.

If the error on the Form W-2 is discovered prior to the submission of the forms to the SSA, the payroll department has the option of voiding out the original Form W-2 and reissuing the form. If the forms are processed on paper, simply mark the void box and reissue the form. If the department has submitted the forms on magnetic media and the payroll system has the capabilities, the Form W-2 could be corrected and a new form issued. If the Forms W-2 have been submitted to the SSA or the payroll department cannot adjust the magnetic media or prefers not to, then a Form W-2c must be created.

The purpose of the Form W-2c is to correct errors discovered on the Form W-2 that has been filed with the SSA. The form is used to correct all forms in the Form W-2 series except Form W-2G. The Form W-2c is also a six-part form like the Form W-2. Copy A is filed with the Social Security Administration, Copies B, C, and 2 are given to the employee, Copy 1 is filed with the state if applicable, and the payroll department retains Copy D for its records. The form is submitted to the SSA accompanied by a Form W-3c. A Form W-3c must be used even if submitting only one Form W-2c. If 250 or more Forms W-2c need to be submitted, then magnetic media must be used.

The Form W-2c was revised by the IRS as of December 2002. The payroll department must make sure that the most current version of the form is used. Substitute forms are permitted if they comply with the rules in Pub. 1223.

The Form W-2c is a correction form but not a replacement form. The form is meant only to correct the information that is wrong on the Form W-2, so that when combined with the Form W-2 it creates one correct form. The payroll department should only complete the identifying information in boxes a through g, then only the boxes that contain incorrect information. When using this form, *do not* resend any information that was correct on the original Form W-2 (in other words, "if it ain't broke, don't fix it"). See Exhibits 7.2 through 7.4 showing examples of completed forms.

If the payroll department filed a Form W-2c with the SSA that contained an incorrect address for the employee but all other information on the form was correct, the department should not file a Form W-2c with the SSA to merely correct the address. However, employee name, employee Social Security number, and all wage and tax information does need to be cor-

Exhibit 7.2

Correcting a Form W-2 with an Incorrect Employee Name

Brandy Winer received a Form W-2 for tax year 2004 from the Big Time Company. She was married in July 2004 but did not inform the payroll department until February 2005 that she had changed her name. Her new name on her new Social Security card is Brandy Cupper.

DO NOT CUT, FOLD, OR STAPLE THIS FORM

a Tax year/Form corrected 2004 / W-2	44444	For Official Use Only ▶ OMB No. 1545-0008		
b Employee's correct SSN 126-45-9955		c Corrected name (if checked enter correct name in box e and complete box i) **X**	d Employer's Federal EIN 95-9876542	
e Employee's first name and initial Brandy G.	Last name Cupper	g Employer's name, address, and ZIP code Big Time Company		
777 Winners Circle Drive Las Vegas NV 89121		3311 S. Rainbow Blvd Las Vegas NV 89146		
f Employee's address and ZIP code				
Complete boxes h and/or i only if incorrect on last form filed. ▶	h Employee's **incorrect** SSN	i Employee's name (as **incorrectly** shown on previous form) Brandy G. Winer		

Note: Only complete money fields that are being corrected (except MQGE).

Previously reported	Correct information	Previously reported	Correct information
1 Wages, tips, other compensation	1 Wages, tips, other compensation	2 Federal income tax withheld	2 Federal income tax withheld
3 Social security wages	3 Social security wages	4 Social security tax withheld	4 Social security tax withheld
5 Medicare wages and tips	5 Medicare wages and tips	6 Medicare tax withheld	6 Medicare tax withheld
7 Social security tips	7 Social security tips	8 Allocated tips	8 Allocated tips
9 Advance EIC payment	9 Advance EIC payment	10 Dependent care benefits	10 Dependent care benefits
11 Nonqualified plans	11 Nonqualified plans	12a See instructions for box 12	12a See instructions for box 12
13 Statutory employee / Retirement plan / Third-party sick-pay	13 Statutory employee / Retirement plan / Third-party sick-pay	12b	12b
14 Other (see instructions)	14 Other (see instructions)	12c	12c
		12d	12d

State Correction Information			
Previously reported	Correct information	Previously reported	Correct information
15 State	15 State	15 State	15 State
Employer's state ID number	Employer's state ID number	Employer's state ID number	Employer's state ID number
16 State wages, tips, etc.	16 State wages, tips, etc.	16 State wages, tips, etc.	16 State wages, tips, etc.
17 State income tax	17 State income tax	17 State income tax	17 State income tax

Locality Correction Information			
18 Local wages, tips, etc.	18 Local wages, tips, etc.	18 Local wages, tips, etc.	18 Local wages, tips, etc.
19 Local income tax	19 Local income tax	19 Local income tax	19 Local income tax
20 Locality name	20 Locality name	20 Locality name	20 Locality name

For Privacy Act and Paperwork Reduction Act Notice, see separate instructions.

Copy A — For Social Security Administration

Form **W-2c** (Rev. 12-2002)

Corrected Wage and Tax Statement
0000/1039

Department of the Treasury
Internal Revenue Service

ISA
STF FED9245F.1

Exhibit 7.3

Correcting a Form W-2 with an Incorrect Social Security Number

---

Jeff Conners received a Form W-2 from the Big Time Company for tax year 2004. The Social Security number listed was incorrect. It was listed as 123-45-6777. It should have been 122-45-6777.

DO NOT CUT, FOLD, OR STAPLE THIS FORM

a Tax year/Form corrected 2004 / W-2	44444	For Official Use Only ▶ OMB No. 1545-0008	
b Employee's correct SSN 122-45-6777		c Corrected name (if checked enter correct name in box e and complete box I)	d Employer's Federal EIN 95-9876542
e Employee's first name and initial Jeff J.	Last name Conners		g Employer's name, address, and ZIP code Big Time Company
888 Desert Inn Rd Las Vegas NV 89121			3311 S. Rainbow Blvd Las Vegas NV 89146
f Employee's address and ZIP code			
Complete boxes h and/or i only if incorrect on last form filed. ▶		h Employee's **incorrect** SSN 123-45-6777	i Employee's name (as **incorrectly** shown on previous form)

Note: Only complete money fields that are being corrected (except MQGE).

Previously reported	Correct information	Previously reported	Correct information
1 Wages, tips, other compensation	1 Wages, tips, other compensation	2 Federal income tax withheld	2 Federal income tax withheld
3 Social security wages	3 Social security wages	4 Social security tax withheld	4 Social security tax withheld
5 Medicare wages and tips	5 Medicare wages and tips	6 Medicare tax withheld	6 Medicare tax withheld
7 Social security tips	7 Social security tips	8 Allocated tips	8 Allocated tips
9 Advance EIC payment	9 Advance EIC payment	10 Dependent care benefits	10 Dependent care benefits
11 Nonqualified plans	11 Nonqualified plans	12a See instructions for box 12	12a See instructions for box 12
13 Statutory employee / Retirement plan / Third-party sick-pay	13 Statutory employee / Retirement plan / Third-party sick-pay	12b	12b
14 Other (see instructions)	14 Other (see instructions)	12c	12c
		12d	12d

State Correction Information

Previously reported	Correct information	Previously reported	Correct information
15 State	15 State	15 State	15 State
Employer's state ID number	Employer's state ID number	Employer's state ID number	Employer's state ID number
16 State wages, tips, etc.	16 State wages, tips, etc.	16 State wages, tips, etc.	16 State wages, tips, etc.
17 State income tax	17 State income tax	17 State income tax	17 State income tax

Locality Correction Information

18 Local wages, tips, etc.	18 Local wages, tips, etc.	18 Local wages, tips, etc.	18 Local wages, tips, etc.
19 Local income tax	19 Local income tax	19 Local income tax	19 Local income tax
20 Locality name	20 Locality name	20 Locality name	20 Locality name

For Privacy Act and Paperwork Reduction Act Notice, see separate instructions.

Copy A — For Social Security Administration

Form **W-2c** (Rev. 12-2002)

ISA
STF FED9245F.1

Corrected Wage and Tax Statement
0000/1039

Department of the Treasury
Internal Revenue Service

EXHIBIT 7.4

Correcting Two Forms W-2

There are two ways to prepare a correction for an employee who received more than one Form W-2 under the same employer identification number (EIN) for the tax year.

1. Consider all the Forms W-2 when determining the amounts to enter on Form W-2c as shown in Example 1 below, or
2. File a single Form W-2c to correct only the incorrect Form W-2.

Example 1.

Mary Smith received two Forms W-2 for tax year 2004 under the same EIN. One form incorrectly reported Social Security wages of $30,000 and the second correctly reported Social Security wages of $20,000. A single Form W-2c filed to change the $30,000 to $25,000 (correct amount) would show $50,000 in box 3 under "Previously reported" and $45,000 in box 3 under "Correct information."

DO NOT CUT, FOLD, OR STAPLE THIS FORM

a Tax year/Form corrected			For Official Use Only ▶	
2004 / W-2	44444		OMB No. 1545-0008	

b Employee's correct SSN	c Corrected name (if checked enter correct name in box e and complete box i)	d Employer's Federal EIN
123-45-6789		95-9876542

e Employee's first name and initial	Last name	g Employer's name, address, and ZIP code
Mary	Smith	Big Time Company
123 Main Street		3311 S. Rainbow Blvd
Las Vegas NV 89121		Las Vegas NV 89146

f Employee's address and ZIP code		
Complete boxes h and/or i only if incorrect on last form filed. ▶	h Employee's incorrect SSN	i Employee's name (as incorrectly shown on previous form)

Note: Only complete money fields that are being corrected (except MQGE).

Previously reported	Correct information	Previously reported	Correct information
1 Wages, tips, other compensation	1 Wages, tips, other compensation	2 Federal income tax withheld	2 Federal income tax withheld
3 Social security wages 50,000.00	3 Social security wages 45,000.00	4 Social security tax withheld	4 Social security tax withheld
5 Medicare wages and tips	5 Medicare wages and tips	6 Medicare tax withheld	6 Medicare tax withheld
7 Social security tips	7 Social security tips	8 Allocated tips	8 Allocated tips
9 Advance EIC payment	9 Advance EIC payment	10 Dependent care benefits	10 Dependent care benefits
11 Nonqualified plans	11 Nonqualified plans	12a See instructions for box 12	12a See instructions for box 12
13 Statutory employee / Retirement plan / Third-party sick-pay	13 Statutory employee / Retirement plan / Third-party sick-pay	12b	12b
14 Other (see instructions)	14 Other (see instructions)	12c	12c
		12d	12d

State Correction Information

Previously reported	Correct information	Previously reported	Correct information
15 State	15 State	15 State	15 State
Employer's state ID number	Employer's state ID number	Employer's state ID number	Employer's state ID number
16 State wages, tips, etc.	16 State wages, tips, etc.	16 State wages, tips, etc.	16 State wages, tips, etc.
17 State income tax	17 State income tax	17 State income tax	17 State income tax

Locality Correction Information

18 Local wages, tips, etc.	18 Local wages, tips, etc.	18 Local wages, tips, etc.	18 Local wages, tips, etc.
19 Local income tax	19 Local income tax	19 Local income tax	19 Local income tax
20 Locality name	20 Locality name	20 Locality name	20 Locality name

For Privacy Act and Paperwork Reduction Act Notice, see separate instructions. Copy A — For Social Security Administration

Form **W-2c** (Rev. 12-2002) **Corrected Wage and Tax Statement** Department of the Treasury Internal Revenue Service
ISA
STF FED9245F.1 **0000/1039**

EXHIBIT 7.4 *(CONTINUED)*

Correcting Two Forms W-2

Example 2.

The facts are the same as in the first example. However, the payroll department may choose to correct only the incorrect Form W-2 by filing a Form W-2c that shows $30,000 in box 3 under "Previously reported" and $25,000 in box 3 under "Correct information."

DO NOT CUT, FOLD, OR STAPLE THIS FORM

a Tax year/Form corrected 2004 / W-2	44444	For Official Use Only ▶ OMB No. 1545-0008		
b Employee's correct SSN 123-45-6789		c Corrected name (if checked enter correct name in box e and complete box l)	d Employer's Federal EIN 95-9876542	

e Employee's first name and initial: Mary Last name: Smith

g Employer's name, address, and ZIP code: Big Time Company

123 Main Street
Las Vegas NV 89121

3311 S. Rainbow Blvd
Las Vegas NV 89146

f Employee's address and ZIP code

Complete boxes h and/or i only if incorrect on last form filed. ▶	h Employee's **incorrect** SSN	i Employee's name (as **incorrectly** shown on previous form)

Note: Only complete money fields that are being corrected (except MQGE).

Previously reported	Correct information	Previously reported	Correct information
1 Wages, tips, other compensation	1 Wages, tips, other compensation	2 Federal income tax withheld	2 Federal income tax withheld
3 Social security wages 30,000.00	3 Social security wages 25,000.00	4 Social security tax withheld	4 Social security tax withheld
5 Medicare wages and tips	5 Medicare wages and tips	6 Medicare tax withheld	6 Medicare tax withheld
7 Social security tips	7 Social security tips	8 Allocated tips	8 Allocated tips
9 Advance EIC payment	9 Advance EIC payment	10 Dependent care benefits	10 Dependent care benefits
11 Nonqualified plans	11 Nonqualified plans	12a See instructions for box 12	12a See instructions for box 12
13 Statutory employee Retirement plan Third-party sick-pay	13 Statutory employee Retirement plan Third-party sick-pay	12b	12b
14 Other (see instructions)	14 Other (see instructions)	12c	12c
		12d	12d

State Correction Information

Previously reported	Correct information	Previously reported	Correct information
15 State	15 State	15 State	15 State
Employer's state ID number	Employer's state ID number	Employer's state ID number	Employer's state ID number
16 State wages, tips, etc.	16 State wages, tips, etc.	16 State wages, tips, etc.	16 State wages, tips, etc.
17 State income tax	17 State income tax	17 State income tax	17 State income tax

Locality Correction Information

18 Local wages, tips, etc.	18 Local wages, tips, etc.	18 Local wages, tips, etc.	18 Local wages, tips, etc.
19 Local income tax	19 Local income tax	19 Local income tax	19 Local income tax
20 Locality name	20 Locality name	20 Locality name	20 Locality name

For Privacy Act and Paperwork Reduction Act Notice, see separate instructions. Copy A — For Social Security Administration

Form **W-2c** (Rev. 12-2002) **Corrected Wage and Tax Statement** Department of the Treasury
ISA 0000/1039 Internal Revenue Service
STF FED9245F.1

rected with SSA if an error is discovered. If the employee's address was incorrect on the Form W-2, the payroll department must do one of the following:

- Issue a new, corrected Form W-2 to the employee including the new address. Indicate "REISSUED STATEMENT" on the new copies. Do not send Copy A to the SSA.

- Issue a Form W-2c to the employee showing the correct address in box f and all other correct information. Do not send Copy A to the SSA.

- Mail the Form W-2 with the incorrect address to the employee in an envelope showing the correct address or otherwise deliver it to the employee.

Whenever the payroll department produces a Form W-2c that increases or decreases any of the wages reported or taxes withheld, a correction to the Form 941 or state equivalent will be required.

(d) Duplicate Requests

Once the Forms W-2 have been distributed to the employees, the next task to handle is issuing duplicate forms. It always seems like employees begin asking about how to request duplicate copies of the form even before the original form is mailed out. Section 7.1 discusses how to inform employees of the upcoming new year information. Listed on the memo are the procedures for requesting a duplicate Form W-2. The procedures for this task should be done as soon as the memo is released. Setting up the procedures in early December will relieve the payroll department of having to handle this task during the hectic January–February time frame. If there is one thing that history tells us, it is that employees will always need duplicate Forms W-2, no matter how hard the payroll department has tried to prevent it. The reasons vary greatly, including everything from, "I never received it; are you sure you mailed it out?" or "I thought you knew I moved six months ago!" to "I didn't know that it was my W-2 so I threw it out." Regardless of the reason, the task will go more smoothly if the procedures are in place as soon as possible because when employees want a copy of the form, they want it now.

However, if employees need the copy right now, does payroll have to give it to them *right now*? Actually, the IRS does not have specific regulations for the timing of reissuing duplicate forms. The only requirement is that they be issued in "a reasonable amount of time" but no specifics are given, so the time frame is up to the individual payroll department. That is why it is important to let employees know how long it will take to receive the form once the request has been submitted.

As mentioned earlier, procedures for requesting duplicate forms should be included in the year-end planning and be part of the "State of the Payroll Address." To assist in creating the procedures, the following questions should be taken into account:

- When can employees begin requesting forms?
- How should they submit the request?
- How long until the employee receives the new form?

Regarding the "When Can Employees Begin Requesting the Form?" question: This is up to the payroll department, but here are a few suggestions:

- Make sure that the employee has allowed sufficient time to receive the original form in the mail. It takes at least five days for the U.S. Postal Service to deliver a letter across the country. In addition, if the employee has a moving order in effect, this might add as much as ten additional days.

- Set a date that allows for postal delivery time. Allowing employees to begin requesting duplicates after February 15 would take this processing time into account. Any earlier and the forms may pass in the mail.

- Advertise this date as soon as possible. That is why it should be in the "State of the Payroll Address." Some employees will insist on requesting the form on February 1 when they were mailed on January 31.

- The payroll department should also let it be known that duplicates or pre-issues will not be done just so that employees can have their tax appointments in early January.

The second question to address is "How Should They Submit the Request?" This is a critical point in the procedures. Employees will try all kinds of ways to submit their request that require the least amount of effort on their part. But remember that this is a duplicate of a very sensitive document. It is possible that, in this day and age, someone other than the employee may try to intercept this document. The payroll department would never mail a copy of a payroll record to someone who just requested it over the phone, so why would the Form W-2 be treated any differently?

One of the best ways to handle the request is to have the employee complete and submit a departmental form only. No requests by phone should be accepted. The employee may obtain the form via e-mail if the department has that capability, or by fax, snail mail, or in person. The employee must complete the form and submit identification proving he or she is the employee on the form. This can be accomplished by showing ID in the form of a driver's license or, if the company uses them, a badge or ID card. If the employee is faxing the form, a copy of the ID should be faxed with the form. There are no restrictions against requiring proof of identity to request or receive duplicate forms. A sample request form is shown in Exhibit 7.5.

The last question that needs to be addressed is "How Long Until the Employee Receives the New Form?" The employee, of course, expects the payroll department to drop everything and process his or her duplicate form request immediately. Whatever the time frame, clearly spell it out in the procedures so that employees understand how long it will take to receive the duplicate form once the request has been received by the payroll department. It is best to announce the processing time early in the year. This can be done at the same time as the announcement for the form and the request dates. Payroll

Exhibit 7.5

Request for Duplicate Form W-2 for Tax Year: 2004

Please return this form to: ABC Company, Inc.
Payroll Department M/S 406
1402 Bonny Meadow Road
Anytown, NY 01014
Fax: 123-45-6789 E-mail: payroll@abcco.com

Please issue a duplicate copy of the Wage and Tax Statement (Form W-2) for the following employee:

Employee Name: _____

Social Security No: _____

Badge # (for current employees): _____

Distribution of Form: (Circle One) Pick-Up From Payroll Mail Form

Mail Form To:

_____
Street Address

_____
City   State   ZIP Code

Reason For Request: (circle one)   Never Received   Lost/Misplaced/Destroyed

Signature of Employee: _____

If requesting form be mailed, please provide copy of picture identification such as driver's license (former employees) or ID badge (current employees) along with this request form. If picking up the duplicate Form W-2 in person, please be prepared to show picture ID such as a driver's license (former employees) or your ID badge (current employees). Allow five business days to process your request.

_____

For Payroll Department Use Only:

Date request received: _____ Date form mailed to employee: _____

Received by employee:_____
Signature of Employee

stuffers, blanket e-mails, postings, and year-end memos are common ways to get this information to the employee. Including it on the form will also help to inform the employee of the amount of time to wait before calling to check on the status.

How much time should the payroll department allow to process the request? It depends on the payroll system. If the payroll department has a system that allows for duplicate forms to be requested right from the system or a CD-ROM storage system, then the department will be able to process the form faster than those departments that must actually retype the form. No matter how late the employee sends the request to payroll, the department still has a "reasonable amount of time" to process the request. The employee who requests a duplicate on April 14 should expect no faster turnaround time than the employee who submits the request on February 18.

When issuing the replacement form, the IRS does have one requirement. Any Form W-2 that is reissued must indicate that on the top of the form. The words "Reissued Statement" must appear on the form.

For those departments with older systems, the habit may have been to photocopy the employer copy and give that to the employee. Remember that although the IRS does allow photocopying, the employee must receive the same copies as with the original form that is, copies B, C, and 2. The employee cannot be given three copies of the employer copy D. It is also acceptable to use the forms if the computer system prints the forms without copy identification at all.

If the current payroll system does not have the capabilities of producing the form, there are various other ways to recreate the form. Over the counter simple programs for retyping the form on a PC are available. In addition, payroll information services provide interactive forms that may be used for this purpose. Be advised that these services are generally only available by subscription.

EXHIBIT 7.6

Form 941 to Form W-2 Reconciliation

Form 941
(Rev. January 2004)
Department of the Treasury
Internal Revenue Service (99)

Employer's Quarterly Federal Tax Return
▶ See separate instructions revised January 2004 for information on completing this return.
Please type or print.

		OMB No. 1545-0029

Name (as distinguished from trade name) | Date quarter ended

Trade name, if any | Employer identification number

Address (number and street) | City, state, and ZIP code

Line 2 should match box 1
(see page 2 of separate instructions).

| T |
| FF |
| FD |
| FP |
| I |
| T |

IRS Use

1 1 1 1 1 1 1 1 1   2   3 3 3 3 3 3 3   4 4 4   5 5 5

Line 3 should match box 2

6   7   8 8 8 8 8 8 8   9 9 9 9 9   10 10 10 10 10 10 10 10 10 10

ave to file returns in the future, check here ▶ ☐ and enter date final wages paid ▶
sonal employer, see **Seasonal employers** on page 1 of the instructions and check here ▶ ☐
mployees in the pay period that includes March 12th ▶ 1

2 Total wages and tips, plus other compensation (see separate instructions) . . . . . | 2
3 Total income tax withheld from wages, tips, and sick pay . . . . | 3
4 Adjustment of withheld income tax for preceding quarters of **this calendar year** . . . | 4
5 Adjusted total of income tax withheld (line 3 as adjusted by line 4) . . . . . . | 5
6 Taxable social security wages . . . . | 6a | × 12.4% (.124) = | 6b
   Taxable social security tips . . . . . | 6c | × 12.4% (.124) = | 6d
7 Taxable Medicare wages and tips . . . | 7a | × 2.9% (.029) = | 7b
8 Total social security and Medicare taxes (add lines 6b, 6d, and 7b). Check here if wages
   are not subject to social security and/or Medicare tax . . . . ▶ ☐ | 8
9 Adjustment of social security and Medicare taxes (see instructions for required explanation)
   Sick Pay $ _____ ± Fractions of Cents $ _____ ± Other $ _____ = | 9
10 Adjusted total of social security and Medicare taxes (line 8 as adjusted by line 9) . . . | 10
11 **Total taxes** (add lines 5 and 10) . . | 11
12 Advance earned income credit (EIC) payments made to employees (see instructions) . | 12
13 Net taxes ... column (d) | 13
14 Total depos... om a prior quarter . . . . . | 14
15 **Balance du**...s . . . . | 15
16 **Overpayme**...here ▶ $ _____
   and check if to be: ☐ Applied to next return **or** ☐ Refunded.

Lines 6a and 6b match to boxes 3 and 4 and lines 7a and 7b match to 5 and 6, allowing for employer match and fractions and tips

• **All filers:** If line 13 is less than $2,500, **do not** complete line 17 or Schedule B (Form 941).
• **Semiweekly schedule depositors:** Complete Schedule B (Form 941) and check here . . . . ▶ ☐
• **Monthly schedule depositors:** Complete line 17, columns (a) through (d), and check here. . . . . ▶ ☐

17	**Monthly Summary of Federal Tax Liability.** (Complete Schedule B (Form 941) instead, if you were a semiweekly schedule depositor.)			
	(a) First month liability	(b) Second month liability	(c) Third month liability	(d) Total liability for quarter

Third Party Designee | Do you want to allow another person to discuss this return with the IRS (see separate instructions)? ☐ **Yes.** Complete the following. ☐ **No**
Designee's name ▶ | Phone no. ▶ ( ) | Personal identification number (PIN) ▶ ☐☐☐☐☐

Sign Here | Under penalties of perjury, I declare that I have examined this return, including accompanying schedules and statements, and to the best of my knowledge and belief, it is true, correct, and complete.
Signature ▶ | Print Your Name and Title ▶ | Date ▶

For Privacy Act and Paperwork Reduction Act Notice, see back of Payment Voucher. Cat. No. 17001Z Form **941** (Rev. 1-2004)

CHAPTER 8

Payroll and the New Year

8.1 SETTING UP THE PAYROLL SYSTEM FOR THE NEW YEAR

One of the more common tasks that needs to be done in this day and age is to update the computer system for the new year. This is especially true in the payroll department. However, unique to the payroll department is the time frame in which this task needs to be accomplished. Most departments can update their systems when they have time after the first of the year. However, payroll has a very short window of opportunity to complete this task. It must be done after the last payroll of the current year, but before the first payroll of the new year. In some payroll departments, this time frame could be as short as a few days. With just a little fore-thought and planning, this task can be streamlined, which will help to get it done on time and more efficiently.

(a) New Wage Bases and Rates

The wage base amounts and rates for taxes may need to be updated for the new year. It depends on the tax itself. The Social Security wage base changes each year but the rate does not. The Medicare wage base and rate both have remained constant since the wage base went to unlimited in the 1990s. The Federal Unemployment Tax (FUTA) wage base remains at $7,000 with a fixed rate, but many states change their State Unemployment Insurance (SUI) wage bases and rates as is needed by the state budget.

To assist in organizing this update process, a spreadsheet should be created that lists all taxes handled by the payroll department and the current rates and wage bases. Then as each wage base is announced or rate is received, it should be entered onto the spreadsheet. That way, when it is possible to update the system, the spreadsheet will expedite the process.

If the payroll processing or tax preparation is outsourced to a third party vendor, this spreadsheet may be furnished by the vendor. If not, it should still be created in order to streamline relaying the information to the vendor, which will ensure an accurate first payroll.

The spreadsheet should be started as soon as possible. This is not a task that needs to wait until the hectic year-end period begins. It can be created in June with the current rates and wage bases inserted. Then as the information is released by the federal and state governments, it can be updated to reflect the new year information.

(b) New Benefit Charts or Deduction Amounts

The charts or tables in the system that reflect benefit amounts or deduction amounts for such items as health insurance or garnishments also must be updated before the first payroll of the new year. The payroll department needs to set up a coordination effort with human resources and/or benefits to ensure that this information is received in a timely manner. Many times the other departments are unaware of the time restraints payroll faces in order to ensure that the first payroll of the year is processed correctly.

(c) Establishing New Benefits on the Computer System

If the company is offering new benefits in the upcoming year, this information must be relayed to payroll as soon as the decision is made to offer the benefit. Payroll must have time to set up the computer system to accept and process the benefit and/or the deduction. To keep on top of this process, the payroll department should periodically check with the appropriate departments to see if new benefits or major changes to current benefits will be occurring in the new year.

8.2 SETTING UP THE PAYROLL DEPARTMENT FOR THE NEW YEAR

To use a sports analogy to describe the payroll year, completing the Forms W-2 is like the Super Bowl or the World Series of payroll. But like any sports team knows, you don't win the championship by waiting until the day before the big game to plan a strategy. This same theory applies to payroll. In order for a payroll department to run smoothly throughout the entire "season" and have a winning year end, the game plan must be made right up front. For payroll, the game plan is organizing the department for the entire year before the first payroll even gets processed. This organization consists of ordering new forms, publications, establishing a payroll calendar, and setting up new files and spreadsheets.

(a) Order New Forms

Sometimes it seems as if the payroll department runs on forms—Forms W-4 and W-5, address change forms, specialty forms for expatriates, direct deposit forms, and many more. This is why when running an efficient payroll department, the task of updating forms for the new year should be done in early December at the latest to ensure a smooth transition to the new year. The IRS and other government agencies usually release most of the upcoming year's forms during the last weeks of November and into early December. (Of course, there have been exceptions to this rule, but it is the normal course for the agencies.) With modern technology, such as the Internet, payroll departments no longer have to complete order forms and wait weeks to receive most forms therefore, the task has become much easier and quicker to perform.

To order the forms the payroll department will need, first create a checklist of all the forms the department uses. This can be a simple handwritten list, however, setting it up in an electronic format, such as an Excel spreadsheet, will allow staff to simply edit the list in subsequent years. This list should include IRS forms, DOL forms, in-house or company-specific forms, and of course, any state forms that the department uses. A sample checklist is included in Exhibit 8.1. The reason the

EXHIBIT 8.1

Sample Spreadsheet for Ordering Forms			
Year: (insert year)	New Year Forms Order Worksheet		
Form Number or Form Name	Agency or Source of Form	Form Reviewed	Date Ordered, Downloaded, or Printed
W-4	IRS		12/4
W-5	IRS		12/4
DE 4	EDD CA		12/15
New Hire Forms (paper stock only)	Internal	11/2	11/15
Set Up New Direct Deposit	Internal	12/9	
Address Change Form	Internal	12/10	

list includes internal forms is very simple. These forms should be reviewed each year and this is an excellent time for that review. When reviewing, include queries such as: Can the form be improved? Can the form be combined with other forms for ease of use by employees or the department? Is the form too cumbersome to use and does it need to be streamlined? If the form works well and no changes need to be made, note this by placing the review date at the bottom of the form to keep track of when the last update was done.

Once the checklist is completed and the internal forms have been reviewed and updated, the next step is to download, print, or order the forms from outside agencies. With the Internet, most payroll departments do not need to print huge quantities of IRS or other government agency forms, as these forms are readily available at a moment's notice. Printing out one or two month's supply each time should cover the department's needs and keep enough of a supply on hand for employees to use.

The main point to remember is that no form should be used in a year that differs from the year on the form. For example, the Form W-4 that is dated for the tax year 2004 should be used only in the year 2004. Once the last payroll is run in 2004, the remaining form stock should be destroyed and replaced with the Form W-4 for 2005.

Offsite locations and the disaster backup site should also receive the new forms. It is a common problem within a payroll department to receive old forms from the field offices or remote sites that do not remember to update forms or that refuse to take the time to do so. It saves time and energy to simply send the remote sites the new forms with instructions to destroy any old stock immediately.

If any of the internal forms are paper stock only (multiple-part forms used for disbursement to different departments) this is also an excellent time to reorder the forms for the new year.

(b) Ordering Publications

As with ordering forms, the first task that should be done is to make a checklist. The forms checklist can, of course, be combined with the publications checklist to cut down on excess files, if desired. Many of the publications may be received automatically through the mail, especially the IRS Publication 15, Circular E, or state employer guides. These should still be listed on the checklist to make sure they are indeed received. This is also an excellent time to order updated versions of any publications that are purchased on a subscription basis each year. These should be added to the list as well but always remember to record the reorder dates.

(c) Establishing the New Processing Calendar

This is an absolute must for all payroll departments and is a standard task during the month of December. In fact, if the department has an outside vendor processing the payroll, the vendor mandates that a processing calendar be set up prior to the new year. However, that type of calendar just outlines when the payroll will be run. The type of calendar discussed in this section includes not only the actual processing of the payroll but also coordinates all the other facets of producing a payroll during the cycle and is useful in coordinating the needs of payroll with other departments.

Many payroll departments have a set schedule in which the payroll is processed and they do not feel that a payroll calendar is necessary, especially if the payroll is processed in house. They believe that just to coordinate with the systems staff is all that is needed. However, it is important to remember that this type of calendar not only helps the payroll department run efficiently but it has a variety of other useful purposes to the department. First, it is an excellent tool to demonstrate to superiors and other departments the tasks that are needed to produce a payroll on time and why scarce company resources should be allocated to the payroll department. What better way to drive the need home, especially during budget discussions, than by showing exactly what has to be done and the short time frame in which it needs to happen in order to pay the company's employees?

Still another excellent reason to create a payroll calendar lies strictly in appearances. Though the department produces payrolls in an efficient and timely manner, having created and disbursed the calendar adds a tremendous amount of credibility to the department. With the calendar, other departments can see that paychecks are not just pulled out of thin air or done magically overnight but are accomplished through a lot of hard work and tough deadlines. The calendar clearly shows how much actually goes into producing a payroll every pay cycle.

And finally, use the payroll calendar to communicate payroll processing needs to other departments. This clearly demonstrates that not only is the information required by payroll vital to complete the processing, but the deadlines are not arbitrary and are, in fact, necessary to ensure that all employees are paid correctly and on time.

What exactly should this important payroll calendar include? Basically, every single task the payroll department needs to accomplish should be listed. In smaller companies that operate in just one state, this is possible to do using only the master calendar and a processing checklist. However, for some larger companies, this calendar could be a huge project too unruly to use efficiently. That is where subcalendars come into play. A subcalendar is a calendar that is for only one facet of the payroll processing cycle. Examples of subcalendars include:

- *Data Input Calendar.* Describes what input is needed for payroll processing and the deadline dates to receive and input such items as time sheets, new hire information, benefit changes, Form W-4 changes, and so on.

- *Processing Calendar.* Describes which processes need to be accomplished to run and complete the payroll cycle and includes the dates for such items as requesting the payroll, printing reports and checks or receiving payroll from an outside vendor, or distributing reports and checks.

- *Tax Deposit Calendar.* This calendar reflects the due dates for all tax deposits for federal and all appropriate state and local tax agencies. Some payroll departments also include third-party checks on this calendar such as for garnishments and disability payments.

- *Quarter-End Calendar.* This reflects all tasks that need to be accomplished to close the quarter. This could include running any extra payrolls to process manual or voided checks (these would also be listed on the processing calendar), reconciling Form W-2 to Form 941, and completing Form 941 and all state equivalents. Note: Tax deposits that are only made quarterly may be noted on this calendar but should be included on the tax calendar as well for consistency.

- *Year-End Calendar.* This calendar will be done by the year-end team and transferred over. It is necessary to have it included on the master calendar to make sure that year end and the current payroll are both being accomplished simultaneously.

- *Year Beginning Calendar.* All the tasks that need to be done at the beginning of the year also need to be listed on the master calendar to make sure they are not overlooked.

But how do the master calendar and the subcalendars work together? Very easily. The subcalendar lists all the tasks and the dates needed and so forth. The only item that is listed on the master calendar is the name of the subcalendar for the date in question. That notation tells the payroll department that a task on the subcalendar needs to be accomplished on that day. The subcalendar is then referenced for exactly what needs to be accomplished. For example, on the master calendar it lists "Tax Calendar" on Tuesday. On the tax deposit subcalendar for that same Tuesday it reads: "Tax deposit for AZ SIT due" and "Tax deposit for HI SIT due." For that same Tuesday, the master calendar could indicate: "Processing calendar." The processing calendar then shows "Print payroll reports" and "E-mail 401(k) plan report to administrator" on that same Tuesday. For large companies, especially those operating in many states, subcalendars will help make the master calendar easier to read and less cluttered, and therefore more useful. For smaller companies, just one or two subcalendars, if any, may be needed.

The subcalendars also make communication with other departments easier. For example, suppose the payroll department needs to coordinate with the human resources department on the input of new hires, pay raises, and benefit changes. This input is done by human resources and fed to the payroll system. The payroll department needs to make sure that all the input is done by the Monday prior to the payroll processing Tuesday, every other week. One way to reflect this need is to show that date on the data input calendar and make sure this calendar is shared with human resources. With this method, human resources is given a clear deadline by which the input must be sent to payroll.

The master calendar also helps in budgeting time during busy intervals such as quarter end. Being able to see all the tasks that need to be done ahead of time (such as a year at a glance) gives perspective on how much time can be allotted to each project during the year. It also assists in juggling the last-minute, ad hoc projects that are sometimes given to the payroll department.

The calendar is a great tool for payroll managers or supervisors in helping to delegate duties and oversee the entire workload of the department. Though each employee in the department may have his or her own personal calendar, the master calendar dictates what needs to be done and when it must be done. This helps keep individual employees from setting their own agenda when it comes to processing payroll or other tasks. This is also helpful when an employee goes on vacation or is absent due to illness or an emergency. Essential tasks that need to be covered can be readily ascertained by checking the master calendar.

Examples of a master calendar and three subcalendars are shown in Exhibit 8.2.

(d) Setting Up New Files and Spreadsheets

This task, on the surface, appears to be so obvious that it should not have to be mentioned. But the reality is that because it is so simple and obvious, it can be and often is overlooked. Many payroll departments omit this task at the beginning of the year and try to catch up around April or May, leaving filing to pile up and reconciliations pending. But spreadsheets and files, such as tax reconciliations and basic file folders, can and indeed do help promote and maintain the department's efficiency.

How can the payroll department find the time needed to create, update, or copy spreadsheet files or make labels for manila folders while racing around producing Forms W-2 and payrolls? The answer is very simple—it cannot! In late December and especially in January, the payroll department does not have the time to devote to these simple but crucial tasks. But who ever said that new year tasks have to be done during that time? During certain times of the year every payroll department has slower periods, such as late August, when there are limited reporting requirements, or early November, before the holidays and the year-end rush begins. This is an excellent time to accomplish these tasks.

For electronic spreadsheets already in use, just simply update a copy of each of the files to be used in the new year, create a new folder with the new year as its name, and store the new files in that folder on your computer, safe and sound until they are needed in January.

The physical files needed at the beginning of the year can be done in one of two ways:

1. Create a set of labels for the files and store them in the new year folder on your computer. This method has a couple of advantages. First, the labels can be used over

Exhibit 8.2

Master Calendar Sample

Our sample company in this exhibit has a biweekly payroll and is a next day depositor. Payday is on Friday and processing begins on Monday. They are located in California, Hawaii, Arizona, and New York. The input for new hires, pay raises, and benefits is done by human resources.

Master Calendar
March 20 × 5

Monday	Tuesday	Wednesday	Thursday	Friday	Saturday /Sunday
	1	2	3	4 DIC	5
6	7 DIC PC	8 PC	9 PC	10 **Payday** PC TC	11
12	13 PC	14	15	16 DIC	17
18	19 DIC PC	20 PC	21 PC	22 **Payday** PC TC	21
24	25 PC	26	27	28 DIC	29
30	31 DIC				

Data Input Calendar
March 20 × 5

Monday	Tuesday	Wednesday	Thursday	Friday	Saturday /Sunday
	1	2	3	4 All changes must be received by 5 pm	5
6	7 Complete data entry by 5pm	8	9	10 **Payday**	11
12	13	14	15	16 All changes must be received by 5 pm	17
18	19 Complete data entry by 5pm	20	21	22 **Payday**	21
24	25	26	27	28 All changes must be received by 5 pm	29
30	31 Complete data entry by 5pm				

EXHIBIT 8.2 *(CONTINUED)*

Master Calendar Sample

Processing Calendar
March 20 × 5

Monday	Tuesday	Wednesday	Thursday	Friday	Saturday /Sunday
	1	2	3	4 All changes must be received by 5 pm	5
6	7 Complete data entry by 5pm	8	9	10 **Payday**	11
12	13	14	15	16 All changes must be received by 5 pm	17
18	19 Complete data entry by 5pm	20	21	22 **Payday**	21
24	25	26	27	28 All changes must be received by 5 pm	29
30	31 Complete data entry by 5pm				

Tax Calendar
March 20 × 5

Monday	Tuesday	Wednesday	Thursday	Friday	Saturday /Sunday
	1	2	3	4	5
6	7	8	9	10 **Payday** Fed tax deposit CA, HI, AZ, and NY SIT deposits	11
12	13	14	15	16	17
18	19	20	21	22 **Payday** Fed tax deposit CA, HI, AZ, and NY SIT deposits	21
24	25	26	27	28	29
30	31				

and over again for each new year. This saves a lot of work; once the file is created, it only needs to be edited and updated each year. Second, it does not take up precious storage space in the department. However, there is one big disadvantage to this method. One still needs time during the department's busiest rush period to physically create the new folders.

2. Create the actual physical file folders and store them until needed at the beginning of the new year. The disadvantage here is having to store the file folders until they are needed.

Whichever method the payroll department chooses, it is important to make sure that the files are ready for the new year so that the department can keep running efficiently.

(e) Updating Procedure Manuals

Writing procedure manuals is a huge undertaking that each payroll department must complete. And once the manuals are in place and are being utilized by the payroll staff, they are a tremendous help in maintaining an efficient department. But what good does it do to take the valuable time to create first-rate procedure manuals if they are allowed to become obsolete because no one takes the time to keep them updated? A review and/or update of the procedure manuals should be done annually to ensure total accuracy. The beginning of the year is an excellent time to begin this process. Once again, the question arises as to timing. Does the payroll department *have* to do this task at such a hectic time? Not necessarily, or at least, not entirely. Procedures, such as those discussed back in Section 2.1, should be constantly updated as a process is changed or adjusted. The review at the beginning of the year should be reserved for items such as forms that have been updated or changed for the new year and new rates or wage bases that may be referenced in the manual. The full review can be done later in the year, when time is available.

CHAPTER 9

Professionalism and the Payroll Department

9.1   WHAT IS A CPP?

Throughout the years, as career fields have grown and matured the need to somehow quantify and qualify the practitioner's knowledge has become increasingly necessary. The modern payroll professional now falls in this category. The pressures of economic and legislative developments on the payroll function have broadened the scope of payroll beyond its original basic function of paying employees. Over the years, payroll has come under a wide array of legislative mandates, from the federal income tax withholding that affects most employees to judgments against individual employees.

The Certified Payroll Professional (CPP) recognition is offered by The American Payroll Association (APA) to recognize those who have achieved a certain level of professional proficiency. Certified Payroll Professional recognition is given by the APA to those who 1) meet the eligibility requirements for admission to the examination, 2) successfully complete the examination, and 3) subscribe to the APA Code of Ethics. Certification is granted for a five-year period, at which time recertification is required.

9.2   WHY BECOME A CPP?

There are countless personal and professional reasons for attaining the CPP designation. But it basically boils down to two main reasons:

1. *Professional.* It raises the standards for the entire profession when criteria for certification are established, accepted, and achieved by members of the profession and the greater business community.

2. *Personal.* The studying and preparation for the test increases the knowledge and skills of the payroll professional.

9.3   STUDYING FOR THE TEST

Once a payroll professional has decided to take the CPP test, the first question that usually arises is how to study for the exam. Actually, there is no one standard study guide, program, or method for this test. The methods for studying vary as greatly as the payroll professionals who take the test each year. However, over the years during which the test has been administered, certain patterns have emerged for studying by those who have successfully passed the exam.

(a) Studying Should Mirror the Format of the Exam

Studying should strictly follow the outline of the exam as provided by the American Payroll Association. (See Exhibit 9.1.) Whatever resources are used, they should be first broken down to follow this outline instead of just beginning to read and memorize. The amount of material covered and the fact that the test requires calculations precludes using the memorization method. This method also ensures that all facets of the information are covered in the course of the study and makes sure that resources are available or have been located for all sections of the exam.

An efficient way to achieve this course of study is to create a study grid or worksheet that identifies each section of the outline and specifies what resources cover that section. An Excel spreadsheet or Word table will work wonderfully for this purpose. An example is shown in Exhibit 9.2.

(b) Time Is Critical

Based on the date of the test, a time frame should be set up to allow sufficient time to study all the necessary information

Exhibit 9.1

Outline of the Certified Payroll Professional Exam

I. Payroll Fundamentals and Operations, 26%

A. Worker status
1. Independent contractors
2. Statutory employees/nonemployees
3. Temporary agency/leased employees

B. FLSA
1. Regular rate of pay
2. Minimum wage
3. Overtime
4. Child labor
5. White-collar exemptions
6. Public sector/hospital special rules
7. Public contracts and other provisions (e.g., compensable time issues, tip credit, public contract laws, sick and vacation time, etc.)

C. Payroll records
- Masterfile components
- Retention requirements

D. Payroll processing and operations
1. Data entry/error correction
2. Balancing input to output
3. Prepare/balance remittances for deductions or funding requests
4. Sorting/distributing output
5. Method and timing of pay
   ○ Direct deposit
   ○ Stop payment and reissuance of paychecks
   ○ Escheat law compliance
   ○ Constructive receipt

E. Customer service
(e.g., problem resolution, vendor relations, confidentiality, payroll forms)

II. Fundamentals for Calculation of Paychecks, 30%

A. Calculation of earnings
(regular, overtime, shift/premium, holiday, bonuses, commissions, tips, etc.)

B. Calculation of special payments
1. Manual or out-of-cycle payments
2. Grossing up
3. Payments after death
4. Other (e.g., severance, workers' compensation, etc.)

C. Calculation of employee benefits
1. IRS-defined (i.e., company automobiles; company aircraft; vacations provided; discounts on property and services; professional memberships; entertainment tickets)
2. Qualified and nonqualified plans
   ○ Pensions
   ○ Deferred compensation
3. Cafeteria and FSA plans
4. Dependent care
5. Relocation
6. Business expense reimbursements
7. Health and welfare plans, including COBRA
8. Stock options
9. Group term life insurance
10. Educational assistance
11. Nontaxable employer-provided benefits (e.g., de minimis, working condition, fringe, etc.)
12. Disability/leaves (e.g., FMLA, etc.)
13. Other (e.g., service awards, gifts, golden parachutes, cash pay-outs, death benefits, adoption assistance, jury and military pay, meals and lodging, etc.)

EXHIBIT 9.1 *(CONTINUED)*

Outline of the Certified Payroll Professional Exam

D. Calculation of employee taxes

1. Federal income tax calculations (e.g., percentage, wage bracket, supplemental)
2. Social Security/Medicare taxes
3. Advance earned income credit
4. Forms (e.g., W-4, W-5, etc.)
5. Resident/nonresident aliens, expatriates, and totalization agreements

E. Calculation of deductions

1. Voluntary (advances, credit union, charity, bonds, etc.)
2. Involuntary (garnishments, support, levies, etc.)

III. Tax and Regulatory Compliance, 10%

A. Employment taxes

1. Federal unemployment tax
2. Social Security and Medicare taxes
3. Federal income tax

B. Tax deposits: methods and timing

C. Reporting requirements

1. Forms (e.g., W-2, W-2c, W-3, 1099, 1042, 940, 941, etc.)
2. Due dates of reports

D. Federal taxation inquiries and notices

1. Penalties
2. Audits
3. Problem resolution

E. Nontax compliance reporting

1. New hires
2. Immigration and Naturalization (I-9)
3. Bureau of Labor Statistics
4. Penalties

F. Payroll penalties

1. FLSA
2. Worker status
3. Payroll records

IV. Accounting, 8%

A. Account classification (assets, liabilities)

B. Account balances (debits, credits)

C. Payroll journal entries

1. Wages/salaries, and other labor cost distribution
2. Accruals, reversals, and adjustments
3. Accounting periods
4. Financial statements

D. Account reconciliation

V. Payroll and Supporting Systems, 16%

A. Feasibility studies, software evaluations, and review

B. Systems implementation, update, enhancement, or upgrade

C. Systems production control (e.g., scheduling, deadlines, system priorities, technical aspects)

D. System edits and balancing

E. Interfaces

F. Security

G. Documentation

H. Backup and disaster recovery

VI. Management and Administration, 10%

A. Policies and procedures

B. Staffing, training, and job descriptions

C. Internal control and audits

D. Management skills and theories

E. Communication

EXHIBIT 9.2

Study Worksheet for the CPP Test

Section of Exam	Topic	Subject	Resource	Page(s)
I. Payroll Fundamentals and Operations	A. Worker Status	1. Independent Contractors	Publication 15-B	Page 3
II. Fundamentals for Calculation of Paychecks				
III. Tax and Regulatory Compliance				
IV. Accounting				
V. Payroll and Supporting Systems				
VI. Management and Administration				

---

including practice tests. The most practical way is to count backwards from the date of the test. It is critical to remember that each section should be given equal time unless calculations are involved, which would require even more time. No section is "easier" than the others or should be given less weight.

(c) Family and Employer Support Is Needed

It is absolutely necessary to have the support of your family and your employer to study successfully for the test. Time must be set aside for studying and practice tests. This requires others in the family to take on responsibilities in order to free up your time for studying. Coworkers or superiors in the office can also help by proctoring quick practice tests during lunch or after hours.

(d) Practice Questions and Tests Are Critical

At least four full practice tests should be taken. These tests will show areas where more studying and/or practice is needed. These tests should be taken in a situation that mirrors the real test. The test questions should be answered without the aid of the resources and on paper or to another person. This prevents the tendency to "kind of answer" the question and then see if the answer is right. At least 100 calculation questions should be attempted prior to taking the actual exam.

(e) Study Groups

Many chapters of the APA hold ad hoc or organized study groups. For payroll professionals who need the support of a group study program, this is an excellent option.

(f) Resources Available

There are dozens of resources available to study for the test. These include guides or books sold on the open market and information available from government agencies such as the IRS or the Department of Labor. A list of the more popular resources for purchase is included in Exhibit 9.3. The public domain information is listed in Exhibit 9.4.

EXHIBIT 9.3

Open Market Publication

Source	Publication
American Payroll Association	*The Payroll Source*
www.americanpayroll.org	*Basic Guide to Payroll*
	Guide to Successful Direct Deposit
	Guide to Global Payroll Management
BNA	*Payroll Administration Guide*
www.bna.com/payroll	
Lambert and Associates	Testing Tutor Cards
www.vickimlambert.com	
RIA	*Principles of Payroll Administration*
www.riahome.com	

EXHIBIT 9.4

Public Domain Publications

Source	Publication Number	Publication Name
Internal Revenue Service	15	Circular E
www.irs.gov	15-A	Employer's Supplemental Tax Guide
	15-B	Employer's Tax Guide to Fringe Benefits
	521	Moving Expenses
	525	Taxable and Nontaxable Income
	531	Reporting Tip Income
	596	Earned Income Credit
	Form Instructions	Form W-2 and W-3
		Form SS-8
		Form W-4
		Form W-5
Department of Labor	1262	Bulletin on Overtime Compensation
www.dol.gov	1281	Defining the Terms—Executive, Administrative, Professional and Outside Sales
	1312	Hours Worked Under the FLSA
	1318	The FLSA of 1938 as amended
	1325	Overtime Compensation Under the FLSA
	Fact Sheets	The Department has numerous fact sheets and one-page publications that assist in studying for the test.

(g) Training Courses

There are also training courses available to assist in learning the knowledge needed to pass the test. This training is offered by the APA, local APA chapters, local universities and community colleges, and online. Payroll professionals wishing to enroll in these types of training courses should check with their local community colleges or universities directly to find the appropriate training.

9.4   ONGOING TRAINING

To keep payroll skills sharp and knowledge current, payroll professionals need to keep training on an ongoing basis. This is true especially if the CPP designation has been earned. But training does not constitute just an organized six- to eight-hour lecture at some hotel across town. To keep training relevant and to optimize the time spent doing it, the payroll professional must use the same efficient methods utilized in processing payroll or organizing the department. This means the most relevant information should be garnered through the shortest, most direct method.

There are various means of obtaining this training using today's technology. The following are a sample of methods now available to receive training right in the payroll office:

- Electronic updates
- Web or audio seminars
- Online training
- Monthly meetings of professional organizations

(a) Electronic Updates

Yes, updates can be considered training. This is a great method for keeping up to date with the latest changes in all areas of payroll. The update comes to your e-mail address in a quick and easy-to-read format. The topics are listed as bullet points or e-mail links in most updates. All that needs to be done is to scan the list for any points or topics that are relevant and just concentrate on reading those articles. One more point needs to be stressed regarding this type of training. Most updates, especially government ones, are free.

(b) Web or Audio Seminars

This is one of the newest and best ways to obtain quick training on a single topic. Instead of sitting captive in a hotel meeting room for six or eight hours listening to information on dozens of topics, the audio seminar covers one topic in depth for 90 minutes. This type of seminar is done on the web or over the phone so the biggest advantage is the lack of travel time required to attend. Come to the office, work on payroll, stop for the seminar, and get right back to payroll processing once the seminar is over. No time is lost stuck in traffic or traveling.

(c) Online Training

Online training is a less formal method of training but an excellent source for wholesale coverage of a payroll topic or topics. This method requires the student to sign on to a website or download manuals, follow the assignments, submit assignments to the instructor, and take the final test all over the Internet or via e-mail. This type of training allows the payroll professional to work at his or her own pace and time frame.

(d) Monthly Meetings of Professional Organizations

One excellent source for quick, efficient training is the local monthly meeting of professional organizations such as those listed in Section 9.5. Usually an hour or two long and in a convenient section of town, the meeting features informative speakers and excellent networking opportunities. In addition to those organizations listed, the payroll professional can also learn about useful topics at local Chamber of Commerce meetings.

9.5 PROFESSIONAL ORGANIZATIONS

The payroll profession has grown and matured over the years. With this maturity comes the need for professional organizations to help practitioners of the art maintain knowledge, grow in the career field, and cultivate professional contacts. The following sections list the professional organizations that might be useful to the payroll professional. Currently it is possible for the payroll professional to be affiliated with the accounting department, finance department, or human resources department. For this reason, organizations that cross over into these areas but still cover pertinent payroll information have been included on the list. The list includes the organization's name, website, and mission statement.

(a) American Payroll Association

The American Payroll Association is the professional society for payroll professionals. The association pursues the following objectives:

- To increase the payroll professional's skill level through education and mutual support
- To obtain recognition for payroll work as practiced in today's business and legislative environments and as a professional discipline
- To represent the payroll professional on the federal, state, and local level
- To provide public service education on payroll and employment issues

Anyone engaged in payroll administration and/or related fields is eligible for APA membership. APA represents a cross section of the payroll profession made up predominantly of payroll managers from all 50 states, Washington D.C., and Puerto Rico, with a growing constituency in Canada and other foreign nations. The Association has local chapters in most major cities. Their website is www.americanpayroll.org.

(b) American Compensation Association

The American Compensation Association is located within the WorldatWork umbrella. WorldatWork is the world's leading not-for-profit professional association dedicated to knowledge leadership in compensation, benefits, and total rewards. Founded in 1955, WorldatWork focuses on human resources disciplines associated with attracting, retaining, and motivating employees. Their website is www.worldatwork.org.

(c) Canadian Payroll Association

The Canadian Payroll Association (CPA), founded in 1978, is the national association representing the payroll community in Canada. There are more than 10,000 members and delegates in Canada, the United States, and abroad. More than 18 million

(75 percent) of Canadian employees are paid through member companies. Their website is www.payroll.ca.

(d) Society for Human Resource Management

The Society for Human Resource Management (SHRM) is the world's largest association devoted to human resource management. Representing more than 180,000 individual members, the Society's mission is to serve the needs of HR professionals by providing the most essential and comprehensive resources available. As an influential voice, the Society's mission is also to advance the human resource profession to ensure that HR is recognized as an essential partner in developing and executing organizational strategy. Founded in 1948, SHRM currently has more than 500 affiliated chapters within the United States and members in more than 100 countries. Their website is located at www.shrm.org.

(e) National Association of Tax Reporting and Payroll Management

NATRPM is a nonprofit corporation organized to address the tax reporting and payroll industries' international, federal, state, and local legislative and regulatory issues; technical tax issues; technology developments; and operational issues. Their website is located at www.natrpm.org.

Index

W
W-2 Form, 251–265
   Correcting, 255–260
   Distribution, 252–255
   Duplicate, 261–265
   Reconciling, 249–251
W-2c Form, 255–260
W-4 form, 11
   Auditing, 12, 15
   Notices, 107
   Record retention, 21
   Sending to IRS, 19
Websites, 127–128, 189

Y
Year beginning, 247–248, 267–278
Year end, 68, 229–266
   Benefits, 142–148
   Charts and databases, 140–142
   Check lists, 243–248
   Memo, 229–233
   Planning and surviving, 234–240
   Reconciliation, 249–251
   Stress, 240
   To do lists, 241

—